FEMINISM

THE ESSENTIAL
HISTORICAL WRITINGS

FEMINISM

THE ESSENTIAL HISTORICAL WRITINGS

Edited and
with an introduction
and commentaries
by

Miriam Schneir

RANDOM HOUSE NEW YORK

Acknowledgment is gratefully extended for permission to
reprint from the following:
The Letters of George Sand, selected and edited by Veronica
Lucas, first published 1930 by George Routledge & Sons
Ltd., London. Reprinted by permission of Routledge &
Kegan Paul Ltd., London.
The Origin of the Family, Private Property, and the State,
by Friedrich Engels. Copyright, 1942, by International Pub-
lishers Co., Inc. Reprinted by permission of International
Publishers Co., Inc., N.Y.
Woman and the New Race, by Margaret Sanger. Copy-
right, 1920, by Brentano's Inc.; copyright, 1940, by Margaret
Sanger. Permission to reprint by Grant Sanger, M.D., is
gratefully acknowledged.
Reminiscences of Lenin, by Clara Zetkin. Copyright, 1934,
by International Publishers Co., Inc. Reprinted by permission
of International Publishers Co., Inc., N.Y.
A Room of One's Own, by Virginia Woolf. Copyright,
1929, by Harcourt Brace Jovanovich, Inc.; copyright, 1957,
by Leonard Woolf. Reprinted by permission of Harcourt
Brace Jovanovich, Inc., N.Y., and The Hogarth Press Ltd.,
London.

Manufactured in the United States of America
by Haddon Craftsmen, Scranton, Pa.
9 7 5 3 2 4 6 8

First Edition

We who like the children of Israel have been wandering in the wilderness of prejudice and ridicule for forty years feel a peculiar tenderness for the young women on whose shoulders we are about to leave our burdens. . . . The younger women are starting with great advantages over us. They have the results of our experience; they have superior opportunities for education; they will find a more enlightened public sentiment for discussion; they will have more courage to take the rights which belong to them. . . . Thus far women have been the mere echoes of men. Our laws and constitutions, our creeds and codes, and the customs of social life are all of masculine origin.

The true woman is as yet a dream of the future.

ELIZABETH CADY STANTON,
at the age of seventy-two, speaking
to the International
Council of Women, 1888

Contents

IV. MEN AS FEMINISTS

V. TWENTIETH-CENTURY THEMES

Contents

Introduction

❧

The Unknown History of Womankind

Feminism is one of the basic movements for human liberty. To view it in any less serious aspect, to ridicule present-day feminism as the passing fancy of a handful of malcontents, is to display a shocking ignorance of the history of one half the human race. Yet how ignorant we all have been, until very lately!

The vast majority of women are unaware of the great feminist writings of the past; not acquainted with the struggles and achievements of the widespread women's movements in the nineteenth and twentieth centuries; without access to scholarly studies (indeed, how few exist) which describe the part played by women in the French and American Revolutions, the anti-slavery movement, the development of organized labor. In short, women have been deprived of their history—thus, their group identity.

The problem is not a new one. Charles Francis Adams wrote in the preface to his 1876 collection of the letters of his grandparents, Abigail and John Adams: "The heroism of the females of the Revolution has gone from memory with the generation that witnessed it, and nothing, absolutely nothing, remains upon the ear of the young of the present day but the faint echo of an expiring general tradition." *

---

* From a "Memoir" by Charles Francis Adams, editor of the *Familiar Letters of John Adams and His Wife, Abigail Adams, During the Revolution* (New York, 1876).

The Literature, Written and Unwritten

The works in this anthology range from 1776, the earliest, to 1929. These dates pretty well define the boundaries of one phase of feminism, which is sometimes referred to as the "old feminism" to distinguish it from the present movement for women's liberation. The old feminism had its origins in the eighteenth-century democratic revolutions of the propertied middle class, and it ended soon after World War I.

However, long before the inception of this phase—in fact, hundreds of years before the publication in 1792 of Mary Wollstonecraft's epoch-making work *A Vindication of the Rights of Woman*—a literature urging wider opportunities for women existed. The first woman to "take up her pen in defense of her sex," according to Simone de Beauvoir, was Christine de Pisan in the fifteenth century. Feminist writers of the sixteenth century were Cornelius Agrippa, author of *The Superior Excellence of Women Over Men,* and Modesta di Pozzo di Forzi, a Venetian woman. Marie Le Jars de Gournay, a protégée of Montaigne, composed two outspoken feminist essays, *Égalité des hommes et des femmes* in 1622 and four years later, *Grief des dames.* Writing in 1642 in Colonial America, the poet Anne Bradstreet lamented: "Who sayes, my hand a needle better fits"; and Poulain de la Barre wrote *De l'égalité des deux sexes* in 1673.

The decline of feminism after the First World War is attributable at least in part to the eventual concentration of the women's movements on the single narrow issue of suffrage—which was won. Other factors which have been cited are the postwar economic depression; the growing influence of anti-feminist Freudianism; and the development in Germany and the Soviet Union of authoritarian governments which tended to foster male supremacist values. Kate Millet has described the period from 1930 to 1960 as the counter-revolution.

The majority of the selections included here are by Americans, although authors who were born in England, France, Germany, Norway, Scotland, Russia and Poland also appear. Of course, the nationality of the editor (American) has influenced the contents, since works written in English by Americans are most available and best known to me. Yet the emphasis on American writings is justified by the fact that the United States was the world center of the old feminism, except for a brief period prior to the First World War when the focus shifted to the militant English suffragists.

It was in the United States in 1848 that the first organized movement for freedom for women was founded. From then, until after the turn of the century, European feminists observed the American movement closely, copied it, and some made pilgrimages to the United States to attend conventions and meet the American leaders.

Among the American women who led the early movement, there were few who had much formal education or experience in public life. At the very first woman's rights convention at Seneca Falls, New York, no woman present dared to take the chair and preside; a man had to lead the meeting. Two years later there was a convention in the little town of Salem, Ohio, where women were the officers and men were not even allowed to speak. But this exclusion of male speakers was unusual. Most other feminist gatherings of that period were addressed by men, and a number of men were quite active in the woman's movement.

The participation of individuals from outside an oppressed class in the early stages of a liberation movement is not at all unique to feminism. Whites were active in the abolitionist movement (William Lloyd Garrison, Harriet Beecher Stowe and John Brown, for example) and theoreticians from the middle class (such as Lenin, Rosa Luxemburg and Che Guevara) were leaders in worker and peasant revolts. No historical survey of feminist writings would be complete without the works of the men included in this anthology.

A voluminous literature was generated by feminists during the latter half of the nineteenth century and the first few decades of the twentieth, in which the status of women in Western society was defined and analyzed. But there is a vast potential feminist literature from this period that is missing: the women of Eastern nations, black American women, and workingwomen—those multitudes who groaned under the heaviest yokes of bondage—created few writings.

No feminist works emerged from behind the Hindu purdah or out of the Moslem harems; centuries of slavery do not provide a fertile soil for intellectual development or expression. The insights that such writings from outside our own historical-cultural field might have offered can only be guessed at. An item to consider is the fact that today both Ceylon and India have designated women as top national leaders, something that is practically unthinkable in the United States. In no modern European nation—including the socialist states *—has any woman held a political position of the first rank.

As for black women, most were slaves or one step away from slavery during the height of the American woman's movement. Those who were free were primarily concerned with racial rather than sexual discrimination. Similarly, workingwomen tended to be totally absorbed in the struggle for bread as well as in their unremitting domestic responsibilities. When they did lift their heads to look at the larger world, they related mostly to the labor movement rather than the woman's movement. Sadly, there is little feminist writing extant by women of either group.

Themes of the Old Feminism

Contrary to popular belief, suffrage was not the sole concern of the old feminism. Votes for women was only one of a broad range of ideas which were discussed and written

---

* A single exception was Ana Pauker, who served as Rumania's Foreign Minister from 1947 to 1952.

about. In compiling this anthology, I have by-passed writings which deal entirely with the outdated topic of suffrage and have tried instead to select materials which pertain to still-unsolved feminist problems. The continued relevance of these feminist writings of a century or more ago is a measure of the lack of improvement in the basic status of women in society.

In the late eighteenth and early nineteenth centuries many early feminists identified marriage as a primary instrument of woman's oppression. Even under the repressive ethos of the Victorian period, a few brave women continued to cite the conjugal relationship as one fraught with sexual, social and economic inequality (although the organized woman's movement essentially ignored the topic). By the early twentieth century there were a number of "advanced" women who not only denounced marriage, but openly advocated sexual freedom.

Typical of this group was Isadora Duncan, who wrote in her autobiography that she had decided while still a young girl "to fight against marriage and for the emancipation of women and for the right of every woman to have a child or children as it pleased her." Duncan also commented: "Any intelligent woman who reads the marriage contract, and then goes into it, deserves all the consequences." *

Another theme of central importance to the old as well as the new feminism is the economic dependence of women. Many writers have pointed out that women who work often are paid wages below subsistence (the fallacious assumption being that all women are supported at least in part by men). In addition, great numbers of women perform onerous labor in the home which is not remunerated, while others (the ladies) do no work of any sort. Serious feminists of every generation have advocated financial self-sufficiency as a prerequisite for independence, personal fulfillment and socialization of womankind.

* *My Life* by Isadora Duncan (New York, 1927).

Finally, there is the pervasive theme of "selfhood" for women. The dominant male society suppresses woman's individuality, inhibits her intelligence and talent, and forces her to assume standards of appearance and personality that coincide with the masculine ideal of how a woman should behave and look.

Over the years many feminists have wondered: What would women be like if they were free to develop without being pressured to conform to some pattern set by men? This theme was and remains one that lies close to the heart of feminism; it evokes the visionary image of the "true woman."

Carrying on the Struggle

The strategy of the old feminist movement was to reform the unjust laws relating to women. Simultaneously, as the feminist consciousness of a growing number of women was awakened, barriers to educational and vocational advancement were assaulted. Other women took the first tentative steps outside the domestic sphere where custom had so long consigned them. Through this interaction of organizational program and individual deeds stemming from raised aspirations, many impressive advances in women's rights were made before the Civil War.

At present the new feminism is likewise primarily involved with attacking a wide variety of discriminatory laws and customs relating to such matters as abortion, work, divorce and contraception. Sexist practices in educational, religious, military and governmental institutions have been challenged by individuals who are supported and spurred on by the new women's organizations. Work on feminist consciousness-raising is progressing apace.

Without in any way denigrating the solid achievements of the American woman's movement in the years between 1848 and 1860, one may say that it did not attempt to strike at the nerve centers of male supremacy—nor could it possibly have done so. Nevertheless, there was no difficulty in finding out what these centers were; once touched, the nerves would remain sensitive for years.

For example, in 1860 Elizabeth Cady Stanton introduced the subject of liberalizing divorce laws at a woman's rights meeting. Some delegates immediately recognized this as an opening thrust in an attack on marriage. Antoinette Brown Blackwell, a minister, vociferously disagreed with the proposal. Wendell Phillips, formerly a staunch supporter of the woman's cause, not only disagreed but even suggested that the whole issue be struck from the minutes of the convention!

Stanton herself had been awaiting the right moment for this proposal for years. She had written to Susan B. Anthony prophetically in 1853: "I do not know whether the world is quite willing or ready to discuss the question of marriage. . . . I feel, as never before, that this whole question of woman's rights turns on the pivot of the marriage relation, and, mark my word, sooner or later it will be the topic for discussion. I would not hurry it on, nor would I avoid it." And after the 1860 convention debacle, she wrote again to Anthony: "With all his excellence and nobility, Wendell Phillips is a man. His words, tone, and manner came down on me like a clap of thunder. . . . How this marriage question grows on me. It lies at the foundation of all progress." *

After the Civil War some influential feminists decided that a mass organization would afford a power base through which pressure for change might be exerted. To gain mass backing, controversial and potentially divisive ideas—such as Stanton's on divorce—were dropped in favor of concentrating on the single issue of suffrage.

Many intelligent and dedicated feminists believed that attainment of the right to vote in a democratic republic like

---

* *Elizabeth Cady Stanton as Revealed in Her Letters, Diary and Reminiscences,* edited by Theodore Stanton and Harriot Stanton Blatch, Volume 2 (New York, 1922).

the United States would enable women to solve a wide spectrum of problems. (Susan B. Anthony herself finally came to favor this position.) But there remained some few individuals who reminded women that the demand for suffrage was by no means a fundamental issue of feminism. Wrote Tennessee (sometimes known as Tennie C.) Claflin as early as 1871: "If the enfranchised woman should still be compelled to remain the servile, docile, meekly-acquiescent, self-immolated and self-abnegative wife, there would be no difficulty about the voting. At the ballot-box is not where the shoe pinches. . . . It is at home where the husband, as in prehistoric times . . . is the supreme ruler, that the little difficulty arises; he will not surrender this absolute power unless he is compelled." *

Building around the issue of votes for women, a mass suffrage organization was finally achieved in the early twentieth century. However, the woman's movement by then was no longer a potent feminist force in the United States. It had grown more and more exclusive, fostering class, race and political division rather than feminist consciousness.

Inasmuch as true feminism involves a sense of sisterhood between all women, it is inextricably related to the needs of black people, of working-class people, of colonial people. There is no need to force the point; obviously, some women are black, some are workers. Furthermore, since the female sex is an oppressed group, the status of women is closely interconnected with that of all other oppressed people in the society. It seems incredible today that the platform of the leading American woman's organization in the years around the turn of the century rang with speeches that were anti-Negro and jingoistic.

Suffrage was won in the United States not through a consciousness-raising *feminist* struggle, but through a *political* battle, fought on terms defined by men within the male

---

* *Constitutional Equality, A Right of Woman,* by Tennie C. Claflin (New York, 1871).

strongholds of the Congress and state legislatures. The American suffrage movement can be usefully contrasted with the British movement led by Emmeline Pankhurst (whose tactics attracted some imitators in the United States). The Pankhurst group also was organized around a single issue—votes for women—but functioned militantly, as *feminists* and *against* the male-dominated power structure.

The words of one Englishwoman, Ida Alexa Ross Wylie, who worked with the militants, impart the feeling of unity they forged in combat: "To my astonishment, I found that women . . . could at a pinch outrun the average London bobby. Their aim with a little practice became good enough to land ripe vegetables in ministerial eyes, their wits sharp enough to keep Scotland Yard running around in circles and looking very silly. . . . The day that, with a straight left to the jaw, I sent a fair-sized CID officer into the orchestra pit of the theatre where we were holding one of our belligerent meetings, was the day of my own coming of age. . . . For two years of wild and sometimes dangerous adventure, I worked and fought alongside vigorous, happy, well-adjusted women. . . . I slept on hard floors between elderly duchesses, stout cooks, and young shopgirls. We were often tired, hurt and frightened. But we were content as we had never been. We shared a joy of life that we had never known." *

However, after the achievement of suffrage, the British movement, like the American, disintegrated. What the English lacked, despite their sense of togetherness which cut across class lines and political allegiances, was an ideology. Without a clearly defined theoretical position, no cause can weather the storms of disappointment and defeat, nor the sometimes equally devastating effects of victory. Suffrage provided the women's movements with a program, under which mass organization and even a feeling of pride in

* Quoted by Betty Friedan in *The Feminine Mystique* (New York, 1963) from *Harper's* Magazine, November, 1945.

sisterhood might flourish, but which could not supply the intellectual basis to sustain the moment.

The old feminism never, neither in the United States nor in Great Britain and the rest of Europe, moved beyond the stage of advocating reform. Despite the existence of some few ideological works which attempted to elucidate the causes for the prolonged slavery of womankind—such as those by John Stuart Mill and Friedrich Engels—feminism lacked and still has not developed a viable theoretical foundation. Mill and Engels, notwithstanding their evident sincerity, could not speak to the most profound feelings of the opposite sex; moreover, their ideas on feminism, useful though they are, seem an almost incidental extension of social philosophies which were derived from the world of men.

Can the new feminism breach the obstacles in the way of a direct attack on male supremacy? The particular vein of reform presently being mined can be worked productively for a long time. The current movement already has achieved much and is capable of achieving more in this endeavor. To move outside the reformist realm and try to effect fundamental changes in the structure of existing institutions, principally the family, is the dangerous yet exciting mission that today's radical feminists have undertaken.

The concrete facts of woman's existence have undergone profound changes in the last few generations. Improved contraception, safer childbirth and abortion, effective treatment of venereal disease, have made possible woman's control of her own body. Other medical advances, particularly in the areas of infant mortality and diseases of childhood, have resulted in the proliferation of population to the point where it now has become socially useful for women to limit their families to one or two (or no) children. Technological developments have further mechanized domestic chores. Finally, large numbers of women have received higher education and expect a full role in society.

All these factors have greatly affected the perspectives

and attitudes of women. It seems possible that a material basis for profound change in male-female relations and the relation of women to the society may now exist. But an enormous movement of women, whether organized or not, would be required before any such changes could occur. Moreover, a system of ideas—a deepened feminist critique of sexual oppression in present society along with a clear definition of *broad* future goals—would be essential, too.

Meanwhile, millions of women throughout the world are slowly groping their way toward a feminist identity. Acquaintance with the writings of sisters of the past will help in this process. Inevitably, the new forces of women's liberation, like those of the old feminism, are being accused by the organs of public opinion of unnecessary shrillness. Contemplating their long history of servitude, women today may usefully recall the words written nearly two hundred years ago by Mary Wollstonecraft: "I might have expressed this conviction in a lower key, but I am afraid it would have been the whine of affectation, and not the faithful expression of my feelings."

I

EIGHTEENTH-CENTURY REBELS

Abigail Adams

Familiar Letters of John Adams and His Wife, Abigail Adams, During the Revolution

Perhaps nothing can better exemplify the circumscribed position of women in the eighteenth century than the fact that Abigail Smith Adams (1744–1818), daughter of a respected Massachusetts minister, wife of the second President and mother of the sixth, never in her life attended any school. "Female education in the best families," she wrote, "went no further than writing and arithmetic; in some few instances, music and dancing." In failing to provide opportunities for women to obtain formal schooling outside the home, the colonists were adhering to English practice.

In the late eighteenth century political revolutions in America and France were accompanied by momentous social upheavals that put new emphasis on individual rights. The best minds of the age were speaking out in favor of democratic libertarian ideals—for free white males, at any rate. The rights of women (along with black slaves, Indians, and indentured servants) were generally ignored. Inevitably, intelligent and socially aware women like Abigail Adams drew courage from the climate to press their own claims.

In 1776, when the letters reprinted below were exchanged, John Adams was in Philadelphia attending the Continental Congress. Within months after receiving his wife's request that the "new code of laws" give some consideration "to the ladies," he was hard at work, with Thomas Jefferson, Benjamin Franklin and others drafting one of the world's great statements of human liberty—the Declaration of Independence. Yet, for the rights of women, he could summon only a smile.

Abigail Adams addressed her husband in a tone of mock-seriousness. No doubt she hoped thus to soften the effect of such brazenly outspoken remarks by a woman. Yet it is not surprising if she felt she had earned the privilege of requesting that the new government provide greater freedom for women. During her husband's extended absences she took upon herself the sole responsibility for children, home and farm, coping with the manifold deprivations and anxieties of the war. Her letters to him reveal her bravery and patriotism in the face of famine, inflation and smallpox epidemic.

Later Abigail Adams wrote to another outstanding American patriot, Mercy Otis Warren. She described the way she had pleaded the rights of women, particularly married women, in letters to her husband, and noted proudly, "I have helped the sex abundantly"; actually, her intercession on behalf of women came to naught. But eighty years later a speaker at a woman's rights convention prophesied that the best-remembered passage of all Abigail Adams' voluminous correspondence would be the one in which "she points out to her great husband, that while emancipating the world, he still believes in giving men the absolute control over women."

(to John Adams)

31 March, 1776. . . . in the new code of laws which I suppose it will be necessary for you to make, I desire you would remember the ladies and be more generous and favorable to them than your ancestors. Do not put such unlimited power into the hands of the husbands. Remember, all men would be tyrants if they could. If particular care and attention is not paid to the ladies, we are determined to foment a rebellion, and will not hold ourselves bound by any laws in which we have no voice or representation.

That your sex are naturally tyrannical is a truth so thoroughly established as to admit of no dispute; but such of you as wish to be happy willingly give up the harsh title of

master for the more tender and endearing one of friend.
Why, then, not put it out of the power of the vicious and the
lawless to use us with cruelty and indignity with impunity.
Men of sense in all ages abhor those customs which treat us
only as the vassals of your sex.

(to Abigail Adams)
14 April, 1776. As to your extraordinary code of laws, I
cannot but laugh. We have been told that our struggle has
loosened the bonds of government everywhere; that children
and apprentices were disobedient; that schools and colleges
were grown turbulent; that Indians slighted their guardians,
and Negroes grew insolent to their masters. But your letter
was the first intimation that another tribe, more numerous
and powerful than all the rest, were grown discontented.

(to John Adams)
7 May, 1776. I cannot say that I think you are very generous to the ladies; for, whilst you are proclaiming peace
and good-will to men, emancipating all nations, you insist
upon retaining an absolute power over wives. But you must
remember that arbitrary power is like most other things
which are very hard, very liable to be broken; and, notwithstanding all your wise laws and maxims, we have it in our
power, not only to free ourselves, but to subdue our masters,
and, without violence, throw both your natural and legal
authority at our feet;—"Charm by accepting, by submitting
sway, Yet have our humor most when we obey."

Mary Wollstonecraft

A Vindication of the Rights of Woman

❦

It has been said of Mary Wollstonecraft (1759–1797) that her personal history proved the need for a new interpretation of woman's rights as much as anything she wrote. As a child in England, she saw her mother abused by a tyrannical husband who drank too much and squandered what little money the family had. Later she helped a sister escape from a similarly cruel husband. She herself attempted suicide when a man with whom she had had a love affair left her immediately following the birth of their child. Some time afterward she became the mistress of the anarchist-philosopher William Godwin. When she became pregnant, she and Godwin bowed to convention and married, but the two continued to maintain separate domiciles. A daughter was born (she later became Mary Shelley, author of *Frankenstein*). Mary Wollstonecraft died of complications following this childbirth, at the age of thirty-eight.

Brilliant and talented, Wollstonecraft first had to eke out a living at whatever work was then available to a young woman: sewing, teaching, taking care of youngsters as a governess. Finally she made her way as a writer. Her book-length works include nonfiction and fiction; translations from German, French and Dutch; an anthology; collected letters; and a children's book.

Her major work, *A Vindication of the Rights of Woman,* appeared in 1792 in London and in the United States; it was the most important of a number of feminist works published in the latter part of the eighteenth century. In the United States there was *The Gleaner* by Judith Sargent Murray (who wrote under the pen name of "Constantia") and Charles Brockden Brown's *Alcuin: A Dialogue*. In France, Condorcet championed political equality for the female sex, and the playwright Olympe de Gouges proclaimed a *Declaration of the Rights of Women.*

Wollstonecraft concentrated on describing the state of ignorance and servility to which women were condemned by social custom and training. The passionate feeling with which her book is imbued gives it wide appeal and persuasive power. Four American and six English editions were published during the first hundred years of the book's life. In the United States, in the late 1860's, Susan B. Anthony's feminist newspaper *The Revolution* serialized *A Vindication of the Rights of Woman.*

Wollstonecraft's acute question—"how many generations may be necessary to give vigour to the virtue and talents of the freed posterity of abject slaves?"—still has pertinence.

The following excerpts are drawn from Chapters II, III and IV.

Men complain, and with reason, of the follies and caprices of our sex, when they do not keenly satirize our headstrong passions and groveling vices. Behold, I should answer, the natural effect of ignorance! The mind will ever be unstable that has only prejudices to rest on, and the current will run with destructive fury when there are no barriers to break its force. Women are told from their infancy, and taught by the example of their mothers, that a little knowledge of human weakness, justly termed cunning, softness of temper, *outward* obedience, and a scrupulous attention to a puerile kind of propriety, will obtain for them the protection of man; and should they be beautiful, everything else is needless, for, at least, twenty years of their lives. . . .

How grossly do they insult us who thus advise us only to render ourselves gentle, domestic brutes! For instance, the winning softness so warmly, and frequently, recommended, that governs by obeying. What childish expressions, and how insignificant is the being—can it be an immortal one? who will condescend to govern by such sinister methods! . . .

I may be accused of arrogance; still I must declare what I firmly believe, that all the writers who have written on the subject of female education and manners from Rousseau to Dr. Gregory,* have contributed to render women more artificial, weak characters, than they would otherwise have been; and, consequently, more useless members of society. I might have expressed this conviction in a lower key; but I am afraid it would have been the whine of affectation, and not the faithful expression of my feelings, of the clear result, which experience and reflection have led me to draw . . . . [I]n the works of the authors I have just alluded to . . . my objection extends to the whole purport of those books, which tend, in my opinion, to degrade one half of the human species, and render women pleasing at the expense of every solid virtue.

Though, to reason on Rousseau's ground, if man did attain a degree of perfection of mind when his body arrived at maturity, it might be proper, in order to make a man and his wife *one,* that she should rely entirely on his understanding; and the graceful ivy, clasping the oak that supported it, would form a whole in which strength and beauty would be equally conspicuous. But, alas! husbands, as well as their helpmates, are often only overgrown children; nay, thanks to early debauchery, scarcely men in their outward form—and if the blind lead the blind, one need not come from heaven to tell us the consequence. . . .

Rousseau declares that a woman should never, for a moment, feel herself independent, that she should be governed by fear to exercise her *natural* cunning, and made a coquettish slave in order to render her a more alluring object of desire, a *sweeter* companion to man, whenever he chooses to relax himself. He carries the arguments, which he pre-

---

* She refers here to *Émile or A Treatise on Education* by Jean-Jacques Rousseau and to Dr. John Gregory's, *A Father's Legacy to his Daughters.* —Ed.

tends to draw from the indications of nature, still further, and insinuates that truth and fortitude, the corner stones of all human virtue, should be cultivated with certain restrictions, because, with respect to the female character, obedience is the grand lesson which ought to be impressed with unrelenting rigour.

What nonsense! when will a great man arise with sufficient strength of mind to puff away the fumes which pride and sensuality have thus spread over the subject! If women are by nature inferior to men, their virtues must be the same in quality, if not in degree, or virtue is a relative idea; consequently, their conduct should be founded on the same principles, and have the same aim.

Connected with man as daughters, wives, and mothers, their moral character may be estimated by their manner of fulfilling those simple duties; but the end, the grand end of their exertions should be to unfold their own faculties and acquire the dignity of conscious virtue. They may try to render their road pleasant; but ought never to forget, in common with man, that life yields not the felicity which can satisfy an immortal soul. I do not mean to insinuate that either sex should be so lost in abstract reflections or distant views, as to forget the affections and duties that lie before them, and are, in truth, the means appointed to produce the fruit of life; on the contrary, I would warmly recommend them, even while I assert, that they afford most satisfaction when they are considered in their true, sober light.

Probably the prevailing opinion, that woman was created for man, may have taken its rise from Moses's poetical story; yet, as very few, it is presumed, who have bestowed any serious thought on the subject, ever supposed that Eve was, literally speaking, one of Adam's ribs, the deduction must be allowed to fall to the ground; or, only be so far admitted as it proves that man, from the remotest antiquity, found it convenient to exert his strength to subjugate his

companion, and his invention to show that she ought to
have her neck bent under the yoke, because the whole creation was only created for his convenience or pleasure. . . .

To speak disrespectfully of love is, I know, high treason
against sentiment and fine feelings; but I wish to speak the
simple language of truth, and rather to address the head
than the heart. To endeavour to reason love out of the
world, would be to out Quixote Cervantes, and equally of-
fend against common sense; but an endeavour to restrain
this tumultuous passion, and to prove that it should not be
allowed to dethrone superior powers, or to usurp the sceptre
which the understanding should ever coolly wield, appears
less wild.

Youth is the season for love in both sexes; but in those
days of thoughtless enjoyment provision should be made for
the more important years of life, when reflection takes place
of sensation. But Rousseau, and most of the male writers
who have followed his steps, have warmly inculcated that
the whole tendency of female education ought to be directed
to one point:—to render them pleasing.

Let me reason with the supporters of this opinion who
have any knowledge of human nature, do they imagine that
marriage can eradicate the habitude of life? The woman
who has only been taught to please will soon find that her
charms are oblique sunbeams, and that they cannot have
much effect on her husband's heart when they are seen
every day, when the summer is passed and gone. Will she
then have sufficient native energy to look into herself for
comfort, and cultivate her dormant faculties? or, is it not
more rational to expect that she will try to please other
men; and, in the emotions raised by the expectation of new
conquests, endeavour to forget the mortification her love or
pride has received? When the husband ceases to be a lover
—and the time will inevitably come, her desire of pleasing
will then grow languid, or become a spring of bitterness;

and love, perhaps, the most evanescent of all passions, gives place to jealousy or vanity.

I now speak of women who are restrained by principle or prejudice; such women, though they would shrink from an intrigue with real abhorrence, yet, nevertheless, wish to be convinced by the homage of gallantry that they are cruelly neglected by their husbands; or, days and weeks are spent in dreaming of the happiness enjoyed by congenial souls till their health is undermined and their spirits broken by discontent. How then can the great art of pleasing be such a necessary study? it is only useful to a mistress; the chaste wife, and serious mother, should only consider her power to please as the polish of her virtues, and the affection of her husband as one of the comforts that render her task less difficult and her life happier. But, whether she be loved or neglected, her first wish should be to make herself respectable, and not to rely for all her happiness on a being subject to like infirmities with herself.

The worthy Dr. Gregory fell into a similar error. I respect his heart; but entirely disapprove of his celebrated Legacy to his Daughters. . . .

Dr. Gregory . . . actually recommends dissimulation, and advises an innocent girl to give the lie to her feelings, and not dance with spirit, when gaiety of heart would make her feet eloquent without making her gestures immodest. In the name of truth and common sense, why should not one woman acknowledge that she can take more exercise than another? or, in other words, that she has a sound constitution; and why, to damp innocent vivacity, is she darkly to be told that men will draw conclusions which she little thinks of?—Let the libertine draw what inference he pleases; but, I hope, that no sensible mother will restrain the natural frankness of youth by instilling such indecent cautions. . . .

Of the same complexion is Dr. Gregory's advice respecting delicacy of sentiment, which he advises a woman not to acquire, if she have determined to marry. . . .

If all the faculties of woman's mind are only to be cultivated as they respect her dependence on man; if, when a husband be obtained, she have arrived at her goal, and meanly proud rests satisfied with such a paltry crown, let her grovel contentedly, scarcely raised by her employments above the animal kingdom; but, if, struggling for the prize of her high calling, she look beyond the present scene, let her cultivate her understanding without stopping to consider what character the husband may have whom she is destined to marry. Let her only determine, without being too anxious about present happiness, to acquire the qualities that ennoble a rational being, and a rough inelegant husband may shock her taste without destroying her peace of mind. She will not model her soul to suit the frailties of her companion, but to bear with them: his character may be a trial, but not an impediment to virtue. . . .

That a proper education; or, to speak with more precision, a well stored mind, would enable a woman to support a single life with dignity, I grant; but that she should avoid cultivating her taste, lest her husband should occasionally shock it, is quitting a substance for a shadow. To say the truth, I do not know of what use is an improved taste, if the individual be not rendered more independent of the casualties of life; if new sources of enjoyment, only dependent on the solitary operations of the mind, are not opened. . . .

The question is, whether it procures most pain or pleasure? The answer will decide the propriety of Dr. Gregory's advice, and show how absurd and tyrannic it is thus to lay down a system of slavery; or to attempt to educate moral beings by any other rules than those deduced from pure reason, which apply to the whole species.

Gentleness of manners, forbearance and long-suffering, are such amiable God-like qualities. . . . but what a different aspect it assumes when [gentleness] is the submissive demeanour of dependence, the support of weakness that loves, because it wants protection; and is forbearing, because it must silently endure injuries; smiling under the lash at which it dare not snarl. . . .

How women are to exist in that state where there is to be neither marrying or giving in marriage, we are not told. For though moralists have agreed that the tenor of life seems to prove that *man* is prepared by various circumstances for a future state, they constantly concur in advising *woman* only to provide for the present. Gentleness, docility, and a spaniel-like affection are, on this ground, consistently recommended as the cardinal virtues of the sex; and, disregarding the arbitrary economy of nature, one writer has declared that it is masculine for a woman to be melancholy. She was created to be the toy of man, his rattle, and it must jingle in his ears whenever, dismissing reason, he chooses to be amused. . . .

If . . . [women] be really capable of acting like rational creatures, let them not be treated like slaves; or, like the brutes who are dependent on the reason of man, when they associate with him; but cultivate their minds, give them the salutary, sublime curb of principle, and let them attain conscious dignity by feeling themselves only dependent on God. Teach them, in common with man, to submit to necessity, instead of giving, to render them more pleasing, a sex to morals. . . .

These may be termed Utopian dreams. Thanks to that Being who impressed them on my soul, and gave me sufficient strength of mind to dare to exert my own reason, till, becoming dependent only on him for the support of my virtue, I view, with indignation, the mistaken notions that enslave my sex.

I love man as my fellow; but his sceptre, real, or usurped, extends not to me, unless the reason of an individual demands my homage; and even then the submission is to reason, and not to man. In fact, the conduct of an accountable being must be regulated by the operations of its own reason; or on what foundation rests the throne of God?

It appears to me necessary to dwell on these obvious truths, because females have been insulated, as it were; and, while they have been stripped of the virtues that should clothe humanity, they have been decked with artificial graces that enable them to exercise a short-lived tyranny. Love, in their bosoms, taking place of every nobler passion, their sole ambition is to be fair, to raise emotion instead of inspiring respect; and this ignoble desire, like the servility in absolute monarchies, destroys all strength of character. Liberty is the mother of virtue, and if women be, by their very constitution, slaves, and not allowed to breathe the sharp invigorating air of freedom, they must ever languish like exotics, and be reckoned beautiful flaws in nature. . . .

[I]f strength of body be, with some show of reason, the boast of men, why are women so infatuated as to be proud of a defect? Rousseau has furnished them with a plausible excuse, which could only have occurred to a man, whose imagination had been allowed to run wild . . . that they might, forsooth, have a pretext for yielding to a natural appetite without violating a romantic species of modesty, which gratifies the pride and libertinism of man.

Women, deluded by these sentiments, sometimes boast of their weakness, cunningly obtaining power by playing on the *weakness* of men; and they may well glory in their illicit sway, for, like Turkish bashaws, they have more real power than their masters: but virtue is sacrificed to temporary gratifications, and the respectability of life to the triumph of an hour. . . .

And if it be granted that woman was not created merely to gratify the appetite of man, or to be the upper servant, who provides his meals and takes care of his linen, it must follow, that the first care of those mothers or fathers, who really attend to the education of females, should be, if not to strengthen the body, at least, not to destroy the constitution by mistaken notions of beauty and female excellence. . . .

To preserve personal beauty, woman's glory! the limbs and faculties are cramped with worse than Chinese bands, and the sedentary life which they are condemned to live, whilst boys frolic in the open air, weakens the muscles and relaxes the nerves. As for Rousseau's remarks . . . that they have naturally, that is from their birth, independent of education, a fondness for dolls, dressing, and talking—they are so puerile as not to merit a serious refutation. . . .

I have, probably, had an opportunity of observing more girls in their infancy than J. J. Rousseau—I can recollect my own feelings, and I have looked steadily around me; yet, so far from coinciding with him in opinion respecting the first dawn of the female character, I will venture to affirm, that a girl, whose spirits have not been damped by inactivity, or innocence tainted by false shame, will always be a romp, and the doll will never excite attention unless confinement allows her no alternative. Girls and boys, in short, would play harmlessly together, if the distinction of sex was not inculcated long before nature makes any difference. I will go further, and affirm, as an indisputable fact, that most of the women, in the circle of my observation, who have acted like rational creatures, or shown any vigour of intellect, have accidentally been allowed to run wild. . . .

Ah! why do women, I write with affectionate solicitude, condescend to receive a degree of attention and respect from strangers, different from that reciprocation of civility which the dictates of humanity and the politeness of civilization authorize between man and man? And, why do they not discover, when "in the noon of beauty's power," that they are treated like queens only to be deluded by hollow respect, till they are led to resign, or not assume, their natural prereogatives? Confined then in cages like the feathered race, they have nothing to do but to plume themselves, and stalk with mock majesty from perch to perch. It is true they are provided with food and raiment, for which they neither toil nor spin; but health, liberty, and virtue, are given in exchange. . . .

I lament that women are systematically degraded by receiving the trivial attentions, which men think it manly to pay to the sex, when, in fact, they are insultingly supporting their own superiority. It is not condescension to bow to an inferior. So ludicrous, in fact, do these ceremonies appear to me, that I scarcely am able to govern my muscles, when I see a man start with eager, and serious solicitude, to lift a handkerchief, or shut a door, when the *lady* could have done it herself, had she only moved a pace or two.

A wild wish has just flown from my heart to my head, and I will not stifle it though it may excite a horse-laugh. I do earnestly wish to see the distinction of sex confounded in society, unless where love animates the behaviour. For this distinction is, I am firmly persuaded, the foundation of the weakness of character ascribed to woman; is the cause why the understanding is neglected, whilst accomplishments are acquired with sedulous care: and the same cause accounts for their preferring the graceful before the heroic virtues. . . .

Women have seldom sufficient serious employment to silence their feelings; a round of little cares, or vain pursuits frittering away all strength of mind and organs, they become naturally only objects of sense. In short, the whole tenor of female education (the education of society) tends to render the best disposed romantic and inconstant; and the remainder vain and mean. In the present state of society this evil can scarcely be remedied, I am afraid, in the slightest degree; should a more laudable ambition ever gain ground they may be brought nearer to nature and reason, and become more virtuous and useful as they grow more respectable. . . .

With respect to virtue, to use the word in a comprehensive sense, I have seen most in low life. Many poor women maintain their children by the sweat of their brow, and keep together families that the vices of the fathers would have scattered abroad; but gentlewomen are too indolent to be actively virtuous, and are softened rather than refined by civilization. Indeed, the good sense which I have met with, among the poor women who have had few advantages of education, and yet have acted heroically, strongly confirmed me in the opinion that trifling employments have rendered woman a trifler. Man, taking her body, the mind is left to rust; so that while physical love enervates man, as being his favourite recreation, he will endeavour to enslave woman: —and, who can tell, how many generations may be necessary to give vigour to the virtue and talents of the freed posterity of abject slaves?

II

WOMEN ALONE

Frances Wright

Course of Popular Lectures

❦

Frances Wright (1795–1852) addressed mixed male and female audiences from lecture platforms in cities from Boston to New Orleans in the years 1828 and 1829, when such activity by a woman was considered shocking and blatantly immodest. She forthrightly presented her views on many controversial subjects; she was anti-slavery, pro-labor unions, pro-free public education, and firmly in favor of full equality for women. However, it was primarily for her advocacy of sexual freedom and atheism that she was popularly known—and vilified. To be labeled a "Fanny Wrightist" was to be placed beyond the pale of respectability.

Frances Wright was born in Scotland, orphaned in early childhood, and raised by aristocratic relatives in England. As a youngster, she read voraciously about the American Revolution and was excited by the ideas of liberty and republicanism upon which the new nation was founded. A substantial inheritance gave her the freedom to study and to travel; in 1818, at the age of twenty-three, she made her first trip to the United States.

In 1824, Wright returned to the United States as the traveling companion of Lafayette. The General, then past sixty years old, introduced her to some of the great Revolutionary heroes she had long admired from afar, including Thomas Jefferson and James Madison. When Lafayette returned to Europe, she stayed on. She had an idea for gradual emancipation of slaves that she was eager to try out.

She purchased about two thousand acres of mosquito-infested wilderness in Tennessee, near Memphis. The plan was for resident slaves to earn their freedom through labor while at the same time they were educated. She called the community "Nashoba."

The social principles on which Nashoba was based were expounded by Wright in her *Explanatory Notes, respecting the Nature and Object of the Institution at Nashoba,* in which she deplored the "servitude of matrimony" and the "opprobrium stamped upon unlegalized connections" for women and advocated the "amalgamation of the races" through miscegenation. Eventually the experiment at Nashoba had to be abandoned.

Afterward Frances Wright joined Robert Dale Owen, son of the Scotch reformer Robert Owen, in Indiana, where they edited the *New Harmony Gazette.* Then she began her daring lecture career. As if her past as founder of Nashoba were not a sufficient burden to carry before the public, she made organized religion the principal target of her speeches. During this period she lived with Owen in New York and published the *Free Enquirer.* This paper promoted feminist ideas, including birth control. (Owen was the author of a pioneering work in this field, *Moral Physiology.*) The *Free Enquirer* also supported the political activities of the Workingman's Party and many reform issues.

Frances Wright's devotion to rationalism and personal liberty underscored all her utterances. Central to her feminism was the idea that "whenever we establish our own pretensions upon the sacrificed rights of others, we do in fact impeach our own liberties." She appealed for woman's emancipation partly on the basis that men themselves were debased by the ignorance and legal inferiority of their wives and daughters. By her words, she awakened in many the discontent that comes before action; by her life, she demonstrated woman's potential for intellectual development and a widened sphere of activity.

At one lecture in New York's Masonic Hall in 1829, the indignation against Wright expressed itself in the setting of a smoky fire which nearly panicked the large crowd gathered to hear her deliver one of the talks from her *Course of Popular Lectures.* Thus, at subsequent gatherings, she began—as below —by warning the audience of possible false alarms. The following excerpts are taken from the "Introductory Address" and from "Lecture 1, On the Nature of Knowledge" and "Lecture 2, Free Enquiry."

Before we open our discussions of the evening, I would suggest to the audience, the propriety of bearing in mind the circumstances under which we meet, the former futile attempts to disturb our meetings in the Masonic Hall, and the possible presence of some mistaken and misguided individuals, ready to excite false alarm, and to take advantage of any the least disturbance, with a view to the injury of the cause of human improvement, which we are met to promote, and to the injury of the lessees of the building which we now occupy.

In case of any attempt to disturb our meeting, by cries of alarm, I beg the audience to bear in mind, that the house is under vigilant and double police. . . .

It is with delight that I have distinguished, at each successive meeting, the increasing ranks of my own sex. Were the vital principle of human equality universally acknowledged, it would be to my fellow beings without regard to nation, class, sect, or sex, that I should delight to address myself. But until equality prevail in condition, opportunity, and instruction, it is every where to the least favored in these advantages, that I most especially and anxiously incline.

Nor is the ignorance of our sex matter of surprise, when efforts, as violent as unrelaxed, are every where made for its continuance.

It is not as of yore. Eve puts not forth her hand to gather the fair fruit of knowledge. The wily serpent now hath better learned his lesson; and, to secure his reign in the garden, beguileth her *not* to eat. Promises, entreaties, threats, tales of wonder, and, alas! tales of horror, are all poured in her tender ears. Above, her agitated fancy hears the voice of a god in thunders; below, she sees the yawning pit; and, before, behind, around, a thousand phantoms, conjured from the prolific brain of insatiate priestcraft, confound, alarm, and overwhelm her reason!

Oh! were that worst evil withdrawn which now weighs upon our race, how rapid were its progress in knowledge! Oh! were men—and, yet more, women, absolved from fear, how easily and speedily and gloriously would they hold on their course in improvement! The difficulty is not to convince, it is to *win attention.* Could truth only be heard, the conversion of the ignorant were easy. And well do the hired supporters of error understand this fact. Well do they *know,* that if the daughters of the present, and mothers of the future generation, were to drink of the living waters of knowledge, their reign would be ended—"their occupation gone." So well do they know it, that, far from obeying to the letter the command of their spiritual leader, "Be ye fishers of men," we find them every where *fishers of women.* Their own sex, old and young, they see with indifference swim by their nets; but closely and warily are their meshes laid, to entangle the female of every age.

Fathers and husbands! do ye not also understand this fact? Do ye not see how, in the mental bondage of your wives and fair companions, ye yourselves are bound? Will ye fondly sport yourselves in your imagined liberty, and say, "it matters not if our women be mental slaves?" Will ye pleasure yourselves in the varied paths of knowledge, and imagine that women, hoodwinked and unawakened, will make the better servants and the easier playthings? . . .

Which of us have not seen fathers of families pursuing investigations themselves, which they hide from their sons, and, more especially, from their wives and daughters? As if truth could be of less importance to the young than to the old; or as if the sex which in all ages has ruled the destinies of the world, could be less worth enlightening than that which only follows its lead!

The observation I have hazarded may require some explanation. Those who arrogate power usually think themselves superior *de facto* and *de jure.* Yet justly might it be made a question whether those who ostensibly govern are not always unconsciously led. Should we examine closely into the state of things, we might find that, in all countries, the governed decide the destinies of the governors, more than the governors those of the governed; even as the labouring classes influence more directly the fortunes of a nation than does the civil officer, the aspiring statesman, the rich capitalist, or the speculative philosopher.

However novel it may appear, I shall venture the assertion, that, until women assume the place in society which good sense and good feeling alike assign to them, human improvement must advance but feebly. It is in vain that we would circumscribe the power of one half of our race, and that half by far the most important and influential. If they exert it not for good, they will for evil; if they advance not knowledge, they will perpetuate ignorance. Let women stand where they may in the scale of improvement, their position decides that of the race. Are they cultivated?—so is society polished and enlightened. Are they ignorant?—so is it gross and insipid. Are they wise?—so is the human condition prosperous. Are they foolish?—so is it unstable and unpromising. Are they free?—so is the human character elevated. Are they enslaved?—so is the whole race degraded. Oh! that we could learn the advantage of just practice and consistent principles! that we could understand, that every departure from principle, how speciously soever it may appear to administer to our selfish interests, invariably saps their very foundation! that we could learn that what is ruinous to some is injurious to all; and that whenever we establish our own pretentions upon the sacrificed rights of others, we do in fact impeach our own liberties, and lower ourselves in the scale of being! . . .

When, now a twelvemonth since, the friends of liberty and science pointed out to me, in London, the walls of their rising university, I observed, with a smile, that they were beginning at the wrong end: "Raise such an edifice for your young women, and ye have enlightened the nation." It has already been observed, that women, wherever placed, however high or low in the scale of cultivation, hold the destinities of humankind. Men will ever rise or fall to the

level of the other sex; and from some causes in their conformation, we find them, however armed with power or
enlightened with knowledge, still held in leading strings
even by the least cultivated female. Surely, then, if they
knew their interests, they would desire the improvement of
those who, if they do not advantage, will injure them; who,
if they elevate not their minds and meliorate not their hearts,
will debase the one and harden the other; and who, if they
endear not existence, most assuredly will dash it with poison.
How many, how omnipotent are the interests which engage men to break the mental chains of women! How many,
how dear are the interests which engage them to exalt rather
than lower their condition, to multiply their solid acquirements, to respect their liberties, to make them their equals,
to wish them even their superiors! Let them enquire into
these things. Let them examine the relation in which the
two sexes stand, and ever must stand, to each other. Let
them perceive, that, mutually dependent, they must ever be
giving and receiving, or they must be losing;—receiving or
losing in knowledge, in virtue, in enjoyment. Let them perceive how immense the loss, or how immense the gain. Let
them not imagine that they know aught of the delights
which intercourse with the other sex can give, until they
have felt the sympathy of mind with mind, and heart with
heart; until they bring into that intercourse every affection,
every talent, every confidence, every refinement, every respect. Until power is annihilated on one side, fear and obedience on the other, and both restored to their birthright—
equality. Let none think that affection can reign without it;
or friendship, or esteem. Jealousies, envyings, suspicions, re-
serves, deceptions—these are the fruits of inequality. Go,
then! and remove the evil first from the minds of women,
then from their condition, and then from your laws. Think
it no longer indifferent whether the mothers of the rising
generation are wise or foolish. Think it not indifferent
whether your own companions are ignorant or enlightened.

Think it not indifferent whether those who are to form the opinions, sway the habits, decide the destinies, of the species —and that not through their children only, but through their lovers and husbands—are enlightened friends or capricious mistresses, efficient coadjutors or careless servants, reasoning beings or blind followers of superstition.

There is a vulgar persuasion, that the ignorance of women, by favoring their subordination, ensures their utility. 'Tis the same argument employed by the ruling few against the subject many in aristocracies; by the rich against the poor in democracies; by the learned professions against the people in all countries.

George Sand

Indiana

❦

George Sand (1804–1876) was born Aurore Dupin, in Paris. She was wed at eighteen years old to one Baron Dudevant; after about eight years of marriage she suddenly left her husband. Divorce was illegal at that time in France, but she managed to obtain a decree of legal separation and custody of her two children.

As a result of Sand's tradition-shattering abandonment of the protection of home and husband, she was forced to engage in a lifelong struggle to provide a livelihood for herself and her children without the assistance of any man. Occupational opportunities for women were limited, and at first she tried to support herself in Paris by painting decorations on candlesticks and snuff boxes. Then she turned to a literary career, adopting the pen name of George Sand. Her first novel, *Indiana,* was published in 1832 and established her reputation.

Sand's flaunting of convention scandalized her contemporaries. Not only did she leave her husband and assume a masculine name, but she wore masculine attire at times and even smoked cigars. Furthermore, she had many lovers and lived openly with some of them (including Alfred de Musset and Frederic Chopin); the course of her relationships was determined by the desires of herself and the man involved without regard to the laws of church or state. One might call her a lifestyle revolutionary in the cause of freedom for women.

Her fictional works are virtually unread today, but were immensely popular during her lifetime and were known all over the world. Between 1832 and 1836 she wrote a number of romantic novels (*Indiana, Valentine, Lélia*) in which she expressed her reactions to her unhappy years of marriage. The heroine Indiana is a young woman married to a much older man, Colonel Delmare. Although she does not love her husband, Indiana is forever bound to him and subservient to his wishes by custom and by law.

In the scene from *Indiana* reprinted below, the young wife asserts the invincible strength of her individual consciousness and will—the only power of which society has not deprived her.

"Will you condescend to tell me, madam," said he, "where you spent this morning, and perhaps, last night?" . . .

"No, sir!" she answered, "my intention is not to tell you."

Delmare turned pale with surprise and anger. "Indeed!" said he in a trembling voice, "do you hope to hide it from me?"

"I do not care about it;" she resumed in an icy tone, "if I refuse to answer you, it is only for form. I wish to convince you, that you have no right to address me that question."

"I have not the right! who is master here, you or I? Who wears a petticoat, and ought to spin on a distaff? Do you pretend to take the beard from my chin? It would well become you."

"I know that I am a slave, and you are my lord. The law of this country has made you my master. You can bind my body, tie my hands, govern my actions: you are the strongest, and society adds to your power; but with my will, sir, you can do nothing. God alone can restrain it and curb it. Seek then a law, a dungeon, an instrument of torture, by which you can hold it, it as if you wished to grasp the air, and seize vacancy."

"Be silent, foolish and impertinent creature! Your romantic phrases annoy me."

"You may impose silence upon me, but you can not prevent me from thinking."

"Miserable pride! haughty worm! you abuse the pity that

is felt for you! But you will see that this proud spirit can be conquered without much trouble."

"I do not advise you to try. Your repose will suffer, and it will add nothing to your manly dignity. . . . You used violence in keeping me in my chamber. I escaped by my window to show you, that reigning over a woman's will is exercising an imaginary sway; I passed some hours out of your dominion; I have been breathing the air of liberty, to show you that you are not morally my master, and that I depend upon myself alone on this earth. In walking, I reflected that I owed it alike to duty and to conscience, to return to your protection. I did so freely. . . ."

"I pity your mental derangement," said the Colonel, shrugging his shoulder.

Letters of George Sand

The following two letters of George Sand's offer an interesting contrast between the manner in which she discussed her feminist views with a man and with a woman.

The first letter was sent by Sand to the Abbé de Lamennais, a prominent social reformer and newspaper editor. She was writing for his publication—as a contribution without pay—a series of fictional letters addressed to a young woman named "Marcie." Evidently the author wished to use these *Letters to Marcie* as a vehicle for expounding her ideas about the condition of women. However, she was not sure that Lamennais would approve. Her request is expressed diffidently and hesitantly, its seriousness underplayed; one almost feels she is trying to dissociate herself from her own ideas.

(In fact, the Abbé de Lamennais was opposed to having a defense of divorce and other such heretical opinions appear in his paper—despite the flattering and affectionate terms in which Sand addressed him. The publication of the *Letters to Marcie* was suspended.)

In writing to a young woman admirer of hers, Mlle. Leroyer de Chantepie, Sand speaks out frankly and boldly: The relations between men and women are such that woman is either enchained (marriage) or considered a culprit (outside marriage); no happiness for women is possible without the complete reformation of society.

(to the Abbé de Lamennais)
Monsieur and my good friend,*

Without knowing it, you have drawn me into a difficult field of action. When I began these *Letters to Marcie* I

* This letter is undated; it was written about 1836–37.—Ed.

expected them to appear in a less serious form than that in which they now do appear, in spite of myself because I am at the mercy of the invincible will which governs my poor reflections.

I am feeling rather alarmed about it, because during the few short hours in which I have had the joy of listening to you with the respect and veneration with which my heart is overflowing, I have never dreamed of asking your opinion on the questions which are confronting me always.

In the course of the religious and political preoccupations which fill your intellectual activities, I do not even know that you have given any consideration to present conditions of women's existence. The most curious thing to me is the fact that though I have written upon that subject throughout my literary career I hardly know what my own opinion is. . . .

However, I have embarked upon this subject and I feel that I want to extend the scope of *Letters to Marcie* as long as I can bring in questions pertaining to women. I want to touch upon all their duties, on marriage and maternity, etc. On some of these subjects I am afraid of being carried away by my natural petulance, carried further indeed, than you would permit me to go if I could consult you in advance. . . .

To confess my chief audacity briefly, I want divorce established in marriage. Search as I may for the remedies to sore injustice, endless misery, and the incurable passions which trouble the union of the sexes, I can see *no* remedy but the power of breaking and reforming the marriage bond. Of course I do not consider that it ought to be done lightly, and without less reason than those which already make a legal separation possible.

Although for my part, I would rather pass the rest of my life in a dungeon than marry again, I know of love outside marriage which is so lasting, so imperious that nothing even in the ancient civil and religious law can make the bond more solid. . . .

Answer me briefly. If you forbid me to go forward on these lines I will conclude the *Letters to Marcie* at the point they have reached and I will turn to some other task which you may appoint. I am able to keep my own counsel on many subjects and I do not feel any vocation as a reformer of the world. Adieu my father and friend, no one loves and respects you more than I do.

(to Mademoiselle Leroyer de Chantepie)
28 August, 1842. Mademoiselle . . . details of existence only present themselves to me as more or less unhappy romances which all lead to one general conclusion: society must be reformed from top to bottom.

It seems to me that it is given up to the most atrocious disorder and amongst all the iniquities which are consecrated within it, the most outstanding seems to me the relations of men and women which are established in an unjust and absurd manner. I therefore cannot advise anyone to enter into a marriage, sanctioned by the civil law which continues to support the dependence, inferiority and social nullity of the woman. I have spent ten years in reflection upon that subject and after having asked myself why all loves in this world, whether legitimised by society or not, were all more or less unhappy whatever the qualities and virtues of the souls thus associated; I convinced myself of the radical impossibility of perfect happiness and ideal love, in conditions of inequality, inferiority, and of the dependence of one sex upon the other. Whether it be by the law, whether by generally recognised morality, whether by opinion or by prejudice the fact remains that woman having given herself to man is either enchained or considered a culprit.

Now, you ask me if you can be happy through love and marriage. I do not believe that you will be happy through either, I am convinced of it. But if you ask me in what other conditions the happiness of women may be found I should tell you that as I am unable to shatter and remould society entirely, and well knowing that it will last beyond our own short sojourn here in this world, I must place the happiness of women in a future in which I firmly believe, in which we shall go back to better conditions in human life, in the bosom of more enlightened society in which our intentions will be better understood and our dignity better established.

The Intimate Journal of George Sand

๛

The following passage from George Sand's *Intimate Journal* was written at a time when she was involved in a love affair with a well-known Republican lawyer, Michel de Bourges. "Dr. Piffoël" is a literary device, Sand's alter ego, with whom she can "discuss" matters in her diary. In this instance, Sand is considering a question which perpetually claimed her attention: the nature of a love relationship in a society where women are deemed inferior and ruled absolutely by men.

13 June, 1837.

Must a woman be as blind, devoted and tireless toward her lover as a tender mother is to her first-born child?

No, Piffoël, such excessive attention is not required. Besides, it is not even noticed unless she also plies him with flattery.

Piffoël, you imagine that a woman can simply say to the object of her passion, "You are a human being like me. I selected you from among all men because I believed you the finest of them all. Today, since you often make me suffer, I am no longer certain *what* you are. It seems to me that, like other men, you are not without imperfections; after all, no man or woman is perfect. But I don't mind your faults. I don't even mind my suffering. In truth, I prefer your blemishes to other men's virtues. I accept you. You are

mine and I am yours, too, for I give all of myself to you—
my life, my ideas, my actions, my faith. Everything is subordinated to your happiness. . . .

No, no Piffoël!—although a Doctor of Psychology, you
are nothing but a fool. *That* is not the sort of talk a man
wants to hear. Devotion he expects as a matter of course,
as his natural right, for no other reason than that he is his
mother's son. He prides himself on such powers of intellect
and will that he cannot tolerate any independence on the
part of his lover. The more goodness, self-sacrifice, abnegation, and kindness she displays toward him, the more he
scorns her. She must permit herself to be ruled, possessed,
absorbed by him, for the privilege of adoring him as a god.
He is unaware that any man who is adored as a god is de-
ceived, mocked, and flattered.

A man knows when he is necessary to a woman. His self-
assurance then is fatuous. Most women, whether from avarice, or sexual desire, or vanity, are so desperate not to lose
the men they love, that they allow these men to rule their
lives absolutely. There is but one way for a woman to both
hold onto her tyrant and at the same time to lighten her
oppression: by flattering him shamelessly. Her submission,
loyalty, tenderness and devotion are received by him as his
due. Unless a woman treats him this way, he will not deign
to put up with her at all.

Still more, however, is required of her. She must prostrate
herself before him and say—"You are great, you are sublime, you are incomparable! You are more perfect than God.
Your face is radiant; in your footsteps, nectar is distilled;
you are without a single failing and every virtue is yours.
No individual is your equal. . . ."

Immodest creature, you do not want a woman who will
accept your faults, you want one who pretends that you are
faultless—one who will caress the hand that strikes her and
kiss the lips that lie to her.

All right. Since you insist on being worshipped as an idol,

seek your female in the dirt and prevent her every effort to rise from her debased condition. . . .

My dear Piffoël, you had better learn more about life. Then, next time you set about writing a novel, see if you can't show more understanding of the human heart. Never choose as your ideal woman one who is strong-minded, disinterested, brave and honest. The public will despise her and call her by the opprobrious name of Lélia,* the unfit. Unfit, yes, thank heaven! Unfit for servility or baseness, unfit for fawning on or fearing men. Stupid men—you who believe in laws which punish murder by murder and who express vengeance in calumny and defamation! But when a woman shows she is able to live without you, then your vain power gives way to fury. Your fury is punished by a smile, an adieu, and eternal unconcern!

* Lélia is the independent and unconventional heroine of Sand's romantic novel of the same name, published in 1833.—Ed.

Sarah M. Grimke

Letters on the Equality of the Sexes and the Condition of Woman

❧

Sarah Moore Grimké (1792–1873) and her younger sister Angelina (1805–1879) were born in South Carolina, to a slave-holding family. As adults, they left the South and came to Pennsylvania to live. Later, describing the agonies of conscience she had suffered on account of slavery, Sarah Grimké referred to the South as "a wilderness" in which she saw nothing "but desolation and suffering."

The sisters became devout Quakers. Angelina, the more beautiful and eloquent of the two, began to address small groups of women under the auspices of the recently organized Female Anti-Slavery Societies. Her descriptions of slavery as she had seen it quickly attracted larger and larger audiences. Soon she and Sarah were speaking before throngs of both men and women. In 1837 the sisters toured Massachusetts, lecturing on abolitionism.

Where Frances Wright had come to the lecture platform trailing rumor of scandal and attacking the church outright, the religious Grimké sisters seemed eminently respectable in their plain Quaker garb. Nevertheless, they found that the rigid limitations imposed by society on the behavior of women could not be disregarded without consequences.

The Congregationalist Clergy of Massachusetts issued a "Pastoral Letter" which was read from the pulpit of every Congregational church in the state. Without mentioning the Grimkés by name, the letter severely condemned their actions in speaking publicly and abandoning their rightful sphere which God himself had assigned. The Massachusetts clergy warned womankind that there was danger of "permanent injury" to the female character if such unwomanly activities should be pursued.

Sarah Grimké's *Letters on the Equality of the Sexes and the Condition of Woman* were originally designed to present her views on feminism but she used them as a means to answer the churchmen as well. As the datelines of the letters indicate, she wrote them while continuing her lecture tour. The central theme is woman's equal moral responsibility with man to *act* for the good of humanity. The author employs wit and acerbity as formidable weapons: all she asks of her brothers, says Grimké, is that they "take their feet from off our necks"; when women rely on men for protection, she notes sarcastically, they are apt to find "that what they have leaned upon has proved a broken reed at best, and oft a spear." She did not hesitate to declare that the word "husband" was "synonymous with tyrant." She herself never married.

Sarah Grimké's *Letters* first appeared as a series in the *New England Spectator*. Subsequently, in 1838, they were printed in pamphlet form. Below are excerpts from five of the letters, numbers I, II, III, VIII, and XIII.

Addressed to Mary S. Parker, President of the Boston Female Anti-Slavery Society.

Amesbury, 7th Mo. 11th, 1837.

My Dear Friend,—In attempting to comply with thy request to give my views on the Province of Woman, I feel that I am venturing on nearly untrodden ground, and that I shall advance arguments in opposition to a corrupt public opinion, and to the perverted interpretation of Holy Writ, which has so universally obtained. But I am in search of truth; and no obstacle shall prevent my prosecuting that search, because I believe the welfare of the world will be materially advanced by every new discovery we make of the designs of Jehovah in the creation of woman. It is impossible that we can answer the purpose of our being, unless we understand that purpose. It is impossible that we should fulfill our duties, unless we comprehend them; or live up to our privileges, unless we know what they are. . . .

We must first view woman at the period of her creation. 'And God said, Let us make man in our own image, after our likeness; and let them have dominion over the fish of the sea, and over the fowl of the air, and over the cattle, and over all the earth, and over every creeping thing that creepeth upon the earth. So God created man in his own image, in the image of God created he him, male and female created he them.' In all this sublime description of the creation of man, (which is a generic term including man and woman,) there is not one particle of difference intimated as existing between them. They were both made in the image of God; dominion was given to both over every other creature, but not over each other. Created in perfect equality, they were expected to exercise the viceregence intrusted to them by their Maker, in harmony and love. . . .

Here then I plant myself. God created us equal;—he created us free agents;—he is our Lawgiver, our King and our Judge, and to him alone is woman bound to be in subjection, and to him alone is she accountable for the use of those talents with which her Heavenly Father has entrusted her. . . .

Thine for the oppressed in the bonds of womanhood,

Sarah M. Grimké

Newburyport, 7th Mo. 17, 1837.

My Dear Sister,—In my last, I traced the creation and the fall of man and woman from that state of purity and happiness which their beneficent Creator designed them to enjoy. . . . Notwithstanding what has been urged, woman I am aware stands charged to the present day with having brought sin into the world. I shall not repel the charge by any counter assertions, although, as was before hinted, Adam's ready acquiescence with his wife's proposal, does not savor much of that superiority *in strength of mind,* which is arrogated by man. Even admitting that Eve was the greater sinner, it seems to me man might be satisfied with the dominion he has claimed and exercised for nearly six thousand years, and that more true nobility would be manifested by endeavoring to raise the fallen and invigorate the weak, than by keeping woman in subjection. But I ask no favors for my sex. I surrender not our claim to equality. All I ask of our brethren is, that they will take their feet from off our necks and permit us to stand upright on that ground which God designed us to occupy. If he has not given us the rights which have, as I conceive, been wrested from us, we shall soon give evidence of our inferiority, and shrink back into that obscurity, which the high souled magnanimity of man has assigned us as our appropriate sphere. . . .

The lust of dominion was probably the first effect of the fall; and as there was no other intelligent being over whom to exercise it, woman was the first victim of this unhallowed passion. . . . All history attests that man has subjected woman to his will, used her as a means to promote his selfish gratification, to minister to his sensual pleasures, to be instrumental in promoting his comfort; but never has he desired to elevate her to that rank she was created to fill. He has done all he could to debase and enslave her mind; and now he looks triumphantly on the ruin he has wrought, and says, the being he has thus deeply injured is his inferior.

Haverhill, 7th Mo. 17, 1837.

Dear Friend,—When I last addressed thee, I had not seen the Pastoral Letter of the General Association [of Congregational Ministers of Massachusetts]. It has since fallen into my hands, and I must digress from my intention of exhibiting the condition of women in different parts of the world, in order to make some remarks on this extraordinary document. I am persuaded that when the minds of men and women become emancipated from the thraldom of super-

stition and 'traditions of men,' the sentiments contained in
the Pastoral Letter will be recurred to with as much astonishment as the opinions of Cotton Mather and other distinguished men of his day, on the subject of witchcraft; nor
will it be deemed less wonderful, that a body of divines
should gravely assemble and endeavor to prove that woman
has no right to 'open her mouth for the dumb,' than it now is
that judges should have sat on the trials of witches, and
solemnly condemned nineteen persons and one dog to death
for witchcraft.

But to the letter. It says, 'We invite your attention to the
dangers which at present seem to threaten the FEMALE
CHARACTER with widespread and permanent injury.' I
rejoice that they have called the attention of my sex to this
subject, because I believe if woman investigates it, she will
soon discover that danger is impending, though from a
totally different source from that which the Association ap-
prehends,—danger from those who, having long held the
reins of *usurped* authority, are unwilling to permit us to fill
that sphere which God created us to move in, and who have
entered into league to crush the immortal mind of woman. I
rejoice, because I am persuaded that the rights of woman,
like the rights of slaves, need only be examined to be understood and asserted, even by some of those, who are now endeavoring to smother the irrepressible desire for mental and
spiritual freedom which glows in the breast of many, who
hardly dare to speak their sentiments.

'The appropriate duties and influence of women are
clearly stated in the New Testament. Those duties are unobtrusive and private, but the sources of *mighty power*.
When the mild, *dependent*, softening influence of woman
upon the sternness of man's opinions is fully exercised, society feels the effects of it in a thousand ways.' No one can
desire more earnestly than I do, that woman may move exactly in the sphere which her Creator has assigned her; and
I believe her having been displaced from that sphere has introduced confusion into the world. It is, therefore, of vast

importance to herself and to all the rational creation, that she should ascertain what are her duties and her privileges as a responsible and immortal being.

The New Testament has been referred to, and I am willing to abide by its decisions, but must enter my protest against the false translation of some passages by the MEN who did that work, and against the perverted interpretation by the MEN who undertook to write commentaries thereon. I am inclined to think, when we are admitted to the honor of studying Greek and Hebrew, we shall produce some various readings of the Bible a little different from those we now have.

The Lord Jesus defines the duties of his followers in his Sermon on the Mount. He lays down grand principles by which they should be governed, without any reference to sex or condition:—'Ye are the light of the world. A city that is set on a hill cannot be hid. Neither do men light a candle and put it under a bushel, but on a candlestick, and it giveth light unto all that are in the house. Let your light so shine before men, that they may see your good works, and glorify your Father which is in Heaven.' I follow him through all his precepts, and find him giving the same directions to women as to men, never even referring to the distinction now so strenuously insisted upon between masculine and feminine virtues: this is one of the anti-christian 'traditions of men' which are taught instead of the 'commandments of God.' Men and women were CREATED EQUAL; they are both moral and accountable beings, and whatever is *right* for man to do, is *right* for woman.

But the influence of woman, says the Association, is to be private and unobtrusive; her light is not to shine before man like that of her brethren; but she is passively to let the lords of the creation, as they call themselves, put the bushel over it, lest peradventure it might appear that the world has been benefitted by the rays of *her* candle. So that her quenched light, according to their judgment, will be of more use than if it were set on the candlestick. 'Her influence is the source of mighty power.' This has ever been the flattering language of man since he laid aside the whip as a means to keep woman in subjection. He spares her body; but the war he has waged against her mind, her heart, and her soul, has been no less destructive to her as a moral being. How monstrous, how anti-christian, is the doctrine that woman is to be dependent on man! Where, in all the sacred Scriptures, is this taught? Alas! she has too well learned the lesson which MAN has labored to teach her. She has surrendered her dearest RIGHTS, and been satisfied with the privileges which man has assumed to grant her; she has been amused with the show of power, whilst man has absorbed all the reality into himself. He has adorned the creature whom God gave him as a companion, with baubles and gewgaws, turned her attention to personal attractions, offered incense to her vanity, and made her the instrument of his selfish gratification, a plaything to please his eye and amuse his hours of leisure. 'Rule by obedience and by submission sway,' or in other words, study to be a hypocrite, pretend to submit, but gain your point, has been the code of household morality which woman has been taught. The poet has sung, in sickly strains, the loveliness of woman's dependence upon man, and now we find it reechoed by those who profess to teach the religion of the Bible. God says, 'Cease ye from man whose breath is in his nostrils, for wherein is he to be accounted of?' Man says, depend upon me. God says, 'HE will teach us of his ways.' Man says, believe it not, I am to be your teacher. This doctrine of dependence upon man is utterly at variance with the doctrine of the Bible. In that book I find nothing like the softness of woman, nor the sternness of man: both are equally commanded to bring forth the fruits of the Spirit, love, meekness, gentleness, etc.

But we are told, 'the power of woman is in her dependence, flowing from a consciousness of that weakness which

God has given her for her protection.' If physical weakness is alluded to, I cheerfully concede the superiority; if brute force is what my brethren are claiming, I am willing to let them have all the honor they desire; but if they mean to intimate, that mental or moral weakness belongs to woman, more than to man, I utterly disclaim the charge. Our powers of mind have been crushed, as far as man could do it, our sense of morality has been impaired by his interpretation of our duties; but no where does God say that he made any distinction between us, as moral and intelligent beings.

'We appreciate,' say the Association, 'the *unostentatious* prayers and efforts of woman in advancing the cause of religion at home and abroad, in leading religious inquirers TO THE PASTOR for instruction.' Several points here demand attention. If public prayers and public efforts are necessarily ostentatious, then 'Anna the prophetess, (or preacher,) who departed not from the temple, but served God with fastings and prayers night and day,' 'and spake of Christ to all them that looked for redemption in Israel,' was ostentatious in her efforts. Then, the apostle Paul encourages women to be ostentatious in their efforts to spread the gospel, when he gives them directions how they should appear, when engaged in praying, or preaching in the public assemblies. Then, the whole association of Congregational ministers are ostentatious, in the efforts they are making in preaching and praying to convert souls.

But woman may be permitted to lead religious inquirers to the PASTORS for instruction. Now this is assuming that all pastors are better qualified to give instruction than woman. This I utterly deny. I have suffered too keenly from the teaching of man, to lead any one to him for instruction. . . .

The General Association say, that 'when woman assumes the place and tone of man as a public reformer, our care and protection of her seem unnecessary; we put ourselves in self-defence against her, and her character becomes unnatural.' Here again the unscriptural notion is held up, that there is a distinction between the duties of men and women as moral beings; that what is virtue in man, is vice in woman; and women who dare to obey the command of Jehovah, 'Cry aloud, spare not, lift up thy voice like a trumpet, and show my people their transgression,' are threatened with having the protection of the brethren withdrawn. If this is all they do, we shall not even know the time when our chastisement is inflicted; our trust is in the Lord Jehovah, and in him is everlasting strength. The motto of woman, when she is engaged in the great work of public reformation should be,—'The Lord is my light and my salvation; whom shall I fear? The Lord is the strength of my life; of whom shall I be afraid?' She must feel, if she feels rightly, that she is fulfilling one of the important duties laid upon her as an accountable being, and that her character, instead of being 'unnatural,' is in exact accordance with the will of Him to whom, and to no other, she is responsible for the talents and the gifts confided to her. As to the pretty simile, introduced into the 'Pastoral Letter,' 'If the vine whose strength and beauty is to lean upon the trellis work, and half conceal its clusters, thinks to assume the independence and the overshadowing nature of the elm,' etc. I shall only remark that it might well suit the poet's fancy, who sings of sparkling eyes and coral lips, and knights in armor clad; but it seems to me utterly inconsistent with the dignity of a Christian body, to endeavor to draw such an anti-scriptural distinction between men and women. Ah! how many of my sex feel in the dominion, thus unrighteously exercised over them, under the gentle appellation of *protection*, that what they have leaned upon has proved a broken reed at best, and oft a spear.

Thine in the bonds of womanhood,

Sarah M. Grimké

Brookline, 1837.

My Dear Sister, ... During the early part of my life, my lot was cast among the butterflies of the *fashionable* world;

and of this class of women, I am constrained to say, both from experience and observation, that their education is miserably deficient; that they are taught to regard marriage as the one thing needful, the only avenue to distinction; hence to attract the notice and win the attentions of men, by their external charms, is the chief business of fashionable girls. They seldom think that men will be allured by intellectual acquirements, because they find, that where any mental superiority exists, a woman is generally shunned and regarded as stepping out of her 'appropriate sphere,' which, in their view, is to dress, to dance, to set out to the best possible advantage her person, to read the novels which inundate the press, and which do more to destroy her character as a rational creature, than anything else. Fashionable women regard themselves, and are regarded by men, as pretty toys or as mere instruments of pleasure; and the vacuity of mind, the heartlessness, the frivolity which is the necessary result of this false and debasing estimate of women, can only be fully understood by those who have mingled in the folly and wickedness of fashionable life. . . .

There is another and much more numerous class in this country, who are withdrawn by education or circumstances from the circle of fashionable amusements, but who are brought up with the dangerous and absurd idea, that *marriage* is a kind of preferment; and that to be able to keep their husband's house, and render his situation comfortable, is the end of her being. Much that she does and says and thinks is done in reference to this situation; and to be married is too often held up to the view of girls as the sine qua non of human happiness and human existence. For this purpose more than for any other, I verily believe the majority of girls are trained. This is demonstrated by the imperfect education which is bestowed upon them, and the little pains taken to cultivate their minds, after they leave school, by the little time allowed them for reading, and by the idea being constantly inculcated, that although all household concerns should be attended to with scrupulous punctuality at particular seasons, the improvement of their intellectual capacities is only a secondary consideration, and may serve as an occupation to fill up the odds and ends of time. In most families, it is considered a matter of far more consequence to call a girl off from making a pie, or a pudding, than to interrupt her whilst engaged in her studies. This mode of training necessarily exalts, in their view, the animal above the intellectual and spiritual nature, and teaches women to regard themselves as a kind of machinery, necessary to keep the domestic engine in order, but of little value as the *intelligent* companions of men. . . .

There is another way in which the general opinion, that women are inferior to men, is manifested, that bears with tremendous effect on the laboring class, and indeed on almost all who are obliged to earn a subsistence, whether it be by mental or physical exertion—I allude to the disproportionate value set on the time and labor of men and of women. A man who is engaged in teaching, can always, I believe, command a higher price for tuition than a woman—even when he teaches the same branches, and is not in any respect superior to the woman. This I know is the case in boarding and other schools with which I have been acquainted, and it is so in every occupation in which the sexes engage indiscriminately. As for example, in tailoring, a man has twice, or three times as much for making a waistcoat or pantaloons as a woman, although the work done by each may be equally good. In those employments which are peculiar to women, their time is estimated at only half the value of that of men. A woman who goes out to wash, works as hard in proportion as a wood sawyer, or a coal heaver, but she is not generally able to make more than half as much by a day's work. The low remuneration which women receive for their work, has claimed the attention of a few philanthropists, and I hope it will continue to do so until some remedy is applied for this enormous evil. I have known a widow, left with four or five children, to provide for, unable to leave home because her helpless babes demand her attention, compelled to earn a scanty subsistence, by making coarse shirts at 12½ cents a piece, or by taking in washing, for which she was paid by some wealthy persons 12½ cents per dozen. All these things evince the low estimation in which woman is held. There is yet another and more disastrous consequence arising from this unscriptural notion—women being educated, from earliest childhood, to regard themselves as inferior creatures, have not that self-respect which conscious equality would engender, and hence when their virtue is assailed, they yield to temptation with facility, under the idea that it rather exalts than debases them, to be connected with a superior being.

There is another class of women in this country, to whom I cannot refer, without feelings of the deepest shame and sorrow. I allude to our female slaves. Our southern cities are whelmed beneath a tide of pollution; the virtue of female slaves is wholly at the mercy of irresponsible tyrants, and women are bought and sold in our slave markets, to gratify the brutal lust of those who bear the name of Christians. In our slave States, if amid all her degradation and ignorance, a woman desires to preserve her virtue unsullied, she is either bribed or whipped into compliance, or if she dares resist her seducer, her life by the laws of some of the slave States may be, and has actually been sacrificed to the fury of disappointed passion. Where such laws do not exist, the power which is necessarily vested in the master over his property, leaves the defenceless slave entirely at his mercy, and the sufferings of some females on this account, both physical and mental, are intense. Mr. Gholson, in the House of Delegates of Virginia, in 1832, said, 'He really had been under the impression that he owned his slaves. He had lately purchased four women and ten children, in whom he thought he had obtained a great bargain; for he supposed they were his own property, *as were his brood mares.*'. . .

Thine in the bonds of womanhood,

Sarah M. Grimké

Brookline, 9th Mo., 1837.

My Dear Sister,—Perhaps some persons may wonder that I should attempt to throw out my views on the important subject of marriage, and may conclude that I am altogether disqualified for the task, because I lack experience. However, I shall not undertake to settle the specific duties of husbands and wives, but only to exhibit opinions based on the word of God, and formed from a little knowledge of human nature, and close observation of the working of generally received notions respecting the dominion of man over woman. . . .

I have already shown, that man has exercised the most unlimited and brutal power over woman, in the peculiar character of husband,—a word in most countries synonymous with tyrant. . . .

Woman, instead of being elevated by her union with man, which might be expected from an alliance with a superior being, is in reality lowered. She generally loses her individuality, her independent character, her moral being. She becomes absorbed into him, and henceforth is looked at, and acts through the medium of her husband.

In the wealthy classes of society, and those who are in comfortable circumstances, women are exempt from great corporeal exertion, and are protected by public opinion, and by the genial influence of Christianity, from much physical ill treatment. Still, there is a vast amount of secret suffering endured, from the forced submission of women to the opinions and whims of their husbands. Hence they are frequently driven to use deception, to compass their ends. They are early taught that to appear to yield, is the only way to govern. Miserable sophism! I deprecate such sentiments, as being peculiarly hostile to the dignity of woman. If she submits, let her do it openly, honorably, not to gain her point, but as a matter of Christian duty. But let her beware how she permits her husband to be her conscience-keeper. On all moral and religious subjects, she is bound to think and to act for herself. . . .

I have sometimes been astonished and grieved at the servitude of women, and at the little idea many of them seem to have of their own moral existence and responsibilities. A woman who is asked to sign a petition for the abolition of slavery in the District of Columbia, or to join a society for the purpose of carrying forward the annihilation of American slavery, or any other great reformation, not unfrequently replies, 'My husband does not approve of it.' She merges her rights and her duties in her husband. . . .

There is, perhaps, less bondage of mind among the poorer classes, because their sphere of duty is more contracted. . . . But women, among the lowest classes of society, so far as my observation has extended, suffer intensely from the brutality of their husbands. Duty as well as inclination has led me, for many years, into the abodes of poverty and sorrow, and I have been amazed at the treatment which women receive at the hands of those, who arrogate to themselves the epithet of *protectors*. Brute force, the law of violence, rules to a great extent in the poor man's domicil; and woman is little more than his drudge. They are less under the supervision of public opinion, less under the restraints of education, and unaided or unbiased by the refinements of polished society. Religion, wherever it exists, supplies the place of all these; but the real cause of woman's degradation and suffering in married life is to be found in the erroneous notion of her inferiority to man; and never will she be rightly regarded by herself, or others, until this opinion, so derogatory to the wisdom and mercy of God, is exploded, and woman arises in all the majesty of her womanhood, to claim those rights which are inseparable from her existence as an immortal, intelligent and responsible being.

Thine in the bonds of womanhood,

Sarah M. Grimké

Harriet H. Robinson

Early Factory Labor in
New England

❀

In the first decades of the nineteenth century, the introduction of power machinery to the manufacture of textiles resulted in the transfer of the labor of women from the spinning wheel at home to the factory. The ceaseless, lonely and unremunerated home manufacture of cloth and garments had long been the responsibility of women, especially of unmarried economically dependent women—hence, the word "spinster." But with the advent of the power loom, this picture began to change. In the United States at that time, labor was scarce; most men were engaged in agriculture. It was therefore necessary to entice females to work the new machines.

By the 1830's thousands of women were employed in the textile mills of New England. Among them was one, Harriet Hanson Robinson (1825–1911), who subsequently had the opportunity and ability to record their experiences as workers and as women. For she was first a mill operative in Lowell, Massachusetts, for many years and, later, an active feminist.

Lowell was one of the most important of the early mill towns. Female employees outnumbered the men by about three to one. The benevolent dictatorship under which the management supervised the lives of their employees was generally acceptable to these inexperienced young women. Their wages, after the cost of room and board was deducted, averaged about two dollars a week. Initially, the women apparently were very pleased by this pay; domestic employment or teaching paid only about one-sixth as much.

However, by 1834 the first strike relating to wages occurred at Lowell. Robinson herself told of participating in another, two years later. By 1840 the comfortable and rather easygoing working conditions Robinson described were giving way to speeded-up machinery, assignments of additional looms to each worker, and lower pay scales. A decade later, by 1850, with a ready supply of immigrant labor available, living and working conditions at Lowell and the other New England factory towns had deteriorated considerably.

It is interesting to note that throughout this early phase of industrialization, workingwomen made briefly successful efforts to organize in an attempt to improve their conditions. In 1825 female "Tailoresses" in New York staged an all-women strike. In 1844, perhaps with the model of recently formed Female Anti-Slavery Societies before them (as well as the existence of male unions), some women at Lowell founded the Lowell Female Labor Reform Association. The president, Sarah Bagley, was an articulate and militant leader. She helped to encourage the setting up of local chapters in other textile centers and attended the first convention of the New England Workingman's Association in Boston. Of thirty delegates to that meeting, ten were women.

Agitation by the so-called "mill girls," including petition campaigns in favor of limiting the workday to ten hours, led the Massachusetts Legislature to order the first government investigation of labor conditions in the United States. In 1845 six women appeared as witnesses before this investigating committee, meeting at the State House in Boston.

The committee found that the average workday ranged from more than eleven hours to thirteen and a half hours a day, depending on the season. However, they decided to take no action; the remedy, they said, lay in the mill owners' cultivation of "less love for money, and a more ardent love for social happiness"!

Harriet Robinson made the opening address at the 1881 Boston Convention of the National Woman Suffrage Association. Her published works include *Loom and Spindle,* the story of Lowell, and *Massachusetts in the Woman Suffrage Movement,* a history. The following selection is from the fourteenth annual report of the Massachusetts Bureau of Statistics of Labor, originally published in 1883.

In what follows, I shall confine myself to a description of factory life in Lowell, Massachusetts, from 1832 to 1848, since, with that phase of Early Factory Labor in New England, I am the most familiar,—because I was a part of it.

In 1832, Lowell was little more than a factory village. Five "corporations" were started, and the cotton mills belonging to them were building. Help was in great demand and stories were told all over the country of the new factory place, and the high wages that were offered to all classes of work-people; stories that reached the ears of mechanics' and farmers' sons and gave new life to lonely and dependent women in distant towns and farm-houses. Into this Yankee El Dorado these needy people began to pour by the various modes of travel known to those slow old days. The stage-coach and the canal-boat came every day, always filled with new recruits for the army of useful people. The mechanic and machinist came, each with his home-made chest of tools and his wife and little ones. The widow came with her little flock and her scanty housekeeping goods to open a board-ing-house or variety store, and so provided a home for her fatherless children. Troops of young girls came from different parts of New England, and from Canada, and men were employed to collect them at so much a head, and deliver them at the factories.

Some of these were daughters of sea captains (like Lucy Larcom *), of professional men or teachers, whose mothers, left widows, were struggling to maintain the younger children. A few were the daughters of persons in reduced circumstances, who had left home "on a visit" to send their wages surreptitiously in aid of the family purse. And some (like the writer) were the granddaughters of patriots who had fought at Bunker Hill, and had lost the family means in the war for independence. . . . Many farmers' daughters

* Larcom, who later became a teacher and a writer, is the author of *A New England Girlhood,* an autobiographical book in which she described her life as a Lowell factory worker.—Ed.

came to earn money to complete their wedding outfit, or buy the bride's share of housekeeping articles. . . .

At the time the Lowell cotton mills were started the caste of the factory girl was the lowest among the employments of women. In England and in France, particularly, great injustice had been done to her real character. She was represented as subjected to influences that must destroy her purity and self-respect. In the eyes of her overseer she was but a brute, a slave, to be beaten, pinched and pushed about. It was to overcome this prejudice that such high wages had been offered to women that they might be induced to become mill-girls, in spite of the opprobrium that still clung to this degrading occupation. At first only a few came; others followed, and in a short time the prejudice against factory labor wore away, and the Lowell mills became filled with blooming and energetic New England women. They were naturally intelligent, had mother wit, and they fell easily into the ways of their new life. . . .

The early mill-girls were of different ages. Some (like the writer) were not over ten years of age; a few were in middle life, but the majority were between the ages of sixteen and twenty-five. The very young girls were called "doffers." They "doffed," or took off, the full bobbins from the spinning-frames, and replaced them with empty ones. These mites worked about fifteen minutes every hour and the rest of the time was their own. When the overseer was kind they were allowed to read, knit, or go outside the mill-yard to play. They were paid two dollars a week. The working hours of all the girls extended from five o'clock in the morning until seven in the evening, with one-half hour each, for breakfast and dinner. Even the doffers were forced to be on duty nearly fourteen hours a day. This was the greatest hardship in the lives of these children. Several years later a ten-hour law was passed, but not until long after some of these little doffers were old enough to appear before the legislative committee on the subject [in 1847], and plead, by their presence, for a reduction of the hours of labor.

Those of the mill-girls who had homes generally worked from eight to ten months in the year; the rest of the time was spent with parents or friends. A few taught school during the summer months. Their life in the factory was made pleasant to them. In those days there was no need of advocating the doctrine of the proper relation between employer and employed. *Help was too valuable to be ill-treated.* . . .

Except in rare instances, the rights of the mill-girls were secure. They were subject to no extortion, and if they did extra work they were always paid in full. Their own account of labor done by the piece was always accepted. They kept the figures, and were paid accordingly. Though the hours of labor were long, yet they were not overworked. They were obliged to tend no more looms and frames than they could easily take care of, and they had plenty of time to sit and rest. I have known a girl to sit twenty or thirty minutes at a time. They were not driven. They took their work-a-day life easy. They were treated with consideration by their employers, and there was a feeling of respectful equality between them. . . .

It is well to consider, for a moment, some of the characteristics of the early mill-girls. We have seen that they were necessarily industrious. They were also frugal and saving. It was their custom the first of every month, after paying their board bill ($1.25 a week), to put their wages in the savings bank. There the money stayed, on interest, until they withdrew it, to carry home or to use for a special purpose. . . .

Young men and women who had spent their two or three years of probation in the Lowell Mills, often returned to the old place, bought land, built their modest houses, and became new and prosperous heads of families. Some of the mill-girls helped maintain widowed mothers, or drunken, incompetent, or invalid fathers. Many of them educated the younger children of the family and young men were sent to college with the money furnished by the untiring industry of their women relatives.

The most prevailing incentive to labor was to secure the means of education for some *male* member of the family. To make a *gentleman* of a brother or a son, to give him a college education, was the dominant thought in the minds of a great many of the better class of mill-girls. I have known more than one to give every cent of her wages, month after month, to her brother, that he might get the education necessary to enter some profession. I have known a mother to work years in this way for her boy. I have known women to educate young men by their earnings, who were not sons or relatives. There are many men now living who were helped to an education by the wages of the early mill-girls.

(These men, educated by the labor and self-sacrifice of others, sometimes acquired just enough learning to make them look down upon the social position in which their women friends and relatives were forced to remain. . . . The average woman of 40 years ago was very humble in her notions of the sphere of woman. What if she did hunger and thirst after knowledge? She could do nothing with it even if she could get it. So she made a *fetich* of some male relative, and gave him the mental food for which she herself was starving; and devoted all her energies towards helping him to become what she felt, under better conditions, she herself might have been. It was enough in those early days to be the *mother* or *sister* of somebody.) *

It is well to digress here a little, and speak of the influence the possession of money had on the characters of some of these women. We can hardly realize what a change the cot-

* In an appendix to her feminist work *Massachusetts in the Woman Suffrage Movement,* Robinson reprinted several of the paragraphs included here and added the material in parentheses.—Ed.

ton factory made in the status of the working women. Hitherto woman had always been a money *saving* rather than a money earning, member of the community. Her labor could command but small return. If she worked out as servant, or "help," her wages were from 50 cents to $1.00 a week; or, if she went from house to house by the day to spin and weave, or do tailoress work, she could get but 75 cents a week and her meals. As teacher her services were not in demand, and the arts, the professions, and even the trades and industries, were nearly all closed to her.

As late as 1840 there were only seven vocations outside the home into which the women of New England had entered. At this time woman had no property rights. A widow could be left without her share of her husband's (or the family) property, an "incumbrance" to his estate. A father could make his will without reference to his daughter's share of the inheritance. He usually left her a home on the farm as long as she remained single. A woman was not supposed to be capable of spending her own, or of using other people's money. In Massachusetts, before 1840, a woman could not, legally, be treasurer of her own sewing society, unless some man were responsible for her.

The law took no cognizance of woman as a money-spender. She was a ward, an appendage, a relict. Thus it happened, that if a woman did not choose to marry, or, when left a widow, to re-marry, she had no choice but to enter one of the few employments open to her or to become a burden on the charity of some relative.

In almost every New England home could be found one or more of these women sitting "solitary" in the family; sometimes welcome, more often unwelcome; leading joyless, and in many instances, unsatisfactory lives. The cotton factory was a great opening to these lonely and dependent women. From a condition of almost pauperism they were placed at once above want. They could earn money and spend it as they pleased. They could gratify their tastes and desires without restraint and without rendering an account to anybody.

At last they had found a place in the universe, and were no longer obliged to finish out their faded lives a burden to their male relatives. Even the *time* of these women was their own, on Sundays, and in the evening, after the day's work was done. . . .

By reading the weekly newspapers the girls became interested in public events. They knew all about the Mexican war, and the anti-slavery cause had its adherents among them. Lectures on the doctrine of Fourier were read, or listened to, and some of them were familiar with, and discussed the Brook Farm experiment.

Mrs. Bloomer, that pioneer of the modern dress reform, found followers in Lowell; and parlor meetings were held at some of the boarding-houses to discuss the feasibility of this great revolution in the style of woman's dress.

One of the first strikes that ever took place in this country was in Lowell in 1836. When it was announced that the wages were to be cut down, great indignation was felt, and it was decided to strike or "turn out" *en masse*. This was done. The mills were shut down, and the girls went from their several corporations in procession to the grove on Chapel Hill, and listened to incendiary speeches from some early labor reformers.

One of the girls stood on a pump and gave vent to the feelings of her companions in a neat speech, declaring that it was their duty to resist all attempts at cutting down the wages. This was the first time a woman had spoken in public in Lowell, and the event caused surprise and consternation among her audience. One of the number (the writer), a little girl eleven years old, had led the turn-out from the room in which she worked. She was a "little doffer," and they called her a ring-leader.

It is hardly necessary to say that, so far as practical results are concerned, this strike did no good.

The corporations would not come to terms. The girls were soon tired of holding out, and they went back to their work at the reduced rate of wages. The ill-success of this early attempt at resistance on the part of the wage element seems to have made a precedent for the issue of many succeeding strikes. . . .

They [the mill girls] went forth from their *Alma Mater*, the Lowell Factory, carrying with them the independence, the self-reliance taught in that hard school, and they have done their little part towards performing the useful labor of life. Into whatever vocation they entered they made practical use of the habits of industry and perseverance learned during those early years.

Skilled labor teaches something not to be found in books or in colleges. Their early experience developed their characters . . . and helped them to fight well the battle of life.

Thomas Hood

Song of the Shirt

❧

The *Song of the Shirt* by Thomas Hood (1799–1845) first appeared in the Christmas issue of *Punch* in 1843. It was an instant sensation. At the time, in England, there was a good deal of public interest in the plight of workingwomen. The previous year, a government commission had issued its first report on workingwomen and children, which included horrifying testimony regarding the inhuman conditions under which they toiled in the mines. In addition, there was a growing literature depicting the lives of virtual slavery led by thousands of women who labored at home industries for a pittance.

The *Song of the Shirt* was reprinted in the United States in 1851 in a newspaper story concerned with efforts of women seamstresses in New York to form a "Shirt Sewers' Co-Operative Union" and was also included in the published proceedings of that year's Woman's Rights Convention.

When Thomas Hood died, contributions were raised to erect a monument over his grave. The monument reads: "He sang the Song of the Shirt."

With fingers weary and worn,
With eyelids heavy and red,
A woman sat in unwomanly rags,
Plying her needle and thread:
Stitch! stitch! stitch!
In poverty, hunger, and dirt;

And still, with a voice of dolorous pitch,
She sang the "Song of the Shirt"!

Work! work! work!
While the cock is crowing aloof!
And work—work—work,
Till the stars shine through the roof!
It's oh! to be a slave
Along with the barbarous Turk,
Where woman has never a soul to save,
If this is Christian work!

Work—work—work!
Till the brain begins to swim;
Work—work—work!
Till the eyes are heavy and dim!
Seam, and gusset, and band,
Band, and gusset, and seam,
Till over the buttons I fall asleep,
And sew them on in my dreams!

Oh men, with sisters dear!
Oh men, with mothers and wives!
It is not linen you're wearing out,
But human creatures' lives!
Stitch—stitch—stitch!
In poverty, hunger, and dirt,
Sewing at once, with a double thread,
A shroud as well as a shirt!

But why do I talk of death,
That phantom of grisly bone?
I hardly fear his terrible shape,
It seems so like my own—
It seems so like my own,
Because of the fasts I keep:
Oh God! that bread should be so dear
And flesh and blood so cheap!

Work—work—work!
My labor never flags;
And what are its wages? A bed of straw,
A crust of bread, and rags;
A shattered roof, and this naked floor,
A table, a broken chair,
And a wall so blank, my shadow I thank
For sometimes falling there!

Work—work—work!
From weary chime to chime;
Work—work—work,
As prisoners work for crime!
Band, and gusset, and seam,
Seam, and gusset, and band,—
Till the heart is sick, and the brain benumbed,
As well as the weary hand!

Work—work—work,
In the dull December light;
And work—work—work,
When the weather is warm and bright;
While underneath the eaves
The brooding swallows cling,
As if to show me their sunny backs
And twit me with the spring.

Oh! but to breathe the breath
Of the cowslip and primrose sweet,
With the sky above my head,
And the grass beneath my feet;
For only one short hour
To feel as I used to feel,
Before I knew the woes of want,
And the walk that costs a meal!

Oh, but for one short hour!
A respite, however brief!—

No blessed leisure for love or hope,
But only time for grief!
A little weeping would ease my heart,
But in their briny bed
My tears must stop, for every drop
Hinders needle and thread!

With fingers weary and worn,
With eyelids heavy and red,
A woman sat in unwomanly rags,
Plying her needle and thread:
Stitch! stitch! stitch!
In poverty, hunger, and dirt;
And still, with a voice of dolorous pitch—
Would that its tone could reach the rich!—
She sang this "Song of the Shirt."

Margaret Fuller

Woman in the Nineteenth Century

֎

Margaret Fuller (1810–1850) had extraordinary intellectual
attainments which brought her to the attention of some of the
outstanding thinkers and writers of her day. She eventually became the "high priestess" of the New England Transcendentalist
group, which included Ralph Waldo Emerson, Bronson Alcott,
and others. For two years, from 1840–1842, she edited the
quarterly journal *The Dial*.

During this period in New England, many women were beginning to move outside the confines of their domestic province.
A few were active on the lecture platforms; some were involved
in political activity through the Female Anti-Slavery Societies;
thousands had entered new avenues of employment outside the
home, such as the textile mills. Moreover, several institutions of
higher education recently had been opened for women.

In this atmosphere, Margaret Fuller launched her famous
series of "conversations" for the women of Boston's intellectual
circles in the West Street Bookshop. With Fuller firmly in command, the women exchanged ideas and information on such
subjects as Classical Mythology and What Is Life? In addition,
the special interests and needs of women were frequently considered during the five years that these discussion groups continued.

In 1844 Fuller left Boston for New York, where she worked
as literary editor for Horace Greeley's New York *Tribune*. She
was the first female editor of a major American newspaper.
The following year her book *Woman in the Nineteenth Century*
was published. (A shorter version entitled "The Great Lawsuit
—Man *versus* Men; Woman *versus* Women" had appeared two

years before in *The Dial.*) The book, which was denounced as immoral and foolish at its publication, was extremely popular. Through this work, Fuller became the most significant influence on the thought of her countrywomen.

In general, Fuller's feminism was based on a belief that "every arbitrary barrier" to woman's full development should be thrown down. In a bewildering mix of mysticism and pragmatism, Fuller predicted that the outcome of such a letting down of barriers would be a "ravishing harmony of the spheres" as well as the emergence of female sea captains. ("I do not doubt there are women well fitted for such an office," she wrote.) Sensing correctly that women were on the threshold of a new day, Fuller advised that they "retire within themselves" to discover their true nature. The favored condition for this period of meditation, as she saw it, was total independence of men, apparently including sexual abstinence.

Of all . . . banners, none has been more steadily upheld, and under none have more valor and willingness for real sacrifices been shown, than that of the champions of the enslaved African. And this band it is, which, partly from a natural following out of principles, partly because many women have been prominent in that cause, makes, just now, the warmest appeal in behalf of Woman.

Though there has been a growing liberality on this subject, yet society at large is not so prepared for the demands of this party, but that its members are, and will be for some time, coldly regarded as the Jacobins of their day.

"Is it not enough," cries the irritated trader, "that you have done all you could to break up the national union, and thus destroy the prosperity of our country, but now you must be trying to break up family union, to take my wife away from the cradle and the kitchen-hearth to vote at polls, and preach from a pulpit? Of course, if she does such things, she cannot attend to those of her own sphere. She is happy enough as she is. She has more leisure than I have,—every means of improvement, every indulgence."

"Have you asked her whether she was satisfied with these *indulgences?*"

"No, but I know she is. She is too amiable to desire what would make me unhappy, and too judicious to wish to step beyond the sphere of her sex. I will never consent to have our peace disturbed by any such discussions."

"Consent—you? It is not consent from you that is in question—it is assent from your wife."

"Am not I the head of my house?"

"You are not the head of your wife. God has given her a mind of her own."

"I am the head, and she the heart."

"God grant you play true to one another, then! I suppose I am to be grateful that you did not say she was only the hand. If the head repress no natural pulse of the heart, there can be no question as to your giving your consent. Both will be of one accord, and there needs but to present any question to get a full and true answer. There is no need of precaution, of indulgence, or consent. But our doubt is whether the heart *does* consent with the head, or only obeys its decrees with a passiveness that precludes the exercise of its natural powers, or a repugnance that turns sweet qualities to bitter, or a doubt that lays waste the fair occasions of life. It is to ascertain the truth that we propose some liberating measures."

Thus vaguely are these questions proposed and discussed at present. But their being proposed at all implies much thought, and suggests more. Many women are considering within themselves what they need that they have not, and what they can have if they find they need it. Many men are considering whether women are capable of being and having more than they are and have, *and* whether, if so, it will be best to consent to improvement in their condition.

This morning, I open the Boston "Daily Mail," and find

in its "poet's corner" a translation of Schiller's "Dignity of Woman." In the advertisement of a book on America, I see in the table of contents this sequence, "Republican Institutions. American Slavery. American Ladies."

I open the *"Deutsche Schnellpost,"* published in New York, and find at the head of a column, . . . "Emancipation of Jews and Women in Hungary."

The past year has seen action in the Rhode Island legislature, to secure married women rights over their own property. . . .

These symptoms of the times have come under my view quite accidentally: one who seeks may, each month or week, collect more. . . .

But to return to the historical progress of this matter. Knowing that there exists in the minds of men a tone of feeling toward women as toward slaves, such as is expressed in the common phrase, "Tell that to women and children;" that the infinite soul can only work through them in already ascertained limits; that the gift of reason, Man's highest prerogative, is allotted to them in much lower degree; that they must be kept from mischief and melancholy by being constantly engaged in active labor, which is to be furnished and directed by those better able to think, etc., etc.,—we need not multiply instances, for who can review the experience of last week without recalling words which imply, whether in jest or earnest, these views, or views like these,—knowing this, can we wonder that many reformers think that measures are not likely to be taken in behalf of women, unless their wishes could be publicly represented by women?

"That can never be necessary," cry the other side. "All men are privately influenced by women; each has his wife, sister, or female friends, and is too much biased by these relations to fail of representing their interests; and, if this is not enough, let them propose and enforce their wishes with the pen. The beauty of home would be destroyed, the delicacy of the sex be violated, the dignity of halls of legislation degraded, by an attempt to introduce them there. Such duties are inconsistent with those of a mother;" and then we have ludicrous pictures of ladies in hysterics at the polls, and senate-chambers filled with cradles.

But if, in reply, we admit as truth that Woman seems destined by nature rather for the inner circle, we must add that the arrangements of civilized life have not been, as yet, such as to secure it to her. Her circle, if the duller, is not the quieter. If kept from "excitement," she is not from drudgery. Not only the Indian squaw carries the burdens of the camp, but the favorites of Louis XIV accompany him in his journeys, and the washerwoman stands at her tub, and carries home her work at all seasons, and in all states of health. Those who think the physical circumstances of Woman would make a part in the affairs of national government unsuitable, are by no means those who think it impossible for negresses to endure field-work, even during pregnancy, or for seamstresses to go through their killing labors.

As to the use of the pen, there was quite as much opposition to Woman's possessing herself of that help to free agency as there is now to her seizing on the rostrum or the desk; and she is likely to draw, from a permission to plead her cause that way, opposite inferences to what might be wished by those who now grant it.

As to the possibility of her filling with grace and dignity any such position, we should think those who had seen the great actresses and heard the Quaker preachers of modern times would not doubt that Woman can express publicly the fulness of thought and creation, without losing any of the peculiar beauty of her sex. What can pollute and tarnish is to act thus from any motive except that something needs to be said or done. Woman could take part in the processions, the songs, the dances of old religion; no one fancied her delicacy was impaired by appearing in public for such a cause.

As to her home, she is not likely to leave it more than

she now does for balls, theaters, meetings for promoting missions, revival meetings, and others to which she flies, in hope of an animation for her existence commensurate with what she sees enjoyed by men. Governors of ladies'-fairs are no less engrossed by such a charge, than the governor of a state by his; presidents of Washingtonian societies no less away from home than presidents of conventions. If men look straitly to it, they will find that, unless their lives are domestic, those of the women will not be. A house is no home unless it contain food and fire for the mind as well as for the body. The female Greek, of our day, is as much in the street as the male to cry, "What news?" We doubt not it was the same in Athens of old. The women, shut out from the market-place, made up for it at the religious festivals. For human beings are not so constituted that they can live without expansion. If they do not get it in one way, they must in another, or perish.

As to men's representing women fairly at present, while we hear from men who owe to their wives not only all that is comfortable or graceful, but all that is wise, in the arrangement of their lives, the frequent remark, "You cannot reason with a woman,"—when from those of delicacy, nobleness, and poetic culture, falls the contemptuous phrase "women and children," and that in no light sally of the hour, but in works intended to give a permanent statement of the best experiences,—when not one man, in the million, shall I say? no, not in the hundred million, can rise above the belief that Woman was made *for Man*,—when such traits as these are daily forced upon the attention, can we feel that Man will always do justice to the interests of Woman? Can we think that he takes a sufficiently discerning and religious view of her office and destiny *ever* to do her justice, except when prompted by sentiment—accidentally or transiently, that is, for the sentiment will vary according to the relations in which he is placed? The lover, the poet, the artist, are likely to view her nobly. The father and the philosopher have some chance of liberality; the man of the world, the legislator for expediency, none.

Under these circumstances, without attaching importance, in themselves, to the changes demanded by the champions of Woman, we hail them as signs of the times. We would have every arbitrary barrier thrown down. We would have every path laid open to Woman as freely as to Man. Were this done, and a slight temporary fermentation allowed to subside, we should see crystallizations more pure and of more various beauty. We believe the divine energy would pervade nature to a degree unknown in the history of former ages, and that no discordant collision, but a ravishing harmony of the spheres, would ensue.

Yet, then and only then will mankind be ripe for this, when inward and outward freedom for Woman as much as for Man shall be acknowledged as a *right,* not yielded as a concession. As the friend of the negro assumes that one man cannot by right hold another in bondage, so should the friend of Woman assume that Man cannot by right lay even well-meant restrictions on Woman. If the negro be a soul, if the woman be a soul, apparelled in flesh, to one Master only are they accountable. There is but one law for souls, and, if there is to be an interpreter of it, he must come not as man, or son of man, but as son of God.

Were thought and feeling once so far elevated that Man should esteem himself the brother and friend, but nowise the lord and tutor, of Woman,—were he really bound with her in equal worship,—arrangements as to function and employment would be of no consequence. What Woman needs is not as a woman to act or rule, but as a nature to grow, as an intellect to discern, as a soul to live freely and unimpeded, to unfold such powers as were given her when we left our common home. If fewer talents were given her, yet if allowed the free and full employment of these, so that she may render back to the giver his own with usury, she will not complain. . . .

Mary Wollstonecraft, like Madame Dudevant (commonly known as George Sand) in our day, was a woman whose existence better proved the need of some new interpretation of Woman's Rights than anything she wrote. Such beings as these, rich in genius, of most tender sympathies, capable of high virtue and a chastened harmony, ought not to find themselves, by birth, in a place so narrow, that, in breaking bonds, they become outlaws. Were there . . . room in the world for such . . . they would not run their heads so wildly against the walls, but prize their shelter rather. They find their way, at last, to light and air, but the world will not take off the brand it has set upon them. The champion of the Rights of Woman found in Godwin, one who would plead that cause like a brother. . . . George Sand smokes, wears male attire, wishes to be addressed as *"Mon frère;"*—perhaps, if she found those who were as brothers indeed, she would not care whether she were brother or sister. . . .

This author, beginning like the many in assault upon bad institutions, and external ills, yet deepening the experience through comparative freedom, sees at last that the only efficient remedy must come from individual character. These bad institutions indeed, it may always be replied, prevent individuals from forming good character, therefore we must remove them. Agreed; yet keep steadily the higher aim in view. Could you clear away all the bad forms of society, it is vain, unless the individual begin to be ready for better. There must be a parallel movement in these two branches of life. And all the rules left by Moses availed less to further the best life than the living example of one Messiah.

Still the mind of the age struggles confusedly with these problems, better discerning as yet the ill it can no longer bear, than the good by which it may supersede it. But women like Sand will speak now and cannot be silenced;

their characters and their eloquence alike foretell an era
when such as they shall easier learn to lead true lives. . . .

If any individual live too much in relations, so that he
becomes a stranger to the resources of his own nature, he
falls, after a while, into a distraction, or imbecility, from
which he can only be cured by a time of isolation, which
gives the renovating fountains time to rise up. With a society it is the same. Many minds, deprived of the tradition-
ary or instinctive means of passing a cheerful existence,
must find help in self-impulse, or perish. It is therefore that,
while any elevation, in the view of union, is to be hailed
with joy, we shall not decline celibacy as the great fact of
the time. It is one from which no vow, no arrangement, can
at present save a thinking mind. For now the rowers are
pausing on their oars; they wait a change before they can
pull together. All tends to illustrate the thought of a wise
contemporary. Union is only possible to those who are units.
To be fit for relations in time, souls, whether of Man or
Woman, must be able to do without them in the spirit.

It is therefore that I would have Woman lay aside all
thought, such as she habitually cherishes, of being taught
and led by men. I would have her, like the Indian girl, dedi-
cate herself to the Sun, the Sun of Truth, and go nowhere if
his beams did not make clear the path. I would have her
free from compromise, from complaisance, from helplessness, because I would have her good enough and strong
enough to love one and all beings, from the fulness, not the
poverty of being.

Men, as at present instructed, will not help this work, because they also are under the slavery of habit. . . .

[M]en do *not* look at both sides, and women must leave
off asking them and being influenced by them, but retire
within themselves, and explore the ground-work of life till
they find their peculiar secret. Then, when they come forth
again, renovated and baptized, they will know how to turn
all dross to gold, and will be rich and free though they live

in a hut, tranquil if in a crowd. Then their sweet singing shall not be from passionate impulse, but the lyrical overflow of a divine rapture, and a new music shall be evolved from this many-chorded world.

Grant her, then, for a while, the armor and the javelin. Let her put from her the press of other minds, and meditate in virgin loneliness. . . .

O men! I speak not to you. . . .

But to you women, American women, a few words may not be addressed in vain. One here and there may listen.

Married Women's Property
Act, New York, 1848

For over seventy years after Abigail Adams complained that the law granted "unlimited power" to husbands, the legal status of married women remained essentially unchanged. The body of laws that most affected the position of women was English common law, described by Robert Dale Owen to the Indiana Legislature as "the barbarous relics of a feudal despotic system."

According to Sir William Blackstone, author of the *Commentaries on the Laws of England* (first published in 1765), "the husband and the wife are one person in law; that is, the very being or legal existence of the woman is suspended during her marriage, or at least, is consolidated into that of her husband." Blackstone, for over a century, was the standard textbook for law students in the United States. Although the provisions of common law might in practice be circumvented by other legal arrangements that took precedence, these provisions nevertheless reflected the prevailing juridical attitudes toward women.

A revised property law for married women was first introduced in the New York State Legislature in 1836. A fortuitous coincidence was the arrival in the United States from England that same year of a young Polish woman, Ernestine Rose. As a teenager in Poland, she had successfully defended in court her right to her deceased mother's estate as against the claim of a spurned fiancé with whom her father had negotiated a marriage contract—with her inheritance as security. Thus, she was especially sensitive to the legal disabilities of women. The very year that she landed in America, she began a door-to-door petition campaign in support of the new property bill.

The solitary campaign that Ernestine Rose began in 1836 was continued by her and others for twelve years. In 1840 Elizabeth Cady Stanton and Paulina Wright Davis joined her in her efforts. The law finally enacted in 1848 was the first of its kind in the nation. Its passage was probably influenced by the agitation of wealthy Dutch landowners in the state (who hated to see property pass out of the hands of daughters) as well as by the petition signatures of numerous women. But the petition campaign had another effect that was, in the long run, far more significant than the passage of the legal measure.

For the first time women had engaged in political activity not on behalf of others (for some years women had been collecting signatures on anti-slavery petitions) but in order to solve their own problems *as women*. Furthermore, this activity had been organized and carried out independently of the guidance or encouragement of men. The three women who were most active in the petitioning were all to play leadership roles in the woman's rights movement.

Said Ernestine Rose of the 1848 Married Women's Property Act, which was designed to protect women of means, it was "not much . . . only for the favored few and not for the suffering many. But it was a beginning and an important step."

The People of the State of New York, represented in Senate and Assembly, do enact as follows:

I The real and personal property of any female who may hereafter marry, and which she shall own at the time of her marriage, and the rents, issues and profits thereof, shall not be subject to the disposal of her husband nor be liable for his debts and shall continue her sole and separate property as if she were a single female.

II The real and personal property and the rents, issues and profits thereof of any female now married shall not be subject to the disposal of her husband; but shall be her sole and separate property as if she were a single female except so far as the same may be liable for the debts of her husband heretofore contracted.

III It shall be lawful for any married female to receive by gift, grant device or bequest, from any person other than her husband and to hold to her sole and separate use, as if she were a single female, real and personal property and the rents, issues and profits thereof, and the same shall not be subject to the disposal of her husband, nor be liable for his debts.

IV All contracts made between persons in contemplation of marriage shall remain in full force after such marriage takes place.

III

AN AMERICAN
WOMAN'S
MOVEMENT

Declaration of Sentiments
and Resolutions,
Seneca Falls

The Seneca Falls Declaration is the single most important document of the nineteenth-century American woman's movement.
It was adopted at a meeting called to consider the "social, civil,
and religious condition and rights of woman," which assembled
at the Wesleyan Chapel at Seneca Falls, New York, on July 19,
1848. The only advertised speaker at the meeting was Lucretia
Mott, of Philadelphia, who was already widely known and experienced in public address through her anti-slavery speeches
and as a Quaker "minister." The impelling force behind the
meeting, however, was Elizabeth Cady Stanton.

Stanton and Mott had first met eight years earlier in London,
at the World's Anti-Slavery Convention. There they witnessed
the exclusion from the convention of all the female delegates,
solely on the basis of sex. Later Stanton wrote that this discrimination against women at the London gathering of reformers "stung many women into new thought and action." She and
Lucretia Mott promised each other at that time to try to do
something to improve woman's lot.

Back in the United States, the newly married Stanton settled
in Boston, where the society of many eminent reformers was
both stimulating and congenial. However, after six years she and
her family moved to Seneca Falls in northern New York State
and there her dissatisfaction with woman's portion was deepened. She felt isolated and burdened with the care of house and
children (eventually there were seven).

She wrote in her memoirs: "My experiences at the World's
Anti-Slavery Convention, all I had read of the legal status of
women, and the oppression I saw everywhere, together swept
across my soul, intensified now by many personal experiences.

. . . In this tempest-tossed condition of mind I received an invitation to spend the day with Lucretia Mott. . . . I poured out the torrent of my long-accumulating discontent with such vehemence and indignation that I stirred myself, as well as the rest of the party."

Then and there the decision was made to call a woman's rights meeting. Only a few days before the convention was scheduled to begin, Stanton, with Lucretia Mott and others, drew up the Seneca Falls Declaration of Sentiments and Resolutions, using the Declaration of Independence as a model.

This use of the Declaration of Independence was particularly appropriate to the time. For in 1848, in England, France, Germany, Austria and elsewhere, people were taking to the streets, seeking the fulfillment of liberal democratic rights proclaimed in the great documents of the French and American Revolutions and, in many instances, demanding new economic rights for workers. Presaging the political and social storms of the future, that very same year Marx and Engels penned and issued the *Communist Manifesto*.

About three hundred persons appeared at the chapel in Seneca Falls on the appointed day. James Mott, husband of Lucretia, chaired the convention. The Declaration of Sentiments was read to the assembly and adopted. Eleven resolutions were adopted unanimously; a twelfth—that pertaining to granting women elective franchise—passed by a narrow margin only after Frederick Douglass stoutly defended it from the floor.

When, in the course of human events, it becomes necessary for one portion of the family of man to assume among the people of the earth a position different from that which they have hitherto occupied, but one to which the laws of nature and of nature's God entitle them, a decent respect to the opinions of mankind requires that they should declare the causes that impel them to such a course.

We hold these truths to be self-evident: that all men and women are created equal; that they are endowed by their Creator with certain inalienable rights; that among these are life, liberty, and the pursuit of happiness; that to secure these rights governments are instituted, deriving their just powers from the consent of the governed. Whenever any form of government becomes destructive of these ends, it is the right of those who suffer from it to refuse allegiance to it, and to insist upon the institution of a new government, laying its foundation on such principles, and organizing its powers in such form, as to them shall seem most likely to effect their safety and happiness. Prudence, indeed, will dictate that governments long established should not be changed for light and transient causes; and accordingly all experience hath shown that mankind are more disposed to suffer, while evils are sufferable, than to right themselves by abolishing the forms to which they were accustomed. But when a long train of abuses and usurpations, pursuing invariably the same object evinces a design to reduce them under absolute despotism, it is their duty to throw off such government, and to provide new guards for their future security. Such has been the patient sufferance of the women under this government, and such is now the necessity which constrains them to demand the equal station to which they are entitled.

The history of mankind is a history of repeated injuries and usurpations on the part of man toward woman, having in direct object the establishment of an absolute tyranny over her. To prove this, let facts be submitted to a candid world.

He has never permitted her to exercise her inalienable right to the elective franchise.

He has compelled her to submit to laws, in the formation of which she had no voice.

He has withheld from her rights which are given to the most ignorant and degraded men—both natives and foreigners.

Having deprived her of this first right of a citizen, the elective franchise, thereby leaving her without representation in the halls of legislation, he has oppressed her on all sides.

He has made her, if married, in the eye of the law, civilly dead.

He has taken from her all right in property, even to the wages she earns.

He has made her, morally, an irresponsible being, as she can commit many crimes with impunity, provided they be done in the presence of her husband. In the covenant of marriage, she is compelled to promise obedience to her husband, he becoming, to all intents and purposes, her master—the law giving him power to deprive her of her liberty, and to administer chastisement.

He has so framed the laws of divorce, as to what shall be the proper causes, and in case of separation, to whom the guardianship of the children shall be given, as to be wholly regardless of the happiness of women—the law, in all cases, going upon a false supposition of the supremacy of man, and giving all power into his hands.

After depriving her of all rights as a married woman, if single, and the owner of property, he has taxed her to support a government which recognizes her only when her property can be made profitable to it.

He has monopolized nearly all the profitable employments, and from those she is permitted to follow, she receives but a scanty remuneration. He closes against her all the avenues to wealth and distinction which he considers most honorable to himself. As a teacher of theology, medicine, or law, she is not known.

He has denied her the facilities for obtaining a thorough education, all colleges being closed against her.

He allows her in Church, as well as State, but a subordinate position, claiming Apolstolic authority for her exclusion from the ministry, and, with some exceptions, from any public participation in the affairs of the Church.

He has created a false public sentiment by giving to the

world a different code of morals for men and women, by which moral delinquencies which exclude women from society, are not only tolerated, but deemed of little account in man.

He has usurped the prerogative of Jehovah himself, claiming it as his right to assign for her a sphere of action, when that belongs to her conscience and to her God.

He has endeavored, in every way that he could, to destroy her confidence in her own powers, to lessen her self-respect, and to make her willing to lead a dependent and abject life.

Now, in view of this entire disfranchisement of one-half the people of this country, their social and religious degradation—in view of the unjust laws above mentioned, and because women do feel themselves aggrieved, oppressed, and fraudulently deprived of their most sacred rights, we insist that they have immediate admission to all the rights and privileges which belong to them as citizens of the United States.

In entering upon the great work before us, we anticipate no small amount of misconception, misrepresentation, and ridicule; but we shall use every instrumentality within our power to effect our object. We shall employ agents, circulate tracts, petition the State and National legislatures, and endeavor to enlist the pulpit and the press in our behalf. We hope this Convention will be followed by a series of Conventions embracing every part of the country.

RESOLUTIONS

WHEREAS, The great precept of nature is conceded to be, that "man shall pursue his own true and substantial happiness." Blackstone in his Commentaries remarks, that this law of Nature being coeval with mankind, and dictated by God himself, is of course superior in obligation to any other. It is binding over all the globe, in all countries and at all times; no human laws are of any validity if contrary to this, and such of them as are valid, derive all their force, and all their validity, and all their authority, mediately and immediately, from this original; therefore,

Resolved, That such laws as conflict, in any way, with the true and substantial happiness of woman, are contrary to the great precept of nature and of no validity, for this is "superior in obligation to any other."

Resolved, That all laws which prevent woman from occupying such a station in society as her conscience shall dictate, or which place her in a position inferior to that of man, are contrary to the great precept of nature, and therefore of no force or authority.

Resolved, That woman is man's equal—was intended to be so by the Creator, and the highest good of the race demands that she should be recognized as such.

Resolved, That the women of this country ought to be enlightened in regard to the laws under which they live, that they may no longer publish their degradation by declaring themselves satisfied with their present position, nor their ignorance, by asserting that they have all the rights they want.

Resolved, That inasmuch as man, while claiming for himself intellectual superiority, does accord to woman moral superiority, it is pre-eminently his duty to encourage her to speak and teach, as she has an opportunity, in all religious assemblies.

Resolved, That the same amount of virtue, delicacy, and refinement of behavior that is required of woman in the social state, should also be required of man, and the same transgressions should be visited with equal severity on both man and woman.

Resolved, That the objection of indelicacy and impropriety, which is so often brought against woman when she addresses a public audience, comes with a very ill-grace from those who encourage, by their attendance, her appearance on the stage, in the concert, or in feats of the circus.

Resolved, That woman has too long rested satisfied in the circumscribed limits which corrupt customs and a perverted application of the Scriptures have marked out for her, and that it is time she should move in the enlarged sphere which her great Creator has assigned her.

Resolved, That it is the duty of the women of this country to secure to themselves their sacred right to the elective franchise.

Resolved, That the equality of human rights results necessarily from the fact of the identity of the race in capabilities and responsibilities.

Resolved, therefore, That, being invested by the Creator with the same capabilities, and the same consciousness of responsibility for their exercise, it is demonstrably the right and duty of woman, equally with man, to promote every righteous cause by every righteous means; and especially in regard to the great subjects of morals and religion, it is self-evidently her right to participate with her brother in teaching them, both in private and in public, by writing and by speaking, by any instrumentalities proper to be used, and in any assemblies proper to be held; and this being a self-evident truth growing out of the divinely implanted principles of human nature, any custom or authority adverse to it, whether modern or wearing the hoary sanction of antiquity, is to be regarded as a self-evident falsehood, and at war with mankind.

[At the last session Lucretia Mott offered and spoke to the following resolution:]

Resolved, That the speedy success of our cause depends upon the zealous and untiring efforts of both men and women, for the overthrow of the monopoly of the pulpit, and for the securing to woman an equal participation with men in the various trades, professions, and commerce.

Frederick Douglass

Editorial from *The North Star*

❦

At the time of the Seneca Falls meeting, Frederick Douglass (1817–1895), born a slave in Maryland, had been a free man for ten years. He was a resident of Rochester, New York, and editor of a weekly abolitionist newspaper, *The North Star,* which was published continuously from 1847 until the time American slaves finally were emancipated.

Douglass wrote in his autobiography: "When the true history of the antislavery cause shall be written, women will occupy a large space in its pages, for the cause of the slave has been peculiarly woman's cause." Just so, Frederick Douglass took the cause of woman's oppression to himself. "Observing woman's agency, devotion, and efficiency in pleading the cause of the slave," he added, "gratitude for this high service early moved me to give favorable attention to the subject of what is called 'woman's rights' and caused me to be denominated a woman's-rights man. I am glad to say that I have never been ashamed to be thus designated."

Frederick Douglass was present at Seneca Falls where he argued effectively in favor of full political rights for women; and in the following decades he was a frequent participant in many other woman's rights conventions. Most American organs of opinion reacted to the founding of a woman's movement with a storm of ridicule and abuse, but Douglass printed the following editorial in *The North Star* of July 28, 1848.

One of the most interesting events of the past week, was the holding of what is technically styled a Woman's Rights Convention at Seneca Falls. The speaking, addresses, and resolutions of this extraordinary meeting were almost wholly conducted by women; and although they evidently felt themselves in a novel position, it is but simple justice to say that their whole proceedings were characterized by marked ability and dignity. No one present, we think, however much he might be disposed to differ from the views advanced by the leading speakers on that occasion, will fail to give them credit for brilliant talents and excellent dispositions. In this meeting, as in other deliberative assemblies, there were frequent differences of opinion and animated discussion; but in no case was there the slightest absence of good feeling and decorum. Several interesting documents setting forth the rights as well as grievances of women were read. Among these was a Declaration of Sentiments, to be regarded as the basis of a grand movement for attaining the civil, social, political, and religious rights of women. We should not do justice to our own convictions, or to the excellent persons connected with this infant movement, if we did not in this connection offer a few remarks on the general subject which the Convention met to consider and the objects they seek to attain. In doing so, we are not insensible that the bare mention of this truly important subject in any other than terms of contemptuous ridicule and scornful disfavor, is likely to excite against us the fury of bigotry and the folly of prejudice. A discussion of the rights of animals would be regarded with far more complacency by many of what are called the *wise* and the *good* of our land, than would be a discussion of the rights of women. It is, in their estimation, to be guilty of evil thoughts, to think that woman is entitled to equal rights with man. Many who have at last made the discovery that the negroes have some rights as well as other members of the human family, have yet to be convinced that women are entitled to any. Eight years ago a number of persons of this description actually abandoned the anti-slavery cause, lest by giving their influence in that direction they might possibly be giving countenance to the dangerous heresy that woman, in respect to rights, stands on an equal footing with man. In the judgment of such persons the American slave system, with all its concomitant horrors, is less to be deplored than this *wicked* idea. It is perhaps needless to say, that we cherish little sympathy for such sentiments or respect for such prejudices. Standing as we do upon the watch-tower of human freedom, we can not be deterred from an expression of our approbation of any movement, however humble, to improve and elevate the character of any members of the human family. While it is impossible for us to go into this subject at length, and dispose of the various objections which are often urged against such a doctrine as that of female equality, we are free to say that in respect to political rights, we hold woman to be justly entitled to all we claim for man. We go farther, and express our conviction that all political rights which it is expedient for man to exercise, it is equally so for woman. All that distinguishes man as an intelligent and accountable being, is equally true of woman; and if that government only is just which governs by the free consent of the governed, there can be no reason in the world for denying to woman the exercise of the elective franchise, or a hand in making and administering the laws of the land. Our doctrine is that "right is of no sex." We therefore bid the women engaged in this movement our humble Godspeed.

William Lloyd Garrison

Intelligent Wickedness

❧

William Lloyd Garrison (1805–1879) was the apostle of immediate and unconditional abolition of slavery. The *Liberator,*
Garrison's anti-slavery paper, which he began publishing in
1831, advocated this point of view—then considered extremely
radical.

In 1840, as the foremost American abolitionist, Garrison
traveled to London for the World's Anti-Slavery Convention.
Arriving a little late, he discovered that Lucretia Mott and other
female delegates from the United States had been barred from
taking their rightful place at the proceedings. Garrison declined
to take his own seat or to participate in the meeting, declaring:
"After battling so many long years for the liberties of African
slaves, I can take no part in a convention that strikes down the
most sacred rights of all women."

Like Frederick Douglass, Garrison became a vigorous supporter of the woman's movement. They along with other abolitionists such as Thomas Wentworth Higginson, Wendell Phillips, Theodore Parker, and Parker Pillsbury, lent their names
and voices to the feminist conventions. Thus, the anti-slavery
movement provided a base of male support for the fledgling
woman's rights movement as well as a training ground for the
female leadership.

The woman's rights conventions were conducted as open
forums, with members of the audience free to participate in discussion and debate of issues. At one convention, in 1853 in
Cleveland, the Seneca Falls Declaration of Sentiments was criticized from the audience by a male speaker because, in his
opinion, that document unfairly blamed men for the condition
of women. Women themselves, said he, were responsible for the
prevailing low public opinion of their sex. Ernestine Rose then

stood and stated that she felt both men and women were to blame.

Garrison apparently could not brook such an approach. He took the floor and, after first praising the Seneca Falls Declaration for its "pertinacity and its power," delivered the following speech extemporaneously.

It was this morning objected to the Declaration of Sentiments, that it implied that man was the only transgressor . . . and our eloquent friend, Mrs. Rose, who stood on this platform . . . told us her creed. She told us she did not blame anybody, really, and did not hold any man to be criminal. . . .

For my own part, I am not prepared to respect that philosophy. I believe in sin, therefore in a sinner; in theft, therefore in a thief; in slavery, therefore in a slaveholder; in wrong, therefore in a wrong-doer; and unless the men of this nation are made by woman to see that they have been guilty of usurpation, and cruel usurpation, I believe very little progress will be made. To say all this has been done without thinking, without calculation, without design, by mere accident, by a want of light; can anybody believe this who is familiar with all the facts in this case? Certainly, for one, I hope ever to lean to the charitable side, and will try to do so. I, too, believe things are done through misconception and misapprehension, which are injurious, yes, which are immoral and unchristian; but only to a limited extent. There is such a thing as intelligent wickedness, a design on the part of those who have the light to quench it, and to do the wrong to gratify their own propensities, and to further their own interests. So, then, I believe, that as man has monopolized for generations all the rights which belong to woman, it has not been accidental, not through ignorance on his part; but I believe that man has done this through calculation, actuated by a spirit of pride, a desire for domination which has made him degrade woman in her own eyes, and thereby tend to make her a mere vassal.

It seems to me, therefore, that we are to deal with the consciences of men. It is idle to say that the guilt is common, that the women are as deeply involved in this matter as the men. Never can it be said that the victims are as much to be blamed as the victimizer; that the slaves are to be as much blamed as the slaveholders and slave-drivers; that the women who have no rights, are to be as much blamed as the men who have played the part of robbers and tyrants. We must deal with conscience. The men of this nation, and the men of all nations, have no just respect for woman. They have tyrannized over her deliberately, they have not sinned through ignorance, but theirs is not the knowledge that saves. Who can say truly, that in all things he acts up to the light he enjoys, that he does not do something which he knows is not the very thing, or the best thing he ought to do? How few there are among mankind who are able to say this with regard to themselves. Is not the light all around us? Does not this nation know how great its guilt is in enslaving one-sixth of its people? Do not the men of this nation know ever since the landing of the pilgrims, that they are wrong in making subject one-half of the people? Rely upon it, it has not been a mistake on their part. It has been sin. It has been guilt; and they manifest their guilt to a demonstration, in the manner in which they receive this movement. Those who do wrong ignorantly, do not willingly continue in it, when they find they are in the wrong. Ignorance is not an evidence of guilt certainly. It is only an evidence of a want of light. They who are only ignorant, will never rage, and rave, and threaten, and foam, when the light comes; but being interested and walking in the light, will always present a manly front, and be willing to be taught and be willing to be told they are in the wrong.

Take the case of slavery: How has the anti-slavery cause been received? Not argumentatively, not by reason, not by entering the free arena of fair discussion and comparing notes; the arguments have been rotten eggs, and brickbats and calumny, and in the southern portion of the country, a spirit of murder, and threats to cut out the tongues of those who spoke against them. What has this indicated on the part of the nation? What but conscious guilt? Not ignorance, not that they had not the light. They had the light and rejected it.

How has this Woman's Rights movement been treated in this country, on the right hand and on the left? This nation ridicules and derides this movement, and spits upon it, as fit only to be cast out and trampled underfoot. This is not ignorance. They know all about the truth. It is the natural outbreak of tyranny. It is because the tyrants and usurpers are alarmed. They have been and are called to judgment, and they dread the examination and exposure of their position and character.

Women of America! you have something to blame yourselves for in this matter, something to account for to God and the world. Granted. But then you are the victims in this land, as the women of all lands are, to the tyrannical power and godless ambition of man; and we must show who are responsible in this matter.

Letter from Prison of
St. Lazare, Paris

Within two weeks after the Seneca Falls convention, another local woman's rights gathering took place in Rochester, New York. Then, after a hiatus of a year and a half, the First National Woman's Rights Convention was called at Worcester, Massachusetts, in 1850. Present at this meeting were many nationally known abolitionists, male and female, white and black. Abby Kelley Foster, a pioneer woman anti-slavery orator, gave voice to a thought that must have been in many minds as they remembered back over the previous decades of lonely struggle on behalf of women. "For fourteen years," she said, "I have advocated this cause by my daily life. Bloody feet, sisters, have worn smooth the path by which you have come up hither."

In 1851 the Second National Convention met at Worcester. To the delight of many present, the infant movement had already excited interest in both England and France. In an article in the *Westminster Review,* Harriet Taylor (a friend of John Stuart Mill and later his wife) complimented American women on their first national convention and noted "indications that the example of America will be followed on this side of the Atlantic." (Actually, feminist activities in England in the 1850's remained quite limited; not until about 1866 were the first suffrage committees formed there.)

In addition, two French feminists addressed a letter to the 1851 convention from a prison cell in Paris, to express their joy at the news of the Seneca Falls Declaration of woman's rights. One, Pauline Roland, was said to have claimed the right to vote in 1848, without success; the other, Jeanne Deroine, had presented herself as a candidate for the Legislative Assembly the following year. Both had been sentenced to six months in St. Lazare Prison because of their activities in connection with the Central Committee of Associative Unions, an outlawed socialist organization. Roland was arrested again shortly after serving her term; she was deported to Algeria, where she died in 1852.

At the conclusion of the reading of the letter, Ernestine Rose —the internationalist of the group by virtue of her foreign birth, travels and linguistic skills—declared: "After having heard the letter read from our poor incarcerated sisters of France, well might we exclaim, Alas, poor France! where is thy glory? Where the glory of the Revolution of 1848?" A few women, including Lucretia Mott, were delegated by the convention to correspond with the French feminists.

June 15, 1851

Dear Sisters:

Your courageous declaration of Woman's Rights has resounded even to our prison, and has filled our souls with inexpressible joy.

In France, reaction has suppressed the cry of liberty of women. . . . The darkness of reaction has obscured the sun of 1848, which seemed to rise so radiantly. Why? Because the revolutionary tempest, in overturning at the same time the throne and the scaffold, in breaking the chain of the black slave, forgot to break the chain of the most oppressed of all—of Woman, the pariah of humanity. . . .

But, while those selected by half of the people—by men alone—evoke force to stifle liberty and forge restrictive laws to establish order by compulsion, woman, guided by fraternity, foreseeing incessant struggles, and in the hope of putting an end to them, makes an appeal to the laborer to found liberty and equality on fraternal solidarity. . . . the laborer recognizes the right of woman, his companion in labor.

The delegates of a hundred and four associations, united, without distinction of sex, elected two women with several of their brothers to participate equally with them in the administration of the interests of labor and in the organization of the work of solidarity. . . .

It is in the name of law framed by man only . . . that the Old World . . . has shut up within the walls of a prison . . . those elected by the laborers. . . .

Sisters of America! your socialist sisters of France are united with you in the vindication of the rights of woman to civil and political equality. We have, moreover, the profound conviction that only by the power of association based on solidarity—by the union of the working classes of both sexes to organize labor—can be acquired, completely and pacifically, the civil and political equality of woman, and the social right for all.

It is in this confidence that, from the depths of the jail which still imprisons our bodies without reaching our hearts, we cry to you, Faith, Love, Hope, and send to you our sisterly salutations.

Jeanne Deroine
Pauline Roland

Sojourner Truth

Ain't I a Woman?

Sojourner Truth (1795–1883) was born into slavery in New York State. She gained her freedom in 1827, when that state emancipated its slaves. At the age of forty-six, after working in New York City as a domestic for some years, she felt that she had been called by the Lord to travel up and down the land testifying to the sins against her people.

Dropping her slave name, Isabella, she took the symbolic name of Sojourner Truth. She spoke at camp meetings, private homes, wherever she could gather an audience. By midcentury she was well known in anti-slavery circles and a frequent speaker at abolitionist gatherings.

Sojourner Truth consistently and actively identified herself with the feminist cause from the early years of the American woman's movement. She attended the First National Woman's Rights Convention in Worcester, Massachusetts, in 1850—the only black woman present. Massachusetts was the center of abolitionist sentiment and the million and a half black women of the South still in slavery were not forgotten by the convention delegates. A resolution was adopted referring to these women— "the most grossly wronged and foully outraged of all women" —and vowing that "in every effort for an improvement in our civilization, we will bear in our heart of hearts the memory of the trampled womanhood of the plantation, and omit no effort to raise it to a share in the rights we claim for ourselves."

The following year Sojourner Truth was a participant in a woman's convention at Akron, Ohio, presided over by Frances D. Gage. Gage later reported that some of the women present were far from happy at seeing Sojourner Truth walk in, and begged the chairman not to let her speak, for fear that "every newspaper in the land will have our cause mixed with abolition."

The Akron convention was marked by the presence of many men of the cloth, most of whom apparently were opposed to the granting of freedom to women. One based his argument in favor of male privilege on man's greater intellect; another on the manhood of Christ; another on the sin of Eve. Finally the atmosphere of the convention became somewhat stormy. As Gage related the scene, "slowly from her seat in the corner rose Sojourner Truth. . . . 'Don't let her speak!' gasped half a dozen in my ear. She moved slowly and solemnly to the front, laid her old bonnet at her feet, and turned her great speaking eyes to me. There was a hissing sound of disapprobation above and below. I rose and announced 'Sojourner Truth,' and begged the audience to keep silence for a few moments."

The simple moving words of Sojourner Truth had an effect on the gathering that Gage described as "magical." Beforehand, the ministers seemed to be getting the better of the women, much to the delight of "the boys in the galleries"; but the speaker had "taken us up in her strong arms and carried us safely over the slough of difficulty turning the whole tide in our favor."

Sojourner Truth never learned to read or write. The speech she delivered at the Akron convention was not officially recorded; it survives because it was written down by Frances Gage. It is reprinted below without the heavy dialect in which Gage recorded the words and without her interjected comments.

Well, children, where there is so much racket there must be something out of kilter. I think that 'twixt the negroes of the South and the women at the North, all talking about rights, the white men will be in a fix pretty soon. But what's all this here talking about?

That man over there says that women need to be helped into carriages, and lifted over ditches, and to have the best place everywhere. Nobody ever helps me into carriages, or over mud-puddles, or gives me any best place! And ain't I a woman? Look at me! Look at my arm! I have ploughed and planted, and gathered into barns, and no man could head me! And ain't I a woman? I could work as much and eat as much as a man—when I could get it—and bear the lash as well! And ain't I a woman? I have borne thirteen children, and seen them most all sold off to slavery, and when I cried out with my mother's grief, none but Jesus heard me! And ain't I a woman?

Then they talk about this thing in the head; what's this they call it? [Intellect, someone whispers.] That's it, honey. What's that got to do with women's rights or negro's rights? If my cup won't hold but a pint, and yours holds a quart, wouldn't you be mean not to let me have my little half-measure full?

Then that little man in black there, he says women can't have as much rights as men, 'cause Christ wasn't a woman! Where did your Christ come from? Where did your Christ come from? From God and a woman! Man had nothing to do with Him.

If the first woman God ever made was strong enough to turn the world upside down all alone, these women together ought to be able to turn it back, and get it right side up again! And now they is asking to do it, the men better let them.

Obliged to you for hearing me, and now old Sojourner ain't got nothing more to say.

What Time of Night It Is

In 1853 Sojourner Truth was in New York for a Woman's Rights Convention at the Broadway Tabernacle. This meeting was dubbed by the authors of the *History of Woman Suffrage* the "Mob Convention." "It was," they wrote, "the first overt exhibition of that public sentiment woman was then combating. The mob represented more than itself; it evidenced that general masculine opinion of woman, which condensed into law, forges the chains which enslave her."

When Sojourner Truth came onto the platform, the frenzy of the crowd grew even greater.

Is it not good for me to come and draw forth a spirit, to see what kind of spirit people are of? I see that some of you have got the spirit of a goose, and some have got the spirit of a snake. I feel at home here. I come to you, citizens of New York, as I suppose you ought to be. I am a citizen of the State of New York; I was born in it, and I was a slave in the State of New York; and now I am a good citizen of this State. I was born here, and I can tell you I feel at home here. I've been lookin' round and watchin' things, and I know a little mite 'bout Woman's Rights, too. I come forth to speak 'bout Woman's Rights, and want to throw in my little mite, to keep the scales a-movin'. I know that it feels a kind o' hissin' and ticklin' like to see a colored woman get up and tell you about things, and Woman's Rights. We have all been thrown down so low that nobody thought we'd ever get up again; but we have been long enough trodden now; we will come up again, and now I am here.

I was a-thinkin', when I see women contendin' for their rights, I was a-thinkin' what a difference there is now, and what there was in old times. I have only a few minutes to speak; but in the old times the kings of the earth would[n't] hear a woman. There was a king in the Scriptures; and then it was the kings of the earth would kill a woman if she come into their presence; but Queen Esther come forth, for she was oppressed, and felt there was a great wrong, and she said I will die or I will bring my complaint before the king. Should the king of the United States be greater, or more crueler, or more harder? But the king, he raised up his sceptre and said: "Thy request shall be granted unto thee— to the half of my kingdom will I grant it to thee!" Then he said he would hang Haman on the gallows he had made up high. But that is not what women come forward to contend. The women want their rights as Esther. She only wanted to explain her rights. And he was so liberal that he said, "the half of my kingdom shall be granted to thee," and he did not wait for her to ask, he was so liberal with her.

Now, women do not ask half of a kingdom, but their rights, and they don't get 'em. When she comes to demand 'em, don't you hear how sons hiss their mothers like snakes, because they ask for their rights; and can they ask for anything less? The king ordered Haman to be hung on the gallows which he prepared to hang others; but I do not want any man to be killed, but I am sorry to see them so short-minded. But we'll have our rights; see if we don't; and you can't stop us from them; see if you can. You may hiss as much as you like, but it is comin'. Women don't get half as much rights as they ought to; we want more, and we will have it. Jesus says: "What I say to one, I say to all— watch!" I'm a-watchin'. God says: "Honor your father and your mother." Sons and daughters ought to behave themselves before their mothers, but they do not. I can see them a-laughin', and pointin' at their mothers up here on the stage. They hiss when an aged woman comes forth. If they'd been brought up proper they'd have known better than hissin' like snakes and geese. I'm 'round watchin' these things, and I wanted to come up and say these few things to you, and I'm glad of the hearin' you give me. I wanted to tell you a mite about Woman's Rights, and so I came out and said so. I am sittin' among you to watch; and every once and awhile I will come out and tell you what time of night it is.

Lucretia Mott

Not Christianity, but Priestcraft

Lucretia Mott (1793–1880) was born into a Quaker family on Nantucket Island. In these circumstances of her birth she was unusually fortunate, for the whalers' wives of Nantucket had a tradition of independence and self-sufficiency, and the Quakers accorded women an equal place with men in their Society. Lucretia Mott's native abilities were encouraged; she attended a Friends' boarding school, where she later taught for a while. At the age of twenty-eight she was honored by being appointed a Minister in the Society of Friends. In this capacity she had the opportunity—rare for a woman—to gain a good deal of experience in public speaking.

When the first Female Anti-Slavery Society was formed in Philadelphia, Mott was a charter member. She spoke widely on behalf of abolitionism and before long was a well-known figure nationally. Her oratorical skills also served the woman's movement from its inception at Seneca Falls until her death.

Typical of contemporary comment about her is Frederick Douglass': "I shall never forget the first time I ever saw or heard Lucretia Mott. . . . In a few moments after she began to speak, I saw before me no more a woman, but a glorified presence, bearing a message of light and love. . . . Whenever and wherever I have listened to her, my heart has always been made better and my spirit raised by her words; and in speaking thus for myself I am sure I am expressing the experience of thousands."

Lucretia Mott had a positive dread of writing, other than informal letters, and most of her recorded speeches fail to convey the effect that her personality evidently imparted to them.

Through her long, active life, Mott seems to have been uniformly described by those who worked with her as saintly in character, serene in countenance, and gentle in manner. Yet she definitely was not a milk-and-water reformer. The views she embraced were radical (regarding slavery, she was a Garrisonian, for example) and she stated them forthrightly. In a letter to an 1850 Woman's Rights Convention in Ohio, she declared that women must "not *ask* as *favor,* but *demand* as *right,* that every civil and ecclesiastical obstacle be removed out of the way."

The following extemporaneous speech was delivered by Mott at a Woman's Rights Convention in Philadelphia in 1854 in answer to the contention made by a minister in the audience that men ought to have authority over women. In fact, clergymen were among the most vociferous antagonists that the women faced. Every scrap of Biblical evidence—especially St. Paul—that they could marshal in favor of male superiority was advanced in convention debates by them. Lucretia Mott, because of her experience as a minister and her familiarity with Scripture, was able to refute the clergymen on their own ground.

It is not Christianity, but priestcraft that has subjected woman as we find her. The Church and State have been united, and it is well for us to see it so. We have had to bear the denunciations of these reverend (irreverend) clergymen . . . of late. But if we look to their authority to see how they expound the text, quite likely we shall find a new reading. . . .

Blame is often attached to the position in which woman is found. I blame her not so much as I pity her. So circumscribed have been her limits that she does not realise the misery of her condition. Such dupes are men to custom that even servitude, the worst of ills, comes to be thought a good, till down from sire to son it is kept and guarded as a sacred thing. Woman's existence is maintained by sufferance. The veneration of man has been misdirected, the pulpit has been prostituted, the Bible has been ill-used. It has been turned over and over as in every reform. The temperance people have had to feel its supposed denunciations. Then the anti-slavery, and now this reform has met, and still continues to meet, passage after passage of the Bible, never intended to be so used. Instead of taking the truths of the Bible in corroboration of the right, the practice has been to turn over its pages to find example and authority for the wrong, for the existing abuses of society. For the usage of drinking wine, the example of the sensualist Solomon, is always appealed to. In reference to our reform, even admitting that Paul did mean preach, when he used that term, he did not say that the recommendation of that time was to be applicable to the churches of all after-time. We have been so long pinning our faith on other people's sleeves that we ought to begin examining these things daily ourselves, to see whether they are so; and we should find on comparing text with text, that a very different construction might be put upon them. Some of our early Quakers not seeing how far they were to be carried, became Greek and Hebrew scholars, and they found that the text would bear other translations as well as other constructions. . . .

It is not so Apostolic to make the wife subject to the husband as many have supposed. It has been done by law and public opinion since that time. There has been a great deal said about sending missionaries over to the East to convert women who are immolating themselves on the funeral pile of the husbands. I know this may be a very good work, but I would ask you to look at it. How many women are there now immolated upon the shrine of superstition and priestcraft, in our very midst, in the assumption that man only has a right to the pulpit, and that if a woman enters it she disobeys God; making woman believe in the misdirection of her vocation, and that it is of divine authority that she should be thus bound. . . .

I do not want to dwell too much upon Scripture authority. We too often bind ourselves by authorities rather than by the truth. We are infidel to truth in seeking examples to overthrow it. The very first act of note that is mentioned when the disciples and apostles went forth after Jesus was removed from them, was the bringing up of an ancient prophecy to prove that they were right in the position they assumed on that occasion, when men and women were gathered together on the holy day of Pentecost, when every man heard and saw those wonderful works which are recorded. Then Peter stood forth—some one has said that Peter made a great mistake in quoting the prophet Joel— but he stated that "the time is come, this day is fulfilled the prophecy, when it is said, I will pour out my spirit upon all flesh, and your sons and your daughters shall prophesy," etc.—the language of the Bible is beautiful in its repetition —"upon my servants and my handmaidens I will pour out my spirit and they shall prophesy." Now can anything be clearer than that?

Lucy Stone

Marriage of Lucy Stone
Under Protest

❧

Lucy Stone (1818–1893) labored all her adult life for the liberation of women. In 1846, while still a student at Oberlin College, one of the few schools of higher education that admitted women, Lucy Stone wrote to her mother about her plans for a future career on the lecture platform: "I expect to plead not for the slave only, but for suffering humanity everywhere. Especially do I mean to labor for the elevation of my sex."

For ten years, from 1847 to 1857, Lucy Stone did just that, traveling about the country from New England to Ohio and beyond. She was speaking under the auspices of the Anti-Slavery Societies, but as she herself admitted, "I was so possessed by the woman's rights idea that I scattered it in every speech." The abolitionists objected to her mingling of the two causes but were appeased when she agreed to speak against slavery on weekends and to confine her arguments on behalf of women to weekdays only.

In 1858 Lucy Stone allowed her household goods to be sold for non-payment of taxes in protest against taxation without representation. In 1867 she and her husband made an arduous tour of Kansas in support of a referendum which would have given women the vote in that state. In 1870 the pair undertook responsibility for the publication of the *Woman's Journal,* the longest-lived of the woman's movement periodicals.

Lucy Stone was extremely reluctant to give up her freedom for marriage. Henry Blackwell, however, was a most persistent suitor and promised her complete equality. When they were married in 1855 in Massachusetts, they had the following protest read and signed as part of the wedding ceremony. In addition, the bride never took her husband's name, preferring to be known instead as "Mrs. Stone."

While acknowledging our mutual affection by publicly assuming the relationship of husband and wife, yet in justice to ourselves and a great principle, we deem it a duty to declare that this act on our part implies no sanction of, nor promise of voluntary obedience to such of the present laws of marriage, as refuse to recognize the wife as an independent, rational being, while they confer upon the husband an injurious and unnatural superiority, investing him with legal powers which no honorable man would exercize, and which no man should possess. We protest especially against the laws which give to the husband:

1. The custody of the wife's person.

2. The exclusive control and guardianship of their children.

3. The sole ownership of her personal, and use of her real estate, unless previously settled upon her, or placed in the hands of trustees, as in the case of minors, lunatics, and idiots.

4. The absolute right to the product of her industry.

5. Also against laws which give to the widower so much larger and more permanent an interest in the property of his deceased wife, than they give to the widow in that of the deceased husband.

6. Finally, against the whole system by which "the legal existence of the wife is suspended during marriage," so that in most States, she neither has a legal part in the choice of her residence, nor can she make a will, nor sue or be sued in her own name, nor inherit property.

We believe that personal independence and equal human rights can never be forfeited, except for crime; that marriage should be an equal and permanent partnership, and so recognized by law; that until it is so recognized, married partners should provide against the radical injustice of present laws, by every means in their power.

We believe that where domestic difficulties arise, no appeal should be made to legal tribunals under existing laws, but that all difficulties should be submitted to the equitable adjustment of arbitrators mutually chosen.

Thus reverencing law, we enter our protest against rules and customs which are unworthy of the name, since they violate justice, the essence of law.

(Signed), Henry B. Blackwell,
Lucy Stone.

Disappointment Is the Lot
of Woman

In 1855 Lucy Stone attended a National Woman's Rights Convention in Cincinnati, Ohio. She responded to a previous speaker with these extemporaneous remarks.

The last speaker alluded to this movement as being that of a few disappointed women. From the first years to which my memory stretches, I have been a disappointed woman. When, with my brothers, I reached forth after the sources of knowledge, I was reproved with "It isn't fit for you; it doesn't belong to women." Then there was but one college in the world where women were admitted, and that was in Brazil. I would have found my way there, but by the time I was prepared to go, one was opened in the young State of Ohio—the first in the United States where women and negroes could enjoy opportunities with white men. I was disappointed when I came to seek a profession worthy an immortal being—every employment was closed to me, except those of the teacher, the seamstress, and the housekeeper. In education, in marriage, in religion, in everything, disappointment is the lot of woman. It shall be the business of my life to deepen this disappointment in every woman's heart until she bows down to it no longer. I wish that women, instead of being walking show-cases, instead of begging of their fathers and brothers the latest and gayest new bonnet, would ask of them their rights.

The question of Woman's Rights is a practical one. The notion has prevailed that it was only an ephemeral idea; that it was but women claiming the right to smoke cigars in the streets, and to frequent bar-rooms. Others have supposed it a question of comparative intellect; others still, of sphere. Too much has already been said and written about woman's sphere. Trace all the doctrines to their source and they will be found to have no basis except in the usages and prejudices of the age. This is seen in the fact that what is tolerated in woman in one country is not tolerated in another. In this country women may hold prayer-meetings, etc., but in Mohammedan countries it is written upon their mosques, "Women and dogs, and other impure animals, are not permitted to enter." Wendell Phillips says, "The best and greatest thing one is capable of doing, that is his sphere." I have confidence in the Father to believe that when He gives us the capacity to do anything He does not make a blunder. Leave women, then, to find their sphere. And do not tell us before we are born even, that our province is to cook dinners, darn stockings, and sew on buttons. We are told woman has all the rights she wants; and even women, I am ashamed to say, tell us so. They mistake the politeness of men for rights—seats while men stand in this hall to-night, and their adultations; but these are mere courtesies. We want rights. The flour-merchant, the house-builder, and the postman charge us no less on account of our sex; but when we endeavor to earn money to pay all these, then, indeed, we find the difference. Man, if he have energy, may hew out for himself a path where no mortal has ever trod, held back by nothing but what is in himself; the world is all before him, where to choose; and we are glad for you, brothers, men, that it is so. But the same society that drives forth the young man, keeps woman at home—a dependent —working little cats on worsted, and little dogs on punc-

tured paper; but if she goes heartily and bravely to give herself to some worthy purpose, she is out of her sphere and
she loses caste. Women working in tailor-shops are paid
one-third as much as men. Some one in Philadelphia has
stated that women make fine shirts for twelve and a half
cents apiece; that no woman can make more than nine a
week, and the sum thus earned, after deducting rent, fuel,
etc., leaves her just three and a half cents a day for bread.
Is it a wonder that women are driven to prostitution? Female teachers in New York are paid fifty dollars a year, and
for every such situation there are five hundred applications.
I know not what you believe of God, but I believe He gave
yearnings and longings to be filled, and that He did not
mean all our time should be devoted to feeding and clothing
the body. The present condition of woman causes a horrible perversion of the marriage relation. It is asked of a
lady, "Has she married well?" "Oh, yes, her husband is
rich." Woman must marry for a home, and you men are the
sufferers by this; for a woman who loathes you may marry
you because you have the means to get money which she
can not have. But when woman can enter the lists with you
and make money for herself, she will marry you only for
deep and earnest affection.

I am detaining you too long, many of you standing, that
I ought to apologize, but women have been wronged so long
that I may wrong you a little. . . . I have seen a woman at
manual labor turning out chair-legs in a cabinet-shop, with
a dress short enough not to drag in the shavings. I wish
other women would imitate her in this. It made her hands
harder and broader, it is true, but I think a hand with a
dollar and a quarter a day in it, better than one with a
crossed ninepence. . . . The widening of woman's sphere is
to improve her lot. Let us do it, and if the world scoff, let it
scoff—if it sneer, let it sneer—but we will go on emulating
the example of the sisters Grimké and Abby Kelley. When
they first lectured against slavery they were not listened to

as respectfully as you listen to us. So the first female physician meets many difficulties, but to the next the path will be made easy.

Lucretia Mott has been a preacher for years; her right to do so is not questioned among Friends. But when Antoinette Brown felt that she was commanded to preach, and to arrest the progress of thousands that were on the road to hell; why, when she applied for ordination they acted as though they had rather the whole world should go to hell, than that Antoinette Brown should be allowed to tell them how to keep out of it.

Elizabeth Cady Stanton

Address to the New York State Legislature, 1854

Elizabeth Cady Stanton (1815–1902) originated the Seneca
Falls convention and went on to become the leading woman
theorist and writer of the movement. A few years after the
Seneca Falls meeting, she wrote to a co-worker that she was "at
the boiling point" on the woman question. She felt that if she
could not steal more time from her family responsibilities to
speak and write about it she would "die of an intellectual repression, a woman's rights convulsion."

Fortunately, no such fate awaited Stanton. Although she never
wrote the full-length work on feminism that her wide-ranging
perceptions and passionate feelings might have produced, her
pen was seldom inactive during the years when speeches, resolutions, letters, calls, and petitions were the very life breath of the
growing movement.

Stanton was by temperament and inclination in the vanguard
of the movement; her intellectual and tactical boldness challenged the courage of others on many occasions. At Seneca Falls,
when the question of "rights" was uppermost, Stanton sailed in
with a resolution asking female suffrage. Even the brave Lucretia
Mott was thrown into consternation: "Thou will make us ridiculous," she warned.

As an early participant in the petition-gathering campaign
prior to the passage of the Married Women's Property Act of
1848, Stanton was well aware of the limitations of that measure.
As the daughter of a judge and the wife of a lawyer, she was
keenly sensitive to and knowledgeable about the legal disabilities
of women. She delivered the following speech on that subject
before the Joint Judiciary Committee of the New York State

Legislature in 1854; at the same time six thousand petition signatures were submitted.

The tyrant, Custom, has been summoned before the bar of Common-Sense. His majesty no longer awes the multitude —his sceptre is broken—his crown is trampled in the dust —the sentence of death is pronounced upon him. All nations, ranks, and classes have, in turn, questioned and repudiated his authority; and now, that the monster is chained and caged, timid woman, on tiptoe, comes to look him in the face, and to demand of her brave sires and sons, who have struck stout blows for liberty, if, in this change of dynasty, she, too, shall find relief. Yes, gentlemen, in republican America, in the nineteenth century, we, the daughters of the revolutionary heroes of '76, demand at your hands the redress of our grievances—a revision of your State Constitution—a new code of laws. Permit us then, as briefly as possible, to call your attention to the legal disabilities under which we labor.

1st. Look at the position of woman as woman. It is not enough for us that by your laws we are permitted to live and breathe, to claim the necessaries of life from our legal protectors—to pay the penalty of our crimes; we demand the full recognition of all our rights as citizens of the Empire State. We are persons; native, free-born citizens; property-holders, tax-payers; yet are we denied the exercise of our right to the elective franchise. We support ourselves, and, in part, your schools, colleges, churches, your poor-houses, jails, prisons, the army, the navy, the whole machinery of government, and yet we have no voice in your councils. We have every qualification required by the Constitution, necessary to the legal voter, but the one of sex. . . .

Again we demand in criminal cases that most sacred of all rights, trial by a jury of our own peers. The establish-

ment of trial by jury is of so early a date that its beginning
is lost in antiquity; but the right of trial by a jury of one's
own peers is a great progressive step of advanced civilization. No rank of men have ever been satisfied with being
tried by jurors higher or lower in the civil or political scale
than themselves; for jealousy on the one hand, and contempt on the other, has ever effectually blinded the eyes of
justice. Hence, all along the pages of history, we find the
king, the noble, the peasant, the cardinal, the priest, the lay-
man, each in turn protesting against the authority of the
tribunal before which they were summoned to appear.
Charles the First refused to recognize the competency of the
tribunal which condemned him: For how, said he, can subjects judge a king? The stern descendants of our Pilgrim
Fathers refused to answer for their crimes before an English
Parliament. For how, said they, can a king judge rebels?
And shall woman here consent to be tried by her liege lord,
who has dubbed himself law-maker, judge, juror, and sher-
iff too?—whose power, though sanctioned by Church and
State, has no foundation in justice and equity, and is a bold
assumption of our inalienable rights. . . . It is not to be denied that the interests of man and woman in the present
undeveloped state of the race, and under the existing social
arrangements, are and must be antagonistic. The nobleman
can not make just laws for the peasant; the slaveholder for
the slave; neither can man make and execute just laws for
woman, because in each case, the one in power fails to apply
the immutable principles of right to any grade but his own
. . . . listen to our just demands and make such a change in
your laws as will secure to every woman tried in your courts,
an impartial jury. At this moment among the hundreds of
women who are shut up in prisons in this State, not one has
enjoyed that most sacred of all rights—that right which you
would die to defend for yourselves—trial by a jury of one's
peers.

2d. Look at the position of woman as wife. Your laws

relating to marriage—founded as they are on the old common law of England, a compound of barbarous usages, but partially modified by progressive civilization—are in open violation of our enlightened ideas of justice, and of the holiest feelings of our nature. If you take the highest view of marriage, as a Divine relation, which love alone can constitute and sanctify, then of course human legislation can only recognize it. Men can neither bind nor loose its ties, for that prerogative belongs to God alone, who makes man and woman, and the laws of attraction by which they are united. But if you regard marriage as a civil contract, then let it be subject to the same laws which control all other contracts. Do not make it a kind of half-human, half-divine institution, which you may build up, but can not regulate. Do not, by your special legislation for this one kind of contract, involve yourselves in the grossest absurdities and contradictions. . . .

The wife who inherits no property holds about the same legal position that does the slave on the Southern plantation. She can own nothing, sell nothing. She has no right even to the wages she earns; her person, her time, her services are the property of another. She can not testify, in many cases, against her husband. She can get no redress for wrongs in her own name in any court of justice. She can neither sue nor be sued. She is not held morally responsible for any crime committed in the presence of her husband, so completely is her very existence supposed by the law to be merged in that of another. . . .

But the wife who is so fortunate as to have inherited property, has, by the new law in this State [the Married Women's Property Act of 1848], been redeemed from her lost condition. She is no longer a legal nonentity. . . .

3d. Look at the position of woman as widow. . . . Behold the magnanimity of the law in allowing the widow to retain a life interest in one-third of the landed estate, and one-half the personal property of her husband, and taking the lion's share to itself! Had she died first, the house and land would all have been the husband's still. . . . The husband has the absolute right to will away his property as he may see fit. . . . The man who leaves his wife the sole guardian of his property and children is an exception to the general rule. . . .

4th. Look at the position of woman as mother. . . . The father may apprentice his child, bind him out to a trade, without the mother's consent—yea, in direct opposition to her most earnest entreaties, prayers and tears. . . . Moreover, the father, about to die, may bind out all his children wherever and to whomsoever he may see fit, and thus, in fact, will away the guardianship of all his children from the mother. . . . Thus, by your laws, the child is the absolute property of the father, wholly at his disposal in life or at death.

In case of separation, the law gives the children to the father; no matter what his character or condition. At this very time we can point you to noble, virtuous, well-educated mothers in this State, who have abandoned their husbands for their profligacy and confirmed drunkenness. All these have been robbed of their children, who are in the custody of the husband, under the care of his relatives, whilst the mothers are permitted to see them but at stated intervals. . . .

Many times and oft it has been asked us, with unaffected seriousness, "What do you women want? What are you aiming at?" Many have manifested a laudable curiosity to know what the wives and daughters could complain of in republican America, where their sires and sons have so bravely fought for freedom and gloriously secured their independence, trampling all tyranny, bigotry, and caste in the dust, and declaring to a waiting world the divine truth that all men are created equal. What can woman want under such a government? Admit a radical difference in sex, and you demand different spheres—water for fish, and air for birds.

It is impossible to make the Southern planter believe that his slave feels and reasons just as he does—that injustice

and subjection are as galling as to him—that the degradation of living by the will of another, the mere dependence
on his caprice, at the mercy of his passions, is as keenly felt
by him as his master. If you can force on his unwilling
vision a vivid picture of the negro's wrongs, and for a moment touch his soul, his logic brings him instant consolation. He says, the slave does not feel this as I would. Here,
gentlemen, is our difficulty: When we plead our cause before the law-makers and savants of the republic, they can
not take in the idea that men and women are alike; and so
long as the mass rest in this delusion, the public mind will
not be so much startled by the revelations made of the
injustice and degradation of woman's position as by the fact
that she should at length wake up to a sense of it.

If you, too, are thus deluded, what avails it that we show
by your statute books that your laws are unjust—that
woman is the victim of avarice and power? What avails it
that we point out the wrongs of woman in social life; the
victim of passion and lust? You scorn the thought that she
has any natural love of freedom burning in her breast, any
clear perception of justice urging her on to demand her
rights.

Would to God you could know the burning indignation
that fills woman's soul when she turns over the pages of your
statute books, and sees there how like feudal barons you
freemen hold your women. Would that you could know the
humiliation she feels for [her] sex, when she thinks of all the
beardless boys in your law offices, learning these ideas of
one-sided justice—taking their first lessons in contempt for
womankind—being indoctrinated into the incapacities of
their mothers, and the lordly, absolute rights of man over
all women, children, and property, and to know that these
are to be our future presidents, judges, husbands, and
fathers. . . .

In conclusion, then, let us say, in behalf of the women of
this State, we ask for all that you have asked for yourselves

in the progress of your development, since the *Mayflower* cast anchor beside Plymouth rock; and simply on the ground that the rights of every human being are the same and identical. You may say that the mass of the women of this State do not make the demand; it comes from a few sour, disappointed old maids and childless women.

You are mistaken; the mass speak through us. . . . the laboring women who are loudly demanding remuneration for their unending toil; those women who teach in our seminaries, academies, and public schools for a miserable pittance; the widows who are taxed without mercy; the unfortunate ones in our work-houses, poor-houses, and prisons. Who are they that we do not now represent? But a small class of the fashionable butterflies, who, through the short summer days, seek the sunshine and the flowers; but the cool breezes of autumn and the hoary frosts of winter will soon chase all these away; then they, too, will need and seek protection, and through other lips demand in their turn justice and equity at your hands.

Elizabeth Cady Stanton

Address to the New York
State Legislature, 1860

❦

After the defeat of the 1854 women's property measure, it was
six years before another opportunity for an all-out effort in the
New York State Legislature presented itself. Susan B. Anthony,
who was forever goading the harried and somewhat self-indulgent
Elizabeth Cady Stanton to greater efforts, told her that the salvation of the women of the Empire State depended upon her
power to move "the hearts of our law-makers at this time."
Anthony, moreover, came to stay at Stanton's house to work
along with her on this crucial speech and to pitch in with household tasks.

The joint efforts of Anthony and Stanton on the following
speech and on dozens of other writings are best described by
Stanton herself:

"In thought and sympathy we were one, and in the division
of labor we exactly complimented each other. I am the better
writer, she the better critic. She supplied the facts and statistics,
I the philosophy and rhetoric, and, together, we have made arguments that stood unshaken through the storms of long years;
arguments that no one has answered. Our speeches may be considered the united product of our two brains."

Speaking on the very eve of the Civil War, Elizabeth Cady
Stanton asserted that "The prejudice against color . . . is no
stronger than that against sex."

You who have read the history of nations, from Moses
down to our last election, where have you ever seen one
class looking after the interests of another? Any of you can

readily see the defects in other governments, and pronounce sentence against those who have sacrificed the masses to themselves; but when we come to our own case, we are blinded by custom and self-interest. Some of you who have no capital can see the injustice which the laborer suffers; some of you who have no slaves, can see the cruelty of his oppression; but who of you appreciate the galling humiliation, the refinements of degradation, to which women (the mothers, wives, sisters, and daughters of freemen) are subject, in this the last half of the nineteenth century? How many of you have ever read even the laws concerning them that now disgrace your statute-books? In cruelty and tyranny, they are not surpassed by any slaveholding code in the Southern States; in fact they are worse, by just so far as woman, from her social position, refinement, and education, is on a more equal ground with the oppressor.

Allow me just here to call the attention of that party now so much interested in the slave of the Carolinas, to the similarity in his condition and that of the mothers, wives, and daughters of the Empire State. The negro has no name. He is Cuffy Douglas or Cuffy Brooks, just whose Cuffy he may chance to be. The woman has no name. She is Mrs. Richard Roe or Mrs. John Doe, just whose Mrs. she may chance to be. Cuffy has no right to his earnings; he can not buy or sell, or lay up anything that he can call his own. Mrs. Roe has no right to her earnings; she can neither buy nor sell, make contracts, nor lay up anything that she can call her own. Cuffy has no right to his children; they can be sold from him at any time. Mrs. Roe has no right to her children; they may be bound out to cancel a father's debts of honor. The unborn child, even, by the last will of the father, may be placed under the guardianship of a stranger and a foreigner. Cuffy has no legal existence; he is subject to restraint and moderate chastisement. Mrs. Roe has no legal existence; she has not the best right to her own person.

The husband has the power to restrain, and administer moderate chastisement.

Blackstone [author of *Commentaries on the Laws of England*] declares that the husband and wife are one, and learned commentators have decided that that one is the husband. In all civil codes, you will find them classified as one. Certain rights and immunities, such and such privileges are to be secured to white male citizens. What have women and negroes to do with rights? What know they of government, war, or glory?

The prejudice against color, of which we hear so much, is no stronger than that against sex. It is produced by the same cause, and manifested very much in the same way. The negro's skin and the woman's sex are both *prima facie* evidence that they were intended to be in subjection to the white Saxon man. The few social privileges which the man gives the woman, he makes up to the negro in civil rights. The woman may sit at the same table and eat with the white man; the free negro may hold property and vote. The woman may sit in the same pew with the white man in church; the free negro may enter the pulpit and preach. Now, with the black man's right to suffrage, the right unquestioned, even by Paul, to minister at the altar, it is evident that the prejudice against sex is more deeply rooted and more unreasonably maintained than that against color. . . .

Just imagine an inhabitant of another planet entertaining himself some pleasant evening in searching over our great national compact, our Declaration of Independence, our Constitutions, or some of our statute-books; what would he think of those "women and negroes" that must be so fenced in, so guarded against? Why, he would certainly suppose we were monsters, like those fabulous giants or Brobdingnagians of olden times, so dangerous to civilized man, from our size, ferocity, and power. Then let him take up our poets, from Pope down to Dana; let him listen to our Fourth of July toasts, and some of the sentimental adultations of social life, and no logic could convince him that this creature of the law, and this angel of the family altar, could be one and the same being. Man is in such a labyrinth of contradictions with his marital and property rights; he is so befogged on the whole question of maidens, wives, and mothers, that from pure benevolence we should relieve him from this troublesome branch of legislation. We should vote, and make laws for ourselves. Do not be alarmed, dear ladies! You need spend no time reading Grotius, Coke, Puffendorf, Blackstone, Bentham, Kent, and Story to find out what you need. We may safely trust the shrewd selfishness of the white man, and consent to live under the same broad code where he has so comfortably ensconced himself. Any legislation that will do for man, we may abide by most cheerfully. . . .

Now do not think, gentlemen, we wish you to do a great many troublesome things for us. We do not ask our legislators to spend a whole session in fixing up a code of laws to satisfy a class of most unreasonable women. We ask no more than the poor devils in the Scripture asked, "Let us alone." In mercy, let us take care of ourselves, our property, our children, and our homes. True, we are not so strong, so wise, so crafty as you are, but if any kind friend leaves us a little money, or we can by great industry earn fifty cents a day, we would rather buy bread and clothes for our children than cigars and champagne for our legal protectors. There has been a great deal written and said about protection. We, as a class, are tired of one kind of protection, that which leaves us everything to do, to dare, and to suffer, and strips us of all means for its accomplishment. We would not tax man to take care of us. No, the Great Father has endowed all his creatures with the necessary powers for self-support, self-defense, and protection. We do not ask man to represent us; it is hard enough in times like these for man to carry backbone enough to represent himself. So long as the mass of men spend most of their time on the fence, not knowing which way to jump, they are surely in no condition to tell us where we had better stand. In pity for man, we would no longer hang like a mill-stone round his neck. Undo what man did for us in the dark ages, and strike out all special legislation for us; strike the words "white male" from all your constitutions, and then, with fair sailing, let us sink or swim, live or die, survive or perish together.

Married Women's Property
Act, New York, 1860

A month after Elizabeth Cady Stanton's address to the Legislature, the New York State Married Women's Property Act of 1860 became law. As the excerpts printed below indicate, the Act represented a considerable advance in the legal position of women. It guaranteed a woman the right to keep her own earnings; the right to equal powers with her husband as joint guardian of their children; and property rights as a widow equal to those her husband would have in the event of her prior death.

The People of the State of New York, represented in Senate and Assembly, do enact as follows:

Section 1. The property, both real and personal, which any married woman now owns, as her sole and separate property; that which comes to her by descent, devise, bequest, gift or grant; that which she acquires by her trade, business, labor, or services, carried on or performed on her sole or separate account; that which a woman married in this State owns at the time of her marriage, and the rents, issues and proceeds of all such property, shall notwithstanding her marriage, be and remain her sole and separate property, and may be used, collected, and invested by her in her own name, and shall not be subject to the interference or control of her husband, or liable for his debts, except such debts as may have been contracted for the support of herself or her children, by her as his agent.

2. A married woman may bargain, sell, assign, and transfer her separate personal property, and carry on any trade or business, and perform any labor or services on her sole and separate account, and the earnings of any married woman from her trade, business, labor, or services shall be her sole and separate property, and may be used or invested by her in her own name.

3. Any married woman possessed of real estate as her separate property may bargain, sell and convey such property, and enter into any contract in reference to the same; but no such conveyance or contract shall be valid without the assent, in writing, of her husband, except as hereinafter provided. . . .

7. Any married woman may, while married, sue and be sued in all matters having relation to her property, which may be her sole and separate property, or which may hereafter come to her by descent, devise, bequest, or the gift of any person except her husband, in the same manner as if she were sole. And any married woman may bring and maintain an action in her own name, for damages against any person or body corporate, for any injury to her person or character, the same as if she were sole; and the money received upon the settlement of any such action, or recovered upon a judgment, shall be her sole and separate property.

8. No bargain or contract made by any married woman, in respect to her sole and separate property . . . shall be binding upon her husband, or render him or his property in any way liable therefor.

9. Every married woman is hereby constituted and declared to be the joint guardian of her children, with her husband, with equal powers, rights, and duties in regard to them, with the husband.

10. At the decease of husband or wife, leaving no minor child or children, the survivor shall hold, possess, and enjoy

life estate in one-third of all the real estate of which the husband or wife died seized.

11. At the decease of the husband or wife intestate, leaving minor child or children, the survivor shall hold, possess, and enjoy all the real estate of which the husband or wife died seized, and all the rents, issues, and profits thereof during the minority of the youngest child, and one-third thereof during his or her natural life.

Ernestine L. Rose

Petitions Were Circulated

❧

Ernestine L. Potowski Rose (1810–1892) was born in Poland, the daughter of a rabbi. She came to the United States at the age of twenty-six, and for the over thirty years that she lived there, agitated for a variety of unpopular ideas. She was a free-thinker (also known in those days as an infidel); an abolitionist; a socialist of the Robert Owen school; and a staunch advocate of woman's rights.

For twelve years she worked for the improvement of women's property rights. After the passage of a first property law in 1848 and, the same year, the beginnings of an organized woman's movement, Rose participated in most of the national woman's conventions, delivering major speeches at many of them and acting as president at one. She was a close associate of Susan B. Anthony's and one of her chief lieutenants in the New York State petition campaigns and canvasses—a herculean task that Anthony directed annually between 1854 and 1860.

The women at the convention of 1860 were jubilant over the victory of the married women's property bill in New York. Ernestine Rose viewed the accomplishment from the perspective of one who knew first-hand the years of work that lay behind it. She declared: "Freedom, my friends, does not come from the clouds, like a meteor; it does not bloom in one night; it does not come without great efforts and great sacrifices; all who love liberty, have to labor for it."

In this excerpt from Ernestine Rose's 1860 convention speech, she reminded her listeners of the tremendous changes in public opinion that had occurred in the United States in a little over twenty years.

Frances Wright was the first woman in this country who spoke on the equality of the sexes. She had indeed a hard task before her. The elements were entirely unprepared. She had to break up the time-hardened soil of conservatism, and her reward was sure—the same reward that is always bestowed upon those who are in the vanguard of any great movement. She was subjected to public odium, slander, and persecution. But these were not the only things that she received. Oh, she had her reward!—that reward of which no enemies could deprive her, which no slanders could make less precious—the eternal reward of knowing that she had done her duty; the reward springing from the consciousness of right, of endeavoring to benefit unborn generations. . . .

After her, in 1837, the subject of woman's rights was again taken hold of—aye, taken hold of by woman; and the soil having been already somewhat prepared, she began to sow the seeds for the future growth, the fruits of which we now begin to enjoy. Petitions were circulated and sent to our Legislature, and who can tell the hardships that then met those who undertook that great work! I went from house to house with a petition for signatures simply asking our Legislature to allow married women to hold real estate in their own name. What did I meet with? Why, the very name exposed one to ridicule, if not to worse treatment. The women said: "We have rights enough; we want no more"; and the men, as a matter of course, echoed it, and said: "You have rights enough; nay, you have too many already." But by perseverance in sending petitions to the Legislature, and, at the same time, enlightening the public mind on the subject, we at last accomplished our purpose. We had to adopt the method which physicians sometimes use, when they are called to a patient who is so hopelessly sick that he is unconscious of his pain and suffering. We had to describe to women their own position, to explain to them the burdens that rested so heavily upon them, and through these means, as a wholesome irritant, we roused public opinion on the subject, and through public opinion, we acted upon the Legislature, and in 1848–49, they gave us the great boon for which we asked, by enacting that a woman who possessed property previous to marriage, or obtained it after marriage, should be allowed to hold it in her own name. Thus far, thus good; but it was only a beginning, and we went on. In 1848 we had the first Woman's Rights Convention, and then some of our papers thought it only a very small affair, called together by a few "strong-minded women," and would pass away like a nine-days' wonder. They little knew woman! They little knew that if woman takes anything earnestly in her hands, she will not lay it aside unaccomplished. We have continued our Conventions ever since. A few years ago, when we sent a petition to our Legislature, we obtained, with but very little effort, upward of thirteen thousand signatures. What a contrast between this number and the five signatures attached to the first petition, in 1837! Since then, we might have had hundreds of thousands of signatures, but it is no longer necessary. Public opinion is too well known to require a long array of names.

Sojourner Truth

Keeping the Thing Going While Things Are Stirring

☙

The post-Civil War period was a time of division and regrouping in the woman's movement. With the outbreak of hostilities between North and South, women had suspended activities on their own behalf to devote full energy to the Union cause. The contributions of women to the war effort were substantial: they performed nursing service (Clara Barton is noted for her front-line work with Civil War wounded), fund-raising, and even some brave military exploits.

In addition, a National Woman's Loyal League was formed under the leadership of Susan B. Anthony, Elizabeth Cady Stanton, and others, which, in effect, functioned as an arm of the Republican Party's radical wing. In this capacity, the Woman's Loyal League collected hundreds of thousands of petition signatures calling for abolition of slavery.

When enfranchisement of black men became the policy of the very faction of the Republican Party that the League had worked to strengthen, the woman's movement confidently trusted that female suffrage would be granted at the same time. However, bitter disillusionment was in store.

The proposed Fourteenth Amendment to the Constitution (adopted in 1866) gave Negroes the vote but omitted any reference to women, and in its second section, actually introduced the word "male" into the Constitution for the first time. Stanton and Anthony felt betrayed and outraged; but their former abolitionist allies for the most part seemed resigned. It was widely held at the time that this was "the Negro's hour," and that women had no decent course available but to stand aside and wait their turn. Frederick Douglass and Frances Watkins Harper, both black people; Wendell Phillips and Abby Kelley Foster, whites—all long-time supporters of the woman's movement—now argued that the black slave's greater suffering entitled him to prior consideration.

Among faithful feminists, perhaps no one was more torn in her loyalties at this moment than was Lucy Stone. She wrote, ". . . woman has an ocean of wrong too deep for any plummet," yet "the Negro too has an ocean of wrong that cannot be fathomed." Out of this conflict, Lucy Stone concluded that she could not oppose the constitutional amendment but hoped it would be broadened to include women: "I will be thankful in my soul if *any* body can get out of the terrible pit."

Stanton and Anthony, on the other hand, not only could but did openly oppose the constitutional amendments which guaranteed suffrage to the black man but not to women. Both believed that this position was the only one consistent with their feminist principles. "The demand of the hour is equal rights to all," Stanton argued.

Into this strife-torn atmosphere came Sojourner Truth to stand alone for the all but forgotten black woman. Her dedication to feminism and her political acumen is demonstrated by this speech, delivered in 1867. Sojourner Truth was greeted by the audience with loud cheering.

My friends, I am rejoiced that you are glad, but I don't know how you will feel when I get through. I come from another field—the country of the slave. They have got their liberty—so much good luck to have slavery partly destroyed; not entirely. I want it root and branch destroyed. Then we will all be free indeed. I feel that if I have to answer for the deeds done in my body just as much as a man, I have a right to have just as much as a man. There is a great stir about colored men getting their rights, but not a word about the colored women; and if colored men get their rights, and not colored women theirs, you see the colored men will be masters over the women, and it will be just as bad as it was before. So I am for keeping the thing going while things are stirring; because if we wait till it is still, it will take a great while to get it going again. White women are a great deal smarter, and know more than colored women, while colored women do not know scarcely anything. They go out washing, which is about as high as a colored woman gets, and their men go about idle, strutting up and down; and when the women come home, they ask for their money and take it all, and then scold because there is no food. I want you to consider on that, chil'n. I call you chil'n; you are somebody's chil'n, and I am old enough to be mother of all that is here. I want women to have their rights. In the courts women have no right, no voice; nobody speaks for them. I wish woman to have her voice there among the pettifoggers. If it is not a fit place for women, it is unfit for men to be there.

I am above eighty years old; it is about time for me to be going. I have been forty years a slave and forty years free, and would be here forty years more to have equal rights for all. I suppose I am kept here because something remains for me to do; I suppose I am yet to help to break the chain. I have done a great deal of work; as much as a man, but did not get so much pay. I used to work in the field and bind grain, keeping up with the cradler; but men doing no more, got twice as much pay; so with the German women. They work in the field and do as much work, but do not get the pay. We do as much, we eat as much, we want as much. I suppose I am about the only colored woman that goes about to speak for the rights of the colored women. I want to keep the thing stirring, now that the ice is cracked. What we want is a little money. You men know that you get as much again as women when you write, or for what you do. When we get our rights we shall not have to come to you for money, for then we shall have money enough in our own pockets; and may be you will ask us for money. But help us now until we get it. It is a good consolation to know that when we have got this battle once fought we shall not be coming to you any more. You have been having our rights so long, that you think, like a slave-holder, that you own us. I know that it is hard for one who has held the reins for so long to give up; it cuts like a knife. It will feel all the better when it closes up again. I have been in Washington about three years, seeing about these colored people. Now colored men have the right to vote. There ought to be equal rights now more than ever, since colored people have got their freedom. I am going to talk several times while I am here; so now I will do a little singing. I have not heard any singing since I came here.

Susan B. Anthony

The United States of America vs.
Susan B. Anthony

❦

Susan B. Anthony (1820–1906), was brought up in a household of socially conscious Quakers. She learned of the Seneca Falls meeting from her mother and sister, both of whom were present and brought back enthusiastic reports. She herself, then twenty-eight years old and a schoolteacher since the age of fifteen, was engaged in the temperance movement at the time. She attended her first Woman's Rights Convention in Syracuse, New York, in 1852; before long, she was completely committed to the feminist cause.

Anthony insisted that she could neither write nor speak from a platform effectively. With a pen in her hand, she complained, she felt as clumsy as if "mounted on stilts." She confided in her journal in 1860: "It is a terrible martyrdom for me to speak." Her forte was as an organizer. There was no other woman of her time who was her equal in this respect. From Stanton's memoirs comes this vivid picture of Anthony in the early days of the movement:

"[W]henever I saw that stately Quaker girl coming across my lawn, I knew that some happy convocation of the sons of Adam was to be set by the ears, by one of our appeals or resolutions. The little portmanteau, stuffed with facts, was opened, and there we had . . . false interpretations of Bible texts, the statistics of women robbed of their property, shut out of some college, half paid for their work, the reports of some disgraceful trial; injustice enough to turn any woman's thoughts from stockings and puddings. . . . Night after night, by an old-fashioned fireplace, we plotted and planned the coming agitation: how, when, and where each entering wedge could be driven, by which women might be recognized and their rights secured."

In 1854 Anthony organized a state-wide canvass in New York to put pressure on the Legislature for revision of the married women's property statute. For six arduous years this canvass, involving collection of petition signatures, distribution of literature, and lecturing, was conducted annually. Again, during the Civil War, it was she who assumed leadership of the mammoth anti-slavery petitioning effort of the Women's Loyal League.

In the post-Civil War decade, there was an increasing use of militant tactics by women. Sit-ins at polling places occurred in New Jersey and other states; non-payment of taxes was employed by Lucy Stone, by the Smith sisters of Connecticut (who had property sold for a fraction of its value in lieu of taxes), by Abby Kelley Foster (whose home was seized), and by others; there were many cases of taxes paid under protest. For several years, beginning with the presidential election of 1868, women attempted—mostly unsuccessfully—to cast ballots.

In 1872 Susan B. Anthony led fifty women to a polling place in Rochester, New York, her home town, where they registered to vote. She urged women elsewhere in the country to do likewise. On election day she and more than a dozen other Rochester women cast their ballots. Within two weeks Anthony and the other women were arrested and charged with voting illegally under a statute (originally meant to be used against freed Negroes) which carried a possible three-year jail term.

The trial of the United States of America *vs.* Susan B. Anthony opened on June 17, 1873, at the courthouse in Canandaigua, New York. Anthony's defense was that the Fourteenth Amendment defined "citizen" as all *persons* born or naturalized in the United States, which made women eligible to vote. The judge would not allow Anthony to testify on her own behalf. Her attorney and the district attorney presented five hours of argument, after which—without leaving the bench—the judge drew a previously prepared written opinion from his pocket and read it. He ruled that the Fourteenth Amendment was inapplicable and directed the all-male jury to bring in a guilty verdict.

The next day the following scene occurred in court. (Anthony never did pay the fine imposed.)

Judge Hunt. (Ordering the defendant to stand up). Has the prisoner anything to say why sentence shall not be pronounced?

Miss Anthony. Yes, your honor, I have many things to say; for in your ordered verdict of guilty you have trampled under foot every vital principle of our government. My natural rights, my civil rights, my political rights, my judicial rights, are all alike ignored. Robbed of the fundamental privilege of citizenship, I am degraded from the status of a citizen to that of a subject; and not only myself individually but all of my sex are, by your honor's verdict, doomed to political subjection under this so-called republican form of government.

Judge Hunt. The Court can not listen to rehearsal of argument which the prisoner's counsel has already consumed three hours in presenting.

Miss Anthony. May it please your honor, I am not arguing the question, but simply stating the reasons why sentence can not, in justice, be pronounced against me. Your denial of my citizen's right to vote, is the denial of my right of consent as one of the governed, the denial of my right of representation as one of the taxed, the denial of my right to a trial by a jury of my peers as an offender against law; therefore, the denial of my sacred right to life, liberty, property and—

Judge Hunt. The Court can not allow the prisoner to go on.

Miss Anthony. But your honor will not deny me this one and only poor privilege of protest against this high-handed outrage upon my citizen's rights. May it please the Court to remember that, since the day of my arrest last November, this is the first time that either myself or any person of my disfranchised class has been allowed a word of defense before judge or jury—

Judge Hunt. The prisoner must sit down—the Court can not allow it.

Miss Anthony. Of all my prosecutors, from the corner grocery politician who entered the complaint, to the United States marshal, commissioner, district-attorney, district-judge, your honor on the bench—not one is my peer, but each and all are my political sovereigns; and had your honor submitted my case to the jury, as was clearly your duty, even then I should have had just cause of protest, for not one of those men was my peer; but, native or foreign born, white or black, rich or poor, educated or ignorant, sober or drunk, each and every man of them was my political superior; hence, in no sense, my peer. Under such circumstances a commoner of England, tried before a jury of lords, would have far less cause to complain than have I, a woman, tried before a jury of men. Even my counsel, Hon. Henry R. Selden, who has argued my cause so ably, so earnestly, so unanswerably before your honor, is my political sovereign. Precisely as no disfranchised person is entitled to sit upon a jury, and no woman is entitled to the franchise, so none but a regularly admitted lawyer is allowed to practice in the courts, and no woman can gain admission to the bar—hence, jury, judge, counsel, all must be of the superior class.

Judge Hunt. The Court must insist—the prisoner has been tried according to the established forms of law.

Miss Anthony. Yes, your honor, but by forms of law all made by men, interpreted by men, administered by men, in favor of men and against women; and hence your honor's ordered verdict of guilty, against a United States citizen for the exercise of the "citizen's right to vote," simply because that citizen was a woman and not a man. But yesterday, the same man-made forms of law declared it a crime punishable with $1,000 fine and six months' imprisonment to give a cup of cold water, a crust of bread or a night's shelter to a panting fugitive tracking his way to Canada; * and every man or woman in whose veins coursed a drop of human sympathy violated that wicked law, reckless of consequences,

* She is referring to the Fugitive Slave Law, passed in 1850.

and was justified in so doing. As then the slaves who got their freedom had to take it over or under or through the unjust forms of law, precisely so now must women take it to get their right to a voice in this government; and I have taken mine, and mean to take it at every opportunity.

Judge Hunt. The Court orders the prisoner to sit down. It will not allow another word.

Miss Anthony. When I was brought before your honor for trial, I hoped for a broad and liberal interpretation of the Constitution and its recent amendments, which should declare all United States citizens under its protecting aegis —which should declare equality of rights the national guarantee to all persons born or naturalized in the United States. But failing to get this justice—failing, even, to get a trial by a jury *not* of my peers—I ask not leniency at your hands but rather the full rigor of the law.

Judge Hunt. The Court must insist—[Here the prisoner sat down.] The prisoner will stand up. [Here Miss Anthony rose again.] The sentence of the Court is that you pay a fine of $100 and the costs of the prosecution.

Miss Anthony. May it please your honor, I will never pay a dollar of your unjust penalty. All the stock in trade I possess is a debt of $10,000, incurred by publishing my paper —The Revolution—the sole object of which was to educate all women to do precisely as I have done, rebel against your man-made, unjust, unconstitutional forms of law, which tax, fine, imprison and hang women, while denying them the right of representation in the government; and I will work on with might and main to pay every dollar of that honest debt, but not a penny shall go to this unjust claim. And I shall earnestly and persistently continue to urge all women to the practical recognition of the old Revolutionary maxim, "Resistance to tyranny is obedience to God."

Judge Hunt. Madam, the Court will not order you to stand committed until the fine is paid.

Susan B. Anthony

Woman Wants Bread,
Not the Ballot!

❧

During a brief two-year period, from 1868 to 1870, Susan B. Anthony published a weekly newspaper, *The Revolution,* with Elizabeth Cady Stanton and the abolitionist Parker Pillsbury as co-editors. *The Revolution* discussed such "scandalous" issues as divorce, prostitution, and the role of the church in the subjugation of women. The weekly also allied itself with the needs of workingwomen. (Anthony founded a Working Woman's Association of printing trade employees and was their delegate to the 1868 National Labor Congress.) *The Revolution* urged more female workers to join unions and "together say *Equal Pay for Equal Work.*"

Stanton and Anthony's determination to keep the platform of the woman's movement broad and inclusive by speaking out on labor and controversial social issues that affected women's lives, coupled with their earlier decision to oppose any suffrage amendment that did not include females, created grave dissent within the movement. By 1869 the feminist forces split. The National Woman Suffrage Association was organized under the leadership of Stanton and Anthony; the American Woman Suffrage Association was centered in New England, with Lucy Stone and Julia Ward Howe as prominent influences and many former anti-slavery stalwarts as adherents. The American based itself solely on the woman suffrage issue and gradually acquired a large conservative following.

In 1870 *The Revolution* collapsed financially and left Anthony with a $10,000 personal debt. Then fifty years old, Anthony undertook strenuous cross-country speaking tours to earn money; it took six years before she could repay it all. The selection below is from one of her most popular speeches of that period.

By this time Anthony had moved beyond the stage of a mere listing of the wrongs perpetrated against women. She was now

considering how woman might bring about change—what lever-
age, what power does she have? Anthony finally concluded that
women needed political power and that the ballot was the means
to that power.

The title *Woman Wants Bread, Not the Ballot!* is an ironical
comment on the failure of workingwomen in any significant numbers to participate in the suffrage movement. It was Anthony's
favorite speech, combining as it did two themes that greatly
interested her: the economic exploitation of woman and her
need for the vote in a democratic nation in order to assume some
control over the conditions of her life in every sphere. In another
of Anthony's speeches of the seventies, *Social Purity*—a full-
blown endorsement of Victorian morality for both men and
women—she notes that it is idle for women to hope to do battle
"until they shall be armed with weapons equal to those of the
enemy—votes and money."

Wherever, on the face of the globe or on the page of history,
you show me a disfranchised class, I will show you a degraded class of labor. Disfranchisement means inability to
make, shape or control one's own circumstances. The disfranchised must always do the work, accept the wages,
occupy the position the enfranchised assign to them. The
disfranchised are in the position of the pauper. You remember the old adage, "Beggars must not be choosers;" they
must take what they can get or nothing! That is exactly the
position of women in the world of work today; they can not
choose. If they could, do you for a moment believe they
would take the subordinate places and the inferior pay?
Nor is it a "new thing under the sun" for the disfranchised,
the inferior classes weighed down with wrongs, to declare
they "do not want to vote." The rank and file are not philosophers, they are not educated to think for themselves, but
simply to accept, unquestioned, whatever comes.

Years ago in England when the workingmen, starving
in the mines and factories, gathered in mobs and took bread

wherever they could get it, their friends tried to educate them into a knowledge of the causes of their poverty and degradation. At one of these "monster bread meetings," held in Manchester, John Bright said to them, "Working-men, what you need to bring to you cheap bread and plenty of it, is the franchise;" but those ignorant men shouted back to Mr. Bright, precisely as the women of America do to us today, "It is not the vote we want, it is bread." . . .

But at length, through the persistent demands of a little handful of reformers, there was introduced into the British Parliament the "household suffrage" bill of 1867 . . . . the opposition was championed by Robert Lowe, who presented all the stock objections to the extension of the franchise to "those ignorant, degraded working men," as he called them, that ever were presented in this country against giving the ballot to the negroes, and that are today being urged against the enfranchisement of women. . . . But notwithstanding Mr. Lowe's persistent opposition, the bill became a law; and before the session closed, that same individual moved that Parliament, having enfranchised these men, should now make an appropriation for the establishment and support of schools for the education of them and their sons. Now, mark you his reason why! "Unless they are educated," said he, "they will be the means of overturning the throne of England." So long as these poor men in the mines and factories had not the right to vote, the power to make and unmake the laws and lawmakers, to help or hurt the government, no measure ever had been proposed for their benefit although they were ground under the heel of the capitalist to a condition of abject slavery. But the moment this power is placed in their hands, before they have used it even once, this bitterest enemy to their possessing it is the first man to spring to his feet and make this motion for the most beneficient measure possible in their behalf—public schools for the education of themselves and their children. . . .

The great distinctive advantage possessed by the workingmen of this republic is that the son of the humblest citizen, black or white, has equal chances with the son of the richest in the land if he take advantage of the public schools, the colleges and the many opportunities freely offered. It is this equality of rights which makes our nation a home for the oppressed of all the monarchies of the old world.

And yet, notwithstanding the declaration of our Revolutionary fathers, "all men created equal," "governments derive their just powers from the consent of the governed," "taxation and representation inseparable"—notwithstanding all these grand enunciations, our government was founded upon the blood and bones of half a million human beings, bought and sold as chattels in the market. Nearly all the original thirteen States had property qualifications which disfranchised poor white men as well as women and negroes. . . .

It is said women do not need the ballot for their protection because they are supported by men. Statistics show that there are 3,000,000 women in this nation supporting themselves. In the crowded cities of the East they are compelled to work in shops, stores and factories for the merest pittance. In New York alone, there are over 50,000 of these women receiving less than fifty cents a day. Women wage-earners in different occupations have organized themselves into trades unions, from time to time, and made their strikes to get justice at the hands of their employers just as men have done, but I have yet to learn of a successful strike of any body of women. The best organized one I ever knew was that of the collar laundry women of the city of Troy, N.Y., the great emporium for the manufacture of shirts, collars and cuffs. They formed a trades union of several hundred members and demanded an increase of wages. It was refused. So one May morning in 1867, each woman threw down her scissors and her needle, her starch-pan and flat-iron, and for three long months not one returned to the factories. At the end of that time they were literally starved out, and the majority of them were compelled to go back, but not at their old wages, for their employers cut them down to even a lower figure.

In the winter following I met the president of this union, a bright young Irish girl, and asked her, "Do you not think if you had been 500 carpenters or 500 masons, you would have succeeded?" "Certainly," she said, and then she told me of 200 bricklayers who had the year before been on strike and gained every point with their employers. "What could have made the difference? Their 200 were but a fraction of that trade, while your 500 absolutely controlled yours." Finally she said, "It was because the editors ridiculed and denounced us." "Did they ridicule and denounce the bricklayers?" "No." "What did they say about you?" "Why, that our wages were good enough now, better than those of any other workingwomen except teachers; and if we weren't satisfied, we had better go and get married. . . . It must have been because our employers bribed the editors." . . . In the case of the bricklayers, no editor, either Democrat or Republican, would have accepted the proffer of a bribe, because he would have known that if he denounced or ridiculed those men, not only they but all the trades union men of the city at the next election would vote solidly against the nominees advocated by that editor. If those collar laundry women had been voters, they would have held, in that little city of Troy, the "balance of political power". . . .

There are many women equally well qualified with men for principals and superintendents of schools, and yet, while three-fourths of the teachers are women, nearly all of them are relegated to subordinate positions on half or at most two-thirds the salaries paid to men . . . . sex alone settles the question. . . .

And then again you say, "Capital, not the vote, regulates labor." Granted, for the sake of the argument, that capital does control the labor of women . . . but no one with eyes to see and ears to hear, will concede for a moment that capital absolutely dominates the work and wages of the free and enfranchised men of this republic. It is in order to lift the millions of our wage-earning women into a position of as much power over their own labor as men possess that they should be invested with the franchise. This ought to be done not only for the sake of justice to the women, but to the men with whom they compete; for, just so long as there is a degraded class of labor in the market, it always will be used by the capitalists to checkmate and undermine the superior classes.

Now that as a result of the agitation for equality of chances, and through the invention of machinery, there has come a great revolution in the world of economics, so that wherever a man may go to earn an honest dollar a woman may go also, there is no escape from the conclusion that she must be clothed with equal power to protect herself. That power is the ballot, the symbol of freedom and equality, without which no citizen is sure of keeping even that which he hath, much less of getting that which he hath not.

Victoria Woodhull & Tennessee Claflin

Virtue: What It Is, and What It Is Not

❧

Victoria Claflin Woodhull (1838–1927) and her sister Tennessee Claflin (1846–1923) never had been affiliated with the organized woman's movement when they burst upon the scene in 1870 with the publication of their radical feminist newspaper, *Woodhull & Claflin's Weekly*. The editors discussed such topics as prostitution, venereal disease, abortion, and female sexuality, and printed news about workingwomen and their efforts to organize and better their conditions. The *Weekly* advocated spiritualism, socialism (it was the first American periodical to publish the *Communist Manifesto*) and free love (a novel by George Sand was published as a serial).

The resourceful Claflin sisters, whose background included dismal poverty and unsavory careers with a "medical" road show and as clairvoyants, had recently earned a considerable fortune in New York as Wall Street's first female stockbrokers. (Their brokerage firm was bankrolled by Cornelius Vanderbilt, an ardent admirer of Tennessee Claflin.) Their uninhibited sex lives, which they made no attempt to conceal, was the subject of much gossip.

Thus, when Victoria Woodhull showed up in Washington in early 1871, just as Susan B. Anthony was about to open a convention of the National Woman Suffrage Association, her presence was probably a source of embarrassment for some delegates. Opponents of woman's rights had long used the charge of "free love" to discredit the movement, and Woodhull frankly avowed her belief in sexual freedom.

In Washington, Woodhull was invited to address the House Judiciary Committee, a privilege never before accorded a woman. The leaders of the National could not ignore this occasion and came to hear her speak. She made a brilliant presentation, suggesting that female suffrage was already an implied right in the Constitution as a result of the use of the word "person" in the Fourteenth and Fifteenth Amendments. (This was the same argument Susan B. Anthony later employed at her trial.) The women were impressed and invited Woodhull to repeat her congressional address before the suffrage convention that very day.

To criticisms about Woodhull's unconventional sexual behavior, Elizabeth Cady Stanton replied: "We have already women enough sacrificed to this sentimental, hypocritical prating about purity, without going out of our way to increase the number. Women have crucified the Mary Wollstonecrafts, the Fanny Wrights and the George Sands of all ages. . . . Let us end this ignoble record and henceforth stand by womanhood. If this present woman [Woodhull] must be crucified, let men drive the spikes."

For a time Victoria Woodhull became in the press the most talked about figure of the suffrage movement. At a National convention in New York she threatened that unless Congress gave women the vote, they would set up a new government. "We mean treason," she proclaimed; "we mean secession, and on a thousand times grander scale than was that of the South. We are plotting a revolution; we will overthrow this bogus Republic and plant a government of righteousness in its stead." Shortly after announcing publicly "I am a free lover!" Woodhull was on the platform at National's 1872 Washington convention, seated between Elizabeth Stanton and the venerable Lucretia Mott.

Finally, Susan B. Anthony called a halt to Woodhull's spectacular ascent in the movement. By this time Woodhull had convinced Stanton that the National ought to back her as candidate for President of the United States in the 1872 election! Anthony vetoed this idea and expelled Woodhull and her followers from the next suffrage convention when they tried to wrest control of a meeting from her. Wrote Susan Anthony in her journal afterward: "Never did Mrs. Stanton do so foolish a thing. All came near being lost."

The flamboyance and grandiosity of Victoria Woodhull tend to obscure her and her sister's real contribution to the ideas of feminism in their relatively brief association with the American woman's movement. For publicly challenging the dearly held Victorian belief in the purity (that is, asexuality) of women, they were certain to be isolated and silenced. However, there is no doubt that Woodhull and Claflin gave voice to the secret longings and dissatisfactions of great numbers of women. Elizabeth Stanton wrote in her confidential diary, begun at the age of sixty-five, that she had come to the conclusion that "the first great work to be accomplished for woman is to revolutionize the dogma that sex is a crime." Later she added, "a healthy woman has as much passion as a man."

The following excerpts from two articles printed in *Woodhull & Claflin's Weekly* in 1871 and 1872 were written by Tennessee (sometimes written "Tennie C.") Claflin, who was a better writer and clearer thinker than her more famous sister. In the first article Claflin urged women to gain their sexual freedom by defying oppressive social customs; in the second, she pointed out that woman's economic dependence forces her to submerge her own nature and become little more than a sexual snare for men.

Words have different and sometimes contradictory meanings. . . . These different meanings of words . . . reveal a whole history and a whole philosophy. . . . Notably does this happen in respect to the words *free* and *virtuous* as applied to men and to women.

A *free* man is a noble being; a *free* woman is a contemptible being. Freedom for a man is emancipation from degrading conditions which prevent the expansion of his soul into godlike grandeur and nobility, which it is assumed is his natural tendency in freedom. Freedom for a woman is, on the contrary, escape from those necessary restraining conditions which prevent the sinking of her soul into degradation and vice, which it is all unconsciously assumed is her natural tendency. In other terms, the use of this one word, in its two-fold application to men and to woman, reveals the unconscious but ever present conviction in the public mind that men tend, of course, heavenward in their natures and development, and that women tend just as naturally hell-ward . . . . freedom is a condition desirable and favorable for men, because men are naturally good, and require only the opportunity to show that fact; but a condition undesirable and unfavorable for women, because women are naturally bad, and require only the opportunity to show their innate tendency to vice or wickedness.

Insulting as this estimate is to our sex, it is the basis on which the whole question of social freedom is argued by the outside world. It is naively and continually assumed that if social restraints were removed, all women, the mothers and sisters and wives and daughters of our virtuous male citizens, would immediately and incontinently *go to the bad*. Men are every day virtually saying this of their own mothers, and women are thoughtlessly chiming in and pronouncing the ban of reprobation upon the name of their own womanhood. . . .

In the same striking way the two uses of the word *virtue* tell the same sad tale of the popular estimate of the character or nature of the two sexes. The very word *virtue* is, I believe, partly derived from the Latin *vir,* the distinctive name of man, and meant originally "manliness." It was natural in a crude age that all questions of womanliness should be left out of account. Even in respect to man it was the warlike quality of mere physical strength which was first prized, and which first received the name of *virtue*. We retain this general idea of strength or efficiency as the first meaning of *virtue* still, as when we speak of the virtue of a medicine, of a public measure, and the like. But in this more spiritual and cultured age, *virtue,* as applied to *man,* has risen to a higher degree of significance, and now means moral goodness, or a general conformity of the whole life to high moral ideas and purposes. But, applied to *woman,* it is confined to a narrow and insulting specialty. It means that woman has never been approached in a special way by man, and nothing but that. Apart from that special idea of virtue, the woman may have all the nobler qualities of her sex— be a pattern of generosity, inspiration, religious emotion- ality even—and yet she is not virtuous, and never can be- come so; but if she is sound in that matter, she may be a virago, a thief, or a fiend, but she is perfectly virtuous— she possesses that which is "prized above rubies."

All this is simply execrable. It is degrading, insulting mockery to define female virtue in this way, or in any way different from man's virtue. And women are constrained to accept these disparaging discriminations by an organized social opinion which is excessively tyrannical. From the mere imputation of *impropriety* in this one particular women shrink and cower with the most abject terror. This slavery to opinion must be abolished; women must vindicate their right to an absolute freedom in their own conduct, except that they shall have no right to encroach on others. The revolt against any oppression usually goes to an opposite extreme for a time; and that is right and necessary. We cannot render the terms "libertine" and "rake" as op- probrious as men have made "mistress" and "courtesan". . . . Let us, then, resort to the opposite tactics, and take the sting out of these bad words by having a consciousness of rectitude, and then not shrinking from any imputation what- ever. The world enslaves our sex by the mere fear of an epithet; and as long as it can throw any vile term at us, be- fore which we cower, it can maintain our enslavement. It is not "freedom" alone, but every other epithet *intended to degrade,* that woman must grow strong enough to defy be- fore she will be free. I do not mean that she shall be what these words are meant to convey, but merely that she shall let the world know that female virtue means here- after something different—that it means, in a word, *just what would make a man virtuous and good.* He or she who would be free must defy the enemy, and must be *ultra* enough to exhaust the possibilities of the enemy's assault; and it will not be until women can contemplate and accept unconcernedly whatsoever imputation an ignorant, bitter, lying, and persecuting world may heap on them that they will be really free.

Victoria Woodhull & Tennessee Claflin

Which Is to Blame?

❦

With the world generally, the assumption is that women, and women only, are liable to seduction, and that men are entirely free from any such weakness. Now what is the implication in all this? Why, simply that women are weaklings and ninnies, and that they have no opinion, no character, no power of self-defense, but simply the liability to be influenced to their ruin by men. And women consent to and strengthen this implication by conceding the truth of this false notion, by joining in the clamor about seduction, precisely as they concur in the false and insulting discrimination between the virtue of man and the virtue of woman. Now, the fact is that seduction is, and ought to be, mutual. No love is without seduction in its highest sense. But love is not the only attribute of either man or woman. There should also be wisdom, character, purpose, and power of self-regulation and defense on the part of each. If there is any difference, woman is, of the two, the grand seductive force, whether the seduction be legitimate charm or its counterpart. She is, by nature and organization, if the poet speak the truth, "a magazine of enticement and influence and power" over the imagination and conduct of the opposite sex. But even if that were not so, if she stood on the same level of capacity in this respect with the man, the condition into which society has thrust her compels her to make a profession of seduction. It is considered a reproach for a woman to be an "old maid." She must, therefore, by all possible means, lure some man into marriage; and not succeeding in that directly, she is tempted to beguile him into some act which will compromise him and compel marriage subsequently. She has the strongest possible motive, therefore, from this point of view, to be herself the tempter; and if the roofs were lifted off the tops of the houses, if the facts were simply known of what is every day occurring, I believe it would be found that a majority of women exert an undue influence over men.

But it is not merely that the female sex is pre-eminently interested in the whole matter of love . . . nor the fact, which I have alluded to, that she is humiliated and despised by society if she fails to secure a husband; there are still stronger impulses and motives and necessities operating on her. As things are in the world at present, women have not equal chances with men of earning and winning anything; men hold the purse and women are dependents and candidates for election to place. They must entice, and seduce, and entrap men, either in the legitimate or in the illegitimate way, in order to secure their portion of the spoil. It is no fault of theirs if they have to do this. Society condemns them to a condition in which they have no other resource. I am not arguing the rectitude or other wise of that point now. I am merely adverting to the fact as a reason why many women make a business—the great pursuit, in fact, of their lives—of the seduction of men; while with men the betrayal of women is an incident, mostly a sudden temptation perhaps thrown in their way, without suspicion on their part, by the very women who then raise a hubbub of excitement about having been ruined. When people had slaves, they expected that their pigs, chickens, corn, and everything lying loose about the plantation would be stolen. But the planters began by stealing the liberty of their slaves, by stealing their labor, by stealing, in fact, all they had; and the natural result was that the slaves stole back all they could. So in the case of women. Reduced to the condition of dependency and with no other avenue for acquirement or success than the one which lies through their mastery or influence over the opposite sex, their natural powers to charm and seduce are, of course, reinforced by astuteness and trickery, and they not only have the cunning to beguile the men, in the majority of cases, but the astuteness also to throw the blame on the men for betraying them. This is sharp practice; but they are taught in a school of sharp practice which the men have instituted for them; and the result is a natural and necessary one from the present organization of society. The very foundation of our existing social order is mutual deception and all-prevalent hypocrisy; and this will always be the case until we have freedom; until we recognize the rights of nature, until we provide in a normal and proper way for every passion of the human soul. . . .

There are, undoubtedly, women who are weak and silly, and simple, and who are taken advantage of by designing men. Until we have such systems of education as will tend to prevent women from being weak, simple, and silly, it is undoubtedly right to have laws punishing seduction with the utmost severity; but we have also, as I think I have shown, ninnies among men, and ought we not, therefore, to have laws for their protection? An Act of the Legislature entitled "An Act for the Protection of Ninnies against Designing Women" would be refreshing, and, perhaps, logically based upon the reason of the laws for the protection of female virtue.

The Elixir of Life

Victoria Woodhull was elected president of the American Association of Spiritualists. At their annual convention in Chicago in 1873, she spoke on "The Elixir of Life," excerpts from which appear below.

In this speech, with her customary disregard of nineteenth-century proprieties, Woodhull openly labeled wives as "sexual slaves." Even more remarkable for her time was her frank assertion of the central importance of "sexual love" and her insights into the harmful effects of intercourse without pleasure or without orgasm ("consummation").

I have said that this problem of sexual love is the most important one that ever engaged the human mind. . . .

Sexual intercourse that is in accordance with nature, and therefore proper, is that which is based upon mutual love and desire, and that ultimates in reciprocal benefit. . . .

[T]here are several classes [of sexual intercourse not in accordance with nature] which deserve to be enumerated, so that they may be understood wherever any of them may be met. First, that class where it is claimed by legal right; second, that class where the female, to please the male, submits without the proper self desire; third, that class where, for money, or any motive other than love, the female sells the use of her body to the male for his gratification; fourth, that class where mutual love and desire exist, but where there is such want of adaptation as to make mutual consummation impossible.

Now, under either of these conditions, if sexual intercourse be maintained for any considerable length of time, disease and sexual demoralization will surely follow; but the most destructive to health as well as the most numerous, are the first and the last classes, which occur almost altogether in marriage. The wife who submits to sexual intercourse against her wishes or desires, virtually commits suicide; while the husband who compels it, commits murder, and ought just as much to be punished for it, as though he strangled her to death for refusing him.

But this even is not so destructive to health as is that intercourse, carried on habitually, without regard to perfect and reciprocal consummation. And when it is known that three-fourths of all married women, who otherwise might be happily mated, suffer from this cause, the terrible and widespread results may be readily conceived, and the need for amelioration as readily understood. I need not explain to any woman the effect of unconsummated intercourse though she may attempt to deceive herself about it; but every man needs to have it thundered in his ears until he wakes to the fact that he is not the only party to the act, and that the other party demands a return for all that he receives; demands that he shall not be enriched at her expense; demands that he shall not, either from ignorance or selfish desire, carry her impulse forward on its mission only to cast it backward with the mission unfulfilled, to prostrate the impelling power and to breed nervous debility or irritability and sexual demoralization. . . .

It is a fact terrible to contemplate, yet it is nevertheless true, and ought to be pressed upon the world for its recognition: that fully one-half of all women seldom or never experience any pleasure whatever in the sexual act. Now this is an impeachment of nature, a disgrace to our civilization. . . .

I have had hundreds of wives say to me, "I would not endure these conditions for a single moment, were I not dependent upon my husband for a home," or "if society would not ostracize me for leaving him;" or some other equally lamentable excuses. . . . To me this farce of marriage is a public placarding, merely, to this effect: that I, the bearer, am this day sold, to be the sexual slave of the person to whom the law, holding that I do not know enough and am unable to protect myself, has committed the care of my person. Wives may not think they are slaves, and yet be open to this charge. Some may not be; but let the large majority attempt to assert their sexual freedom, and they will quickly come to the realization.

To what does modern marriage amount, if it be not to hold sexual slaves, who otherwise would be free? . . .

Beside the evils of improper sexual relations resulting from legalized prostitution, there are the still more terrible conditions to which they are condemned, who languish in single cursedness. To this very considerable portion of female humanity the right to the exercise and enjoyment of their sexual instincts is absolutely denied, under the penalty of social death. They are condemned to a life of degradation and misery, from which there is no escape. Add to this class who are sexually starved, those who are compelled to undesired relations with the legal owners of their sexual organs, and a sum total of misery is formed which altogether beggars description. . . .

I said in my Steinway Hall speech, "I am a Free Lover. . . ." I will supplement this by saying now: That I will love whom I may; that I will love as long or as short a period as I can; that I will change this love when the conditions to which I have referred indicate that it ought to be changed; and that neither you nor any law you can make shall deter me. I hope everybody will understand just what sort of a Free Lover I am, and never have any more contention over it.

Elizabeth Cady Stanton

Womanliness

❦

In 1890 the two factions of the American woman's movement were reunited as the National American Woman Suffrage Association. Stanton, looking over the proposed constitution of the new organization, felt that dictates of "policy and propriety" had resulted in so narrowing the platform to the single issue of suffrage that the movement would henceforth cease to "point the way." She wrote, "It is germane to our platform to discuss every invidious distinction of sex . . . . covering the whole range of human experience."

Despite this basic disagreement with the goals of the new organization, Stanton was elected first president. In her address to the convention of 1890, Stanton slighted the suffrage issue and spoke on the broader questions that interested her.

Some men tell us we must be patient and persuasive; that we must be womanly. My friends, what is man's idea of womanliness? It is to have a manner which pleases him— quiet, deferential, submissive, approaching him as a subject does a master. He wants no self-assertion on our part, no defiance, no vehement arraignment of him as a robber and a criminal . . . . while every right achieved by the oppressed has been wrung from tyrants by force; while the darkest page on human history is the outrages on women—shall men still tell us to be patient, persuasive, womanly?

What do we know as yet of the womanly? The women we have seen thus far have been, with rare exceptions, the mere echoes of men. Man has spoken in the State, the Church and the Home, and made the codes, creeds and customs which govern every relation in life, and women have simply echoed all his thoughts and walked in the paths he prescribed. And this they call womanly! When Joan of Arc led the French army to victory I dare say the carpet knights of England thought her unwomanly. When Florence Nightingale, in search of blankets for the soldiers in the Crimean War, cut her way through all orders and red tape, commanded with vehemence and determination those who guarded the supplies to "unlock the doors and not talk to her of proper authorities when brave men were shivering in their beds," no doubt she was called unwomanly. To me, "unlock the doors" sounds better than any words of circumlocution, however sweet and persuasive, and I consider that she took the most womanly way of accomplishing her object. Patience and persuasiveness are beautiful virtues in dealing with children and feeble-minded adults, but those who have the gift of reason and understand the principles of justice, it is our duty to compel to act up to the highest light that is in them, and as promptly as possible. . . .

In this way we make ourselves mediums through which the great souls of the past may speak again. The moment we begin to fear the opinions of others and hesitate to tell the truth that is in us, and from motives of policy are silent when we should speak, the divine floods of light and life flow no longer into our souls. Every truth we see is ours to give the world, not to keep for ourselves alone, for in so doing we cheat humanity out of their rights and check our own development.

Elizabeth Cady Stanton

Solitude of Self

The following speech was delivered by Stanton before the House
Judiciary Committee and the National American convention in
1892. By then seventy-six years old and widowed, this was her
last appearance at a national convention, although she continued to send in speeches to be read by Susan B. Anthony.

This address was considered by many at the time to be her
masterpiece. Stanton herself was "much inclined" to think it the
best thing she had ever written. Perhaps a bit diffuse to earn this
distinction, in comparison with some of her earlier incisive writings, "Solitude of Self" is nevertheless an eloquent and mature
plea for the right of every woman to selfhood as well as womanhood.

The point I wish plainly to bring before you on this occasion is the individuality of each human soul—our Protestant
idea, the right of individual conscience and judgment—
our republican idea, individual citizenship. In discussing the
rights of woman, we are to consider, first, what belongs to
her as an individual, in a world of her own, the arbiter of
her own destiny, an imaginary Robinson Crusoe with her
woman Friday on a solitary island. Her rights under such
circumstances are to use all her faculties for her own
safety and happiness. . . .

It is only the incidental relations of life, such as mother,
wife, sister, daughter, which may involve some special duties
and training. In the usual discussion in regard to woman's
sphere . . . her rights and duties as an individual, as a citi-

zen, as a woman, [are uniformly subordinated] to the necessities of these incidental relations, some of which a large class of women may never assume. In discussing the sphere of man we do not decide his rights as an individual, as a citizen, as a man, by his duties as a father, a husband, a brother, or a son, relations some of which he may never fill. Moreover, he would be better fitted for these very relations, and whatever special work he might choose to do to earn his bread, by the complete development of all his faculties as an individual.

Just so with woman. The education that will fit her to discharge the duties in the largest sphere of human usefulness, will best fit her for whatever special work she may be compelled to do.

The isolation of every human soul and the necessity of self-dependence must give each individual the right to choose his own surroundings. The strongest reason for giving woman all the opportunities for higher education, for the full development of her faculties, her forces of mind and body; for giving her the most enlarged freedom of thought and action; a complete emancipation from all forms of bondage, of custom, dependence, superstition; from all the crippling influences of fear; is the solitude and personal responsibility of her own individual life. The strongest reason why we ask for woman a voice in the government under which she lives; in the religion she is asked to believe; equality in social life, where she is the chief factor; a place in the trades and professions, where she may earn her bread, is because of her birthright to self-sovereignty; because, as an individual, she must rely on herself. No matter how much women prefer to lean, to be protected and supported, nor how much men desire to have them do so, they must make the voyage of life alone, and for safety in an emergency they must know something of the laws of navigation. . . .

Nothing strengthens the judgment and quickens the conscience like individual responsibility. Nothing adds such dignity to character as the recognition of one's self-sovereignty; the right to an equal place, everywhere conceded; a place earned by personal merit, not an artificial attainment by inheritance, wealth, family, and position. Seeing, then, that the responsibilities of life rest equally on man and woman, that their destiny is the same, they need the same preparation for time and eternity. The talk of sheltering woman from the fierce storms of life is the sheerest mockery, for they beat on her from every point of the compass, just as they do on man, and with more fatal results, for he has been trained to protect himself, to resist, to conquer.

Whatever the theories may be of woman's dependence on man, in the supreme moments of her life he can not bear her burdens. . . . We may have many friends, love, kindness, sympathy and charity to smooth our pathway in everyday life, but in the tragedies and triumphs of human experience each mortal stands alone.

But when all artificial trammels are removed, and women are recognized as individuals, responsible for their own environments, thoroughly educated for all positions in life they may be called to fill; with all the resources in themselves that liberal thought and broad culture can give; guided by their own conscience and judgment; trained to self-protection by a healthy development of the muscular system and skill in the use of weapons of defense, and stimulated to self-support by a knowledge of the business world and the pleasure that pecuniary independence must ever give; when women are trained in this way they will, in a measure, be fitted for those years of solitude that come to all, whether prepared or otherwise.

IV

MEN AS FEMINISTS

John Stuart Mill

The Subjection of Women

John Stuart Mill (1806–1873) was taken into custody by London police at the age of seventeen for distributing birth-control information. In 1865, when he was elected to Parliament, Mill become the political voice of the recently organized British woman's suffrage movement. His amendment to the 1867 Reform Bill provoked the first Parliamentary debate on votes for women. Moreover, in his famed address to Parliament, Mill went beyond the issue of enfranchisement to argue the larger question of woman's full social equality.

Mill's long essay *The Subjection of Women* was written in 1861 but was not published until 1869. The philosopher's devoted friend of twenty years and later his wife, Harriet Taylor, is known to have had a tremendous influence on this work. (Just how much she may actually have participated in its authorship is today a disputed point.) At the time of Mill's marriage to her in 1851 he issued a formal protest "against the existing law of marriage" which conferred excessive power on the husband over "the freedom of action of the other party." This protest was made several years before that of Lucy Stone and her husband.

Mill regarded women as a subject class. However, he recognized that the state of female bondage in at least one respect was a refinement over that of the black slave: each man wants his woman to be "not a forced slave but a willing one, not a slave merely, but a favourite." In *The Subjection of Women,* he emphasized that subtle and pervasive social conditioning is the means by which women are prepared to accede to roles as the servants of men.

Sigmund Freud criticized Mill's study of women for giving

insufficient consideration to what Freud believed to be inborn temperamental differences between the sexes.

The object of this Essay is to explain as clearly as I am able, the grounds of an opinion which I have held from the very earliest period when I had formed any opinions at all on social or political matters, and which, instead of being weakened or modified, has been constantly growing stronger by the progress of reflection and the experience of life. That the principle which regulates the existing social relations between the two sexes—the legal subordination of one sex to the other—is wrong in itself, and now one of the chief hindrances to human improvement; and that it ought to be replaced by a principle of perfect equality, admitting no power or privilege on the one side, nor disability on the other.

The very words necessary to express the task I have undertaken, show how arduous it is. But it would be a mistake to suppose that the difficulty of the case must lie in the insufficiency or obscurity of the grounds of reason on which my conviction rests. The difficulty is that which exists in all cases in which there is a mass of feeling to be contended against. . . . And there are so many causes tending to make the feelings connected with this subject the most intense and most deeply-rooted of all those which gather round and protect old institutions and customs, that we need not wonder to find them as yet less undermined and loosened than any of the rest by the progress of the great modern spiritual and social transition; nor suppose that the barbarisms to which men cling longest must be less barbarisms than those which they earlier shake off. . . .

In early times, the great majority of the male sex were slaves, as well as the whole of the female. And many ages elapsed, some of them ages of high cultivation, before any

thinker was bold enough to question the rightfulness, and
the absolute social necessity, either of the one slavery or of
the other. By degrees such thinkers did arise; and (the general progress of society assisting) the slavery of the male sex
has, in all the countries of Christian Europe at least (though,
in one of them, only within the last few years) been at length
abolished, and that of the female sex has been gradually
changed into a milder form of dependence. But this dependence, as it exists at present, is not an original institution,
taking a fresh start from considerations of justice and social
expediency—it is the primitive state of slavery lasting on,
through successive mitigations and modifications occasioned
by the same causes which have softened the general manners, and brought all human relations more under the control of justice and the influence of humanity. It has not lost
the taint of its brutal origin. . . .

Less than forty years ago, Englishmen might still by law
hold human beings in bondage as saleable property: within
the present century they might kidnap them and carry them
off, and work them literally to death. This absolutely extreme case of the law of force, condemned by those who can
tolerate almost every other form of arbitrary power, and
which, of all others presents features the most revolting to
the feelings of all who look at it from an impartial position,
was the law of civilised and Christian England within the
memory of persons now living: and in one half of Anglo-
Saxon America three or four years ago, not only did slavery
exist, but the slave-trade, and the breeding of slaves expressly for it, was a general practice between slave-states.
Yet not only was there a greater strength of sentiment
against it, but, in England at least, a less amount either of
feeling or of interest in favour of it, than of any other of the
customary abuses of force: for its motive was the love of
gain, unmixed and undisguised; and those who profited by
it were a very small numerical fraction of the country, while
the natural feeling of all who were not personally interested

in it, was unmitigated abhorrence. So extreme an instance makes it almost superfluous to refer to any other: but consider the long duration of absolute monarchy. In England at present it is the almost universal conviction that military despotism is a case of the law of force, having no other origin or justification. Yet in all the great nations of Europe except England it either still exists, or has only just ceased to exist, and has even now a strong party favourable to it in all ranks of the people, especially among persons of station and consequence. Such is the power of an established system, even when far from universal. . . . How different are these cases from that of the power of men over women! I am not now prejudging the question of its justifiableness. I am showing how vastly more permanent it could not but be, even if not justifiable, than these other dominations which have nevertheless lasted down to our own time. Whatever gratification of pride there is in the possession of power, and whatever personal interest in its exercise, is in this case not confined to a limited class, but common to the whole male sex. Instead of being, to most of its supporters, a thing desirable chiefly in the abstract, or, like the political ends usually contended for by factions, of little private importance to any but the leaders; it comes home to the person and hearth of every male head of a family, and of everyone who looks forward to being so. The clodhopper exercises, or is to exercise, his share of the power equally with the highest nobleman. And the case is that in which the desire of power is the strongest: for everyone who desires power, desires it most over those who are nearest to him, with whom his life is passed, with whom he has most concerns in common, and in whom any independence of his authority is oftenest likely to interfere with his individual preferences. If, in the other cases specified, powers manifestly grounded only on force, and having so much less to support them, are so slowly and with so much difficulty got rid of, much more must it be so with this, even if it rests on no better foundation than those.

We must consider, too, that the possessors of the power have facilities in this case, greater than in any other, to prevent any uprising against it. Every one of the subjects lives under the very eye, and almost, it may be said, in the hands, of one of the masters—in closer intimacy with him than with any of her fellow-subjects; with no means of combining against him, no power of even locally overmastering him, and, on the other hand, with the strongest motives for seeking his favour and avoiding to give him offence. In struggles for political emancipation, everybody knows how often its champions are bought off by bribes, or daunted by terrors. In the case of women, each individual of the subject-class is in a chronic state of bribery and intimidation combined. In setting up the standard of resistance, a large number of the leaders, and still more of the followers, must make an almost complete sacrifice of the pleasures or the alleviations of their own individual lot. If ever any system of privilege and enforced subjection had its yoke tightly riveted on the necks of those who are kept down by it, this has. I have not yet shown that it is a wrong system: but everyone who is capable of thinking on the subject must see that even if it is, it was certain to outlast all other forms of unjust authority. And when some of the grossest of the other forms still exist in many civilised countries, and have only recently been got rid of in others, it would be strange if that which is so much the deepest rooted had yet been perceptibly shaken anywhere. There is more reason to wonder that the protests and testimonies against it should have been so numerous and so weighty as they are. . . .

But, it will be said, the rule of men over women differs from all these others in not being a rule of force: it is accepted voluntarily; women make no complaint, and are consenting parties to it. In the first place, a great number of women do not accept it. Ever since there have been women able to make their sentiments known by their writings (the only mode of publicity which society permits to them), an increasing number of them have recorded protests against their present social condition: and recently many thousands of them, headed by the most eminent women known to the public, have petitioned Parliament for their admission to the Parliamentary Suffrage. The claim of women to be educated as solidly, and in the same branches of knowledge, as men, is urged with growing intensity, and with a great prospect of success; while the demand for their admission into professions and occupations hitherto closed against them, becomes every year more urgent. Though there are not in this country, as there are in the United States, periodical conventions and an organised party to agitate for the Rights of Women, there is a numerous and active society organised and managed by women, for the more limited object of obtaining the political franchise. Nor is it only in our own country and in America that women are beginning to protest, more or less collectively, against the disabilities under which they labour. France, and Italy, and Switzerland, and Russia now afford examples of the same thing. How many more women there are who silently cherish similar aspirations, no one can possibly know; but there are abundant tokens how many *would* cherish them, were they not so strenuously taught to repress them as contrary to the proprieties of their sex. . . .

All causes, social and natural, combine to make it unlikely that women should be collectively rebellious to the power of men. They are so far in a position different from all other subject classes, that their masters require something more from them than actual service. Men do not want solely the obedience of women, they want their sentiments. All men, except the most brutish, desire to have, in the woman most nearly connected with them, not a forced slave but a willing one, not a slave merely, but a favourite. They have therefore put everything in practice to enslave their minds. The masters of all other slaves rely, for maintaining obedience, on fear; either fear of themselves, or religious fears. The masters of women wanted more than simple obedience, and they turned the whole force of education to effect their purpose. All women are brought up from the very earliest years in the belief that their ideal of character is the very opposite to that of men; not self-will, and government by self-control, but submission, and yielding to the control of others. All the moralities tell them that it is the duty of women, and all the current sentimentalities that it is their nature, to live for others; to make complete abnegation of themselves, and to have no life but in their affections. And by their affections are meant the only ones they are allowed to have—those to the men with whom they are connected, or to the children who constitute an additional and indefeasible tie between them and a man. When we put together three things—first, the natural attraction between opposite sexes; secondly, the wife's entire dependence on the husband, every privilege or pleasure she has being either his gift, or depending entirely on his will; and lastly, that the principal object of human pursuit, consideration, and all objects of social ambition, can in general be sought or obtained by her only through him, it would be a miracle if the object of being attractive to men had not become the polar star of feminine education and formation of character. And, this great means of influence over the minds of women having been acquired, an instinct of selfishness made men avail themselves of it to the utmost as a means of holding women in subjection, by representing to them meekness, submissiveness, and resignation of all individual will into the hands of a man, as an essential part of sexual attractiveness. Can it be doubted that any of the other yokes which mankind have succeeded in breaking, would have subsisted till now if the same means had existed, and had been so sedulously used, to bow down their minds to it? If it had been made the object of the life of every young plebeian to find personal favour in the eyes of some patrician, of every young serf with some seigneur; if domestication with him, and a share of his personal affections, had been held out as the prize which they all should look out for, the most gifted and aspiring being able to reckon on the most desirable prizes; and if, when this prize had been obtained, they had been shut out by a wall of brass from all interests not centring in him, all feelings and desires but those which he shared or inculcated; would not serfs and seigneurs, plebeians and patricians, have been as broadly distinguished at this day as men and women are? and would not all but a thinker here and there, have believed the distinction to be a fundamental and unalterable fact in human nature? . . .

At present, in the more improved countries, the disabilities of women are the only case, save one, in which laws and institutions take persons at their birth, and ordain that they shall never in all their lives be allowed to compete for certain things. The one exception is that of royalty. Persons still are born to the throne; no one, not of the reigning family, can ever occupy it, and no one even of that family can, by any means but the course of hereditary succession, attain it. All other dignities and social advantages are open to the whole male sex: many indeed are only attainable by wealth, but wealth may be striven for by anyone, and is actually obtained by many men of the very humblest origin. The difficulties, to the majority, are indeed insuperable without the aid of fortunate accidents; but no male human being is under any legal ban: neither law nor opinion superadd artificial obstacles to the natural ones. . . . The disabilities, therefore, to which women are subject from the mere fact of their birth, are the solitary examples of the kind in modern legislation. In no instance except this, which comprehends half the human race, are the higher social functions closed against anyone by a fatality of birth which no exertions, and no change of circumstances, can overcome. . . .

Neither does it avail anything to say that the *nature* of the two sexes adapts them to their present functions and position, and renders these appropriate to them. Standing on the ground of common sense and the constitution of the human mind, I deny that anyone knows, or can know, the nature of the two sexes, as long as they have only been seen in their present relation to one another. If men had ever been found in society without women, or women without men, or if there had been a society of men and women in which the women were not under the control of the men, something might have been positively known about the mental and moral differences which may be inherent in the nature of each. What is now called the nature of women is an eminently artificial thing—the result of forced repression in some directions, unnatural stimulation in others. It may be asserted without scruple, that no other class of dependents have had their character so entirely distorted from its natural proportions by their relation with their masters; for, if conquered and slave races have been, in some respects, more forcibly repressed, whatever in them has not been crushed down by an iron heel has generally been let alone, and if left with any liberty of development, it has developed itself according to its own laws; but in the case of women, a hothouse and stove cultivation has always been carried on of some of the capabilities of their nature, for the benefit and pleasure of their masters. Then, because certain products of the general vital force sprout luxuriantly and reach a great development in this heated atmosphere and under this active nurture and watering, while other shoots from the same root, which are left outside in the wintry air, with ice purposely heaped all round them, have a stunted growth, and some are burnt off with fire and disappear; men, with that inability to recognize their own work which distinguishes the unanalytic mind, indolently believe that the tree grows of itself in the way they have made it grow, and that it would die if one half of it were not kept in a vapour bath and the other half in the snow. . . .

Hence, in regard to that most difficult question, what are the natural differences between the two sexes—a subject on which it is impossible in the present state of society to obtain complete and correct knowledge—while almost everybody dogmatises upon it, almost all neglect and make light of the only means by which any partial insight can be obtained into it. This is, an analytic study of the most important department of psychology, the laws of the influence of circumstances on character. . . . The profoundest knowledge of the laws of the formation of character is indispensable to entitle anyone to affirm even that there is any difference, much more what the difference is, between the two sexes considered as moral and rational beings; and since no one, as yet, has that knowledge (for there is hardly any subject which, in proportion to its importance, has been so little studied), no one is thus far entitled to any positive opinion on the subject. Conjectures are all that can at present be made. . . . nothing final can be known, so long as those who alone can really know it, women themselves, have given but little testimony, and that little, mostly suborned. . . . The most favourable case which a man can generally have for studying the character of a woman, is that of his own wife: for the opportunities are greater, and the cases of complete sympathy not so unspeakably rare. And in fact, this is the source from which any knowledge worth having on the subject has, I believe, generally come. But most men have not had the opportunity of studying in this way more than a single case: accordingly one can, to an almost laughable degree, infer what a man's wife is like, from his opinions about women in general. To make even this one case yield any result, the woman must be worth knowing, and the man not only a competent judge, but of a character so sympathetic in itself, and so well adapted to hers, that he can either read her mind by sympathetic intuition, or has nothing in himself which makes her shy of disclosing it. Hardly anything, I believe, can be more rare than this conjunction. It often happens that there is the most complete unity of feeling and community of interests as to all external things, yet the one has as little admission into the internal life of the other as if they were common acquaintance. Even with true affection, authority on the one side and subordination on the other prevent perfect confidence. Though nothing may be intentionally withheld, much is not shown. In the analogous relation of parent and child, the corresponding phenomenon must have been in the observation of everyone. As between father and son, how many are the cases in which the father, in spite of real affection on both sides, obviously to all the world does not know, nor suspect, parts of the son's character familiar to his companions and equals. The truth is, that the position of looking up to another is extremely unpropitious to complete sincerity and openness with him. The fear of losing ground in his opinion or in his feelings is so strong, that even in an upright character, there is an unconscious tendency to show only the best side, or the side which, though not the best, is that which he most likes to see: and it may be confidently said that thorough knowledge of one another hardly ever exists, but between persons who, besides being intimates, are equals. How much more true, then, must all this be, when the one is not only under the authority of the other, but has it inculcated on her as a duty to reckon everything else subordinate to his comfort and pleasure, and to let him neither see nor feel anything coming from her, except what is agreeable to him. All these difficulties stand in the way of a man's obtaining any thorough knowledge even of the one woman whom alone, in general, he has sufficient opportunity of studying. When we further consider that to understand one woman is not necessarily to understand any other woman; that even if he could study many women of one rank, or of one country, he would not thereby understand women of other ranks or countries; and even if he did, they are still only the women of a single period of history; we may safely assert that the knowledge which men can acquire of women, even as they have been

and are, without reference to what they might be, is wretch-
edly imperfect and superficial, and always will be so, until
women themselves have told all that they have to tell.

And this time has not come; nor will it come otherwise
than gradually. It is but of yesterday that women have either
been qualified by literary accomplishments, or permitted by
society, to tell anything to the general public. As yet very
few of them dare tell anything, which men, on whom their
literary success depends, are unwilling to hear. . . .

I have dwelt so much on the difficulties which at present
obstruct any real knowledge by men of the true nature of
women, because . . . there is little chance of reasonable
thinking on the matter, while people flatter themselves that
they perfectly understand a subject of which most men know
absolutely nothing, and of which it is at present impossible
that any man, or all men taken together, should have knowledge which can qualify them to lay down the law to women
as to what is, or is not, their vocation. Happily, no such
knowledge is necessary for any practical purpose connected
with the position of women in relation to society and life.
For, according to all the principles involved in modern society, the question rests with women themselves—to be decided by their own experience, and by the use of their own
faculties. There are no means of finding what either one person or many can do, but by trying—and no means by which
anyone else can discover for them what it is for their happiness to do or leave undone. . . .

[I]f men are determined that the law of marriage shall be
a law of despotism, they are quite right, in point of mere
policy, in leaving to women only Hobson's choice ["that or
none"]. But, in that case, all that has been done in the modern world to relax the chain on the minds of women, has
been a mistake. They never should have been allowed to
receive a literary education. Women who read, much more
women who write, are, in the existing constitution of things,

a contradiction and a disturbing element: and it was wrong to bring women up with any acquirements but those of an odalisque, or of a domestic servant. . . .

Whether the institution to be defended is slavery, political absolutism, or the absolutism of the head of a family, we are always expected to judge of it from its best instances; and we are presented with pictures of loving exercise of authority on one side, loving submission to it on the other—superior wisdom ordering all things for the greatest good of the dependents, and surrounded by their smiles and benedictions. All this would be very much to the purpose if anyone pretended that there are no such things as good men. Who doubts that there may be great goodness, and great happiness, and great affection, under the absolute government of a good man? Meanwhile, laws and institutions require to be adapted, not to good men, but to bad. Marriage is not an institution designed for a select few. Men are not required, as a preliminary to the marriage ceremony, to prove by testimonials that they are fit to be trusted with the exercise of absolute power. . . . And how many thousands are there among the lowest classes in every country, who, without being in a legal sense malefactors in any other respect, because in every other quarter their aggressions meet with resistance, indulge the utmost habitual excesses of bodily violence towards the unhappy wife, who alone, at least of grown persons, can neither repel nor escape from their brutality; and towards whom the excess of dependence inspires their mean and savage natures, not with a generous forbearance, and a point of honour to behave well to one whose lot in life is trusted entirely to their kindness, but on the contrary with a notion that the law has delivered her to them as their thing, to be used at their pleasure, and that they are not expected to practise the consideration towards her which is required from them towards everybody else. . . .

It would be tiresome to repeat the commonplaces about

the unfitness of men in general for power, which, after the political discussions of centuries, everyone knows by heart, were it not that hardly anyone thinks of applying these maxims to the case in which above all others they are applicable, that of power, not placed in the hands of a man here and there, but offered to every adult male, down to the basest and most ferocious. . . . If the family in its best forms is, as it is often said to be, a school of sympathy, tenderness, and loving forgetfulness of self, it is still oftener, as respects its chief, a school of wilfulness, overbearingness, unbounded selfish indulgence, and a double-dyed and idealised selfishness, of which sacrifice itself is only a particular form: the care for the wife and children being only care for them as parts of the man's own interests and belongings, and their individual happiness being immolated in every shape to his smallest preferences. What better is to be looked for under the existing form of the institution? . . . the almost unlimited power which present social institutions give to the man over at least one human being—the one with whom he resides, and whom he has always present—this power seeks out and evokes the latent germs of selfishness in the remotest corners of his nature—fans its faintest sparks and smouldering embers—offers to him a licence for the indulgence of those points of his original character which in all other relations he would have found it necessary to repress and conceal. . . .

The family is a school of despotism, in which the virtues of despotism, but also its vices, are largely nourished. . . .

The law of servitude in marriage is a monstrous contradiction to all the principles of the modern world, and to all the experience through which those principles have been slowly and painfully worked out. It is the sole case, now that negro slavery has been abolished, in which a human being in the plenitude of every faculty is delivered up to the tender mercies of another human being, in the hope forsooth that this other will use the power solely for the good of the person subjected to it. Marriage is the only actual bondage known to our law. There remain no legal slaves, except the mistress of every house. . . .

All the selfish propensities, the self-worship, the unjust self-preference, which exist among mankind, have their source and root in, and derive their principal nourishment from, the present constitution of the relation between men and women. Think what it is to a boy, to grow up to manhood in the belief that without any merit or any exertion of his own, though he may be the most frivolous and empty or the most ignorant and stolid of mankind, by the mere fact of being born a male he is by right the superior of all and every one of an entire half of the human race: including probably some whose real superiority to himself he has daily or hourly occasion to feel. . . . What must be the effect on his character of this lesson? And men of the cultivated classes are often not aware how deeply it sinks into the immense majority of male minds. For, among right-feeling and well-bred people, the inequality is kept as much as possible out of sight; above all, out of sight of the children. As much obedience is required from boys to their mother as to their father: they are not permitted to domineer over their sisters, nor are they accustomed to see these postponed to them, but the contrary; the compensations of the chivalrous feeling being made prominent, while the servitude which requires them is kept in the background. Well brought-up youths in the higher classes thus often escape the bad influences of the situation in their early years, and only experience them when, arrived at manhood, they fall under the dominion of facts as they really exist. Such people are little aware, when a boy is differently brought up, how early the notion of his inherent superiority to a girl arises in his mind; how it grows with his growth and strengthens with his strength; how it is inoculated by one schoolboy upon another; how early the youth thinks himself superior to his mother, owing her perhaps forbearance, but no real respect; and how sublime and sultan-like a sense of superiority he feels, above all, over the woman whom he honours by admitting her to a partnership of his life. Is it imagined that all this does not pervert the whole manner of existence of the man, both as an individual and as a social being? It is an exact parallel to the feeling of a hereditary king that he is excellent above others by being born a king, or a noble by being born a noble. The relation between husband and wife is very like that between lord and vassal, except that the wife is held to more un-limited obedience than the vassal was. . . .

The example afforded, and the education given to the sentiments, by laying the foundation of domestic existence upon a relation contradictory to the first principles of social justice, must, from the very nature of man, have a perverting influence of such magnitude, that it is hardly possible with our present experience to raise our imaginations to the con-ception of so great a change for the better as would be made by its removal. All that education and civilisation are doing to efface the influences on character of the law of force, and replace them by those of justice, remains merely on the sur-face, as long as the citadel of the enemy is not attacked. The principle of the modern movement in morals and politics, is that conduct, and conduct alone, entitles to respect: that not what men are, but what they do, constitutes their claim to deference; that, above all, merit, and not birth, is the only rightful claim to power and authority. If no authority, not in its nature temporary, were allowed to one human being over another, society would not be employed in building up propensities with one hand which it has to curb with the other. . . . But so long as the right of the strong to power over the weak rules in the very heart of society, the attempt to make the equal right of the weak the principle of its out-ward actions will always be an uphill struggle; for the law of justice, which is also that of Christianity, will never get pos-session of man's inmost sentiments; they will be working against it, even when bending to it. . . .

When we consider the positive evil caused to the disqualified half of the human race by their disqualification—first in the loss of the most inspiriting and elevating kind of personal enjoyment, and next in the weariness, disappointment, and profound dissatisfaction with life, which are so often the substitute for it; one feels that among all the lessons which men require for carrying on the struggle against the inevitable imperfections of their lot on earth, there is no lesson which they more need, than not to add to the evils which nature inflicts, by their jealous and prejudiced restrictions on one another. Their vain fears only substitute other and worse evils for those which they are idly apprehensive of: while every restraint on the freedom of conduct of any of their human fellow-creatures (otherwise than by making them responsible for any evil actually caused by it), dries up *pro tanto* the principal fountain of human happiness, and leaves the species less rich . . . in all that makes life valuable to the individual human being.

Henrik Ibsen

A Doll's House

Henrik Ibsen (1828–1906), the Norwegian playwright, wrote *A Doll's House* in 1879. The first performance of the play in England is said to have occurred in a Bloomsbury rooming house, with a daughter of Karl Marx acting the part of Nora and Bernard Shaw playing the role of the blackmailer. Within a decade after it was written, the play had been performed in almost every Western country, and its ideas about the infantalization of women in marriage had provoked extensive discussion and analysis in print.

Ibsen himself was not interested in being identified with the organized woman's movement and, speaking before the Norwegian Association for Women's Rights in 1898, he declared that he was "more of a poet and less of a social philosopher" than most people realized and wasn't sure he knew what women's rights really were. Whatever his intentions, however, his play has exerted a profound impact as the best-known dramatic exposition of feminist ideas.

The following excerpt, from the translation by William Archer, is the end of the final scene of the work. Nora, a pampered wife and the mother of three children, had forged a signature on a promissory note years before in order to obtain money for her then ill husband, Torvald Helmer. The owner of the note, having discovered the forgery, is attempting to blackmail her. Nora and Torvald return from a masquerade party and Torvald learns of the situation. Terrified that he will be publicly humiliated and ruined, he reviles Nora as "a hypocrite," "a liar" and "a criminal" unfit to associate with their children. Suddenly Torvald's fury is cut short by the delivery of a note from the blackmailer.

HELMER.   Nora!—Oh! I must read it again.—Yes, yes, it is so. I am saved! Nora, I am saved!

NORA.   And I?

HELMER.   You too, of course; we are both saved, both of us. Look here—he sends you back your promissory note. He writes that he regrets and apologises, that a happy turn in his life—Oh, what matter what he writes! We are saved, Nora! No one can harm you. Oh, Nora, Nora—; but first to get rid of this hateful thing. I'll just see—*(Glances at the I.O.U.)* No, I will not look at it; the whole thing shall be nothing but a dream to me. *(Tears the I.O.U. and both letters in pieces. Throws them into the fire and watches them burn.)* There! It's gone! . . . Don't you hear, Nora? You don't seem able to grasp it. Yes, it's over. What is this set look on your face? Oh, my poor Nora, I understand; you cannot believe that I have forgiven you. But I have, Nora; I swear it. I have forgiven everything. I know that what you did was all for love of me.

NORA.   That is true.

HELMER.   You loved me as a wife should love her husband. It was only the means that, in your inexperience, you misjudged. But do you think I love you the less because you cannot do without guidance? No, no. Only lean on me; I will counsel you, and guide you. I should be no true man if this very womanly helplessness did not make you doubly dear in my eyes. You mustn't dwell upon the hard things I said in my first moment of terror, when the world seemed to be tumbling about my ears. I have forgiven you, Nora —I swear I have forgiven you.

NORA.   I thank you for your forgiveness. *(Goes out, to the right.)*

HELMER.   No, stay—! *(Looking through doorway.)* What are you going to do?

NORA   *(inside).*   To take off my masquerade dress.

HELMER   *(in the doorway).*   Yes, do, dear. Try to calm down, and recover your balance, my scared little songbird. You may rest secure. I have broad wings to shield you. *(Walking up and down near the door.)* Oh, how lovely—how cosy our home is, Nora! Here you are safe; here I can shelter you like a hunted dove whom I have saved from the claws of the hawk. I shall soon bring your poor beating heart to rest; believe me, Nora, very soon. Tomorrow all this will seem quite different—everything will be as before. I shall not need to tell you again that I forgive you; you will feel for yourself that it is true. How could you think I could find it in my heart to drive you away, or even so much as to reproach you? Oh, you don't know a true man's heart, Nora. There is something indescribably sweet and soothing to a man in having forgiven his wife—honestly forgiven her, from the bottom of his heart. She becomes his property in a double sense. She is as though born again; she has become, so to speak, at once his wife and his child. That is what you shall henceforth be to me, my bewildered, helpless darling. Don't be troubled about anything, Nora; only open your heart to me, and I will be both will and conscience to you. *(Nora enters in everyday dress.)* Why, what's this? Not gone to bed? You have changed your dress?

NORA. Yes, Torvald; now I have changed my dress.

HELMER. But why now, so late—?

NORA. I shall not sleep tonight.

HELMER. But, Nora dear—

NORA *(looking at her watch).* It's not so late yet. Sit down, Torvald; you and I have much to say to each other. *(She sits at one side of the table.)*

HELMER. Nora—what does this mean? Your cold, set face—

NORA. Sit down. It will take some time. I have much to talk over with you. *(Helmer sits at the other side of the table.)*

HELMER. You alarm me, Nora. I don't understand you.

NORA. No, that is just it. You don't understand me; and I

have never understood you—till tonight. No, don't interrupt. Only listen to what I say.—We must come to a final settlement, Torvald.

HELMER.   How do you mean?

NORA   *(after a short silence).*   Does not one thing strike you as we sit here?

HELMER.   What should strike me?

NORA.   We have been married eight years. Does it not strike you that this is the first time we two, you and I, man and wife, have talked together seriously?

HELMER.   Seriously! What do you call seriously?

NORA.   During eight whole years, and more—ever since the day we first met—we have never exchanged one serious word about serious things.

HELMER.   Was I always to trouble you with the cares you could not help me to bear?

NORA.   I am not talking of cares. I say that we have never yet set ourselves seriously to get to the bottom of anything.

HELMER.   Why, my dearest Nora, what have you to do with serious things?

NORA.   There we have it! You have never understood me. —I have had great injustice done me, Torvald; first by father, and then by you.

HELMER.   What! By your father and me?—By us, who have loved you more than all the world?

NORA   *(shaking her head).*   You have never loved me. You only thought it amusing to be in love with me.

HELMER.   Why, Nora, what a thing to say!

NORA.   Yes, it is so, Torvald. While I was at home with father, he used to tell me all his opinions, and I held the same opinions. If I had others I said nothing about them, because he wouldn't have liked it. He used to call me his doll-child, and played with me as I played with my dolls. Then I came to live in your house—

HELMER.   What an expression to use about our marriage!

NORA   *(undisturbed).*   I mean I passed from father's hands into yours. You arranged everything according to your taste; and I got the same tastes as you; or I pretended to—I don't know which—both ways, perhaps; sometimes one and sometimes the other. When I look back on it now, I seem to have been living here like a beggar, from hand to mouth. I lived by performing tricks for you, Torvald. But you would have it so. You and father have done me a great wrong. It is your fault that my life has come to nothing.

HELMER.   Why, Nora, how unreasonable and ungrateful you are! Have you not been happy here?

NORA.   No, never. I thought I was; but I never was.

HELMER.   Not—not happy!

NORA.   No; only merry. And you have always been so kind to me. But our house has been nothing but a playroom. Here I have been your doll-wife, just as at home I used to be papa's doll-child. And the children, in their turn, have been my dolls. I thought it fun when you played with me, just as the children did when I played with them. That has been our marriage, Torvald.

HELMER.   There is some truth in what you say, exaggerated and overstrained though it be. But henceforth it shall be different. Playtime is over; now comes the time for education.

NORA.   Whose education? Mine, or the children's?

HELMER.   Both, my dear Nora.

NORA.   Oh, Torvald, you are not the man to teach me to be a fit wife for you.

HELMER.   And you can say that?

NORA.   And I—how have I prepared myself to educate the children?

HELMER.   Nora!

NORA.   Did you not say yourself, a few minutes ago, you dared not trust them to me?

HELMER.   In the excitement of the moment! Why should you dwell upon that?

NORA.   No—you were perfectly right. That problem is beyond me. There is another to be solved first—I must try to educate myself. You are not the man to help me in that. I must set about it alone. And that is why I am leaving you.

HELMER   *(jumping up).*   What—do you mean to say—?

NORA.   I must stand quite alone if I am ever to know myself and my surroundings; so I cannot stay with you.

HELMER.   Nora! Nora!

NORA.   I am going at once. I daresay Christina will take me in for tonight—

HELMER.   You are mad! I shall not allow it! I forbid it!

NORA.   It is of no use your forbidding me anything now. I shall take with me what belongs to me. From you I will accept nothing, either now or afterwards.

HELMER.   What madness is this!

NORA.   Tomorrow I shall go home—I mean to what was my home. It will be easier for me to find some opening there.

HELMER.   Oh, in your blind inexperience—

NORA.   I must try to gain experience, Torvald.

HELMER.   To forsake your home, your husband, and your children! And you don't consider what the world will say!

NORA.   I can pay no heed to that. I only know that I must do it.

HELMER.   This is monstrous! Can you forsake your holiest duties in this way?

NORA.   What do you consider my holiest duties?

HELMER.   Do I need to tell you that? Your duties to your husband and your children.

NORA.   I have other duties equally sacred.

HELMER.   Impossible! What duties do you mean?

NORA.   My duties towards myself.

HELMER.   Before all else you are a wife and a mother.

NORA.   That I no longer believe. I believe that before all

else I am a human being, just as much as you are—or at
least that I should try to become one. I know that most
people agree with you, Torvald, and that they say so in
books. But henceforth I can't be satisfied with what most
people say, and what is in books. I must think things out
for myself, and try to get clear about them.

HELMER.   Are you not clear about your place in your own
home? Have you not an infallible guide in questions like
these? Have you not religion?

NORA.   Oh, Torvald, I don't really know what religion is.

HELMER.   What do you mean?

NORA.   I know nothing but what Pastor Hansen told me
when I was confirmed. He explained that religion was this
and that. When I get away from all this and stand alone,
I will look into that matter too. I will see whether what
he taught me is right, or, at any rate, whether it is right
for me.

HELMER.   Oh, this is unheard-of! And from so young a
woman! But if religion cannot keep you right, let me appeal to your conscience—for I suppose you have some
moral feeling? Or, answer me: perhaps you have none?

NORA.   Well, Torvald, it's not easy to say. I really don't
know—I am all at sea about these things. I only know
that I think quite differently from you about them. I hear,
too, that the laws are different from what I thought, but I
can't believe that they can be right. It appears that a
woman has no right to spare her dying father, or to save
her husband's life! I don't believe that.

HELMER.   You talk like a child. You don't understand the
society in which you live.

NORA.   No, I do not. But now I shall try to learn. I must
make up my mind which is right—society or I.

HELMER.   Nora, you are ill; you are feverish; I almost think
you are out of your senses.

NORA.   I have never felt so much clearness and certainty as
tonight.

HELMER.   You are clear and certain enough to forsake husband and children?

NORA.   Yes, I am.

HELMER.   Then there is only one explanation possible.

NORA.   What is that?

HELMER.   You no longer love me.

NORA.   No; that is just it.

HELMER.   Nora!—Can you say so!

NORA.   Oh, I'm so sorry Torvald; for you've always been so kind to me. But I can't help it. I do not love you any longer.

HELMER   *(mastering himself with difficulty)*.   Are you clear and certain on this point too?

NORA.   Yes, quite. That is why I will not stay here any longer. . . .

HELMER.   I would gladly work for you day and night, Nora —bear sorrow and want for your sake. But no man sacrifices his honour, even for one he loves.

NORA.   Millions of women have done so.

HELMER.   Oh, you think and talk like a silly child.

NORA.   Very likely. But you neither think nor talk like the man I can share my life with. When your terror was over —not for what threatened me, but for yourself—when there was nothing more to fear—then it seemed to you as though nothing had happened. I was your lark again, your doll, just as before—whom you would take twice as much care of in future, because she was so weak and fragile. *(Stands up.)* Torvald—in that moment it burst upon me that I had been living here these eight years with a strange man, and had borne him three children.—Oh, I can't bear to think of it! I could tear myself to pieces!

HELMER   *(sadly)*.   I see it, I see it; an abyss has opened between us.—But, Nora, can it never be filled up?

NORA.   As I now am, I am no wife for you.

HELMER.   I have strength to become another man.

NORA.   Perhaps—when your doll is taken away from you.

HELMER. To part—to part from you! No, Nora, no; I can't grasp the thought.

NORA *(going into the room on the right).* The more reason for the thing to happen. *(She comes back with outdoor things and a small travelling-bag, which she places on a chair.)*

HELMER. Nora, Nora, not now! Wait till tomorrow.

NORA *(putting on cloak).* I can't spend the night in a strange man's house.

HELMER. But can we not live here, as brother and sister—?

NORA *(fastening her hat).* You know very well that wouldn't last long. *(Puts on the shawl.)* Goodbye, Torvald. No, I won't go to the children. I know they are in better hands than mine. As I now am, I can be nothing to them.

HELMER. But some time, Nora—some time—?

NORA. How can I tell? I have no idea what will become of me.

HELMER. But you are my wife, now and always!

NORA. Listen, Torvald—when a wife leaves her husband's house, as I am doing, I have heard that in the eyes of the law he is free from all duties towards her. At any rate I release you from all duties. You must not feel yourself bound, any more than I shall. There must be perfect freedom on both sides. There, I give you back your ring. Give me mine.

HELMER. That too?

NORA. That too.

HELMER. Here it is.

NORA. Very well. Now it is all over. I lay the keys here. The servants know about everything in the house—better than I do. Tomorrow, when I have started, Christina will come to pack up the things I brought with me from home. I will have them sent after me.

HELMER. All over! All over! Nora, will you never think of me again?

NORA.   Oh, I shall often think of you, and the children, and this house.

HELMER.   May I write to you, Nora?

NORA.   No—never. You must not.

HELMER.   But I must send you—

NORA.   Nothing, nothing.

HELMER.   I must help you if you need it.

NORA.   No, I say. I take nothing from strangers.

HELMER.   Nora—can I never be more than a stranger to you?

NORA *(taking her travelling-bag).*   Oh, Torvald, then the miracle of miracles would have to happen—

HELMER.   What is the miracle of miracles?

NORA.   Both of us would have to change so that—Oh, Torvald, I no longer believe in miracles.

HELMER.   But *I* will believe. Tell me! We must so change that—?

NORA.   That communion between us shall be a marriage. Goodbye. *(She goes out by the hall door.)*

HELMER *(sinks into a chair by the door with his face in his hands).*   Nora! Nora! *(He looks round and rises.)* Empty. She is gone. *(A hope springs up in him.)* Ah! The miracle of miracles—? *(From below is heard the reverberation of a heavy door closing.)*

Curtain

Friedrich Engels

The Origin of the Family, Private Property, and the State

❧

Friedrich Engels (1820–1895), German-born co-author of the *Communist Manifesto,* explored the origin of the family "in the light of the researches of Lewis H. Morgan," the American anthropologist. Morgan had challenged the assumption that women had always in all societies, including prehistoric societies, been relegated to an inferior and subservient role. In fact, Morgan deduced from his studies a prehistoric period of matriarchy.

Utilizing Morgan's theory, Engels was free to view the patriarchal family as only one of a number of possible variations. Thus, he not only applied the insights of historical materialism to his analysis of the economic basis of the domination of woman by man, but also identified the existing monogamous family structure as the instrument for the exercise of male supremacy.

The Origin of the Family, Private Property, and the State was first published in 1884. It offers the basic Marxist explanation for the oppression of women. According to Engels, that oppression is rooted in the twin facts of private ownership of property and the exclusion of women from social production. The following excerpts are all drawn from Chapter II, "The Family."

The overthrow of mother-right * was the *world historical defeat of the female sex*. The man took command in the

* Mother-right, according to Engels, was the "reckoning of descent in the female line."—Ed.

home also; the woman was degraded and reduced to servitude, she became the slave of his lust and a mere instrument for the production of children. This degraded position of the woman, especially conspicuous among the Greeks of the heroic and still more of the classical age, has gradually been palliated and glozed over, and sometimes clothed in a milder form; in no sense has it been abolished.

The establishment of the exclusive supremacy of the man shows its effects first in the patriarchal family, which now emerges as an intermediate form. . . .

Its essential features are the incorporation of unfree persons, and paternal power; hence the perfect type of this form of family is the Roman. The original meaning of the word "family" (*familia*) is not that compound of sentimentality and domestic strife which forms the ideal of the present-day philistine; among the Romans it did not at first even refer to the married pair and their children, but only to the slaves. *Famulus* means domestic slave, and *familia* is the total number of slaves belonging to one man. . . . The term was invented by the Romans to denote a new social organism, whose head ruled over wife and children and a number of slaves, and was invested under Roman paternal power with rights of life and death over them all. . . .

Such a form of family shows the transition of the pairing family * to monogamy. In order to make certain of the wife's fidelity and therefore of the paternity of the children, she is delivered over unconditionally into the power of the husband; if he kills her, he is only exercising his rights. . . .

[The monogamous family] . . . develops out of the pairing family . . . its decisive victory is one of the signs that civilization is beginning. It is based on the supremacy of the man, the express purpose being to produce children of undis-

---

* In the pairing family, one man lives with one woman. Polygamy and infidelity are permitted the man, but adultery by the woman is strictly forbidden. The marriage tie is easily dissolved and the children belong to the mother alone.—Ed.

puted paternity; such paternity is demanded because these children are later to come into their father's property as his natural heirs. It is distinguished from pairing marriage by the much greater strength of the marriage tie, which can no longer be dissolved at either partner's wish. As a rule, it is now only the man who can dissolve it, and put away his wife. The right of conjugal infidelity also remains secured to him, at any rate by custom. . . .

We meet this new form of the family in all its severity among the Greeks. While the position of the goddesses in their mythology, as Marx points out, brings before us an earlier period when the position of women was freer and more respected, in the heroic age we find the woman already being humiliated by the domination of the man and by competition from girl slaves. Note how Telemachus in the *Odyssey* silences his mother. In Homer young women are booty and are handed over to the pleasure of the conquerors, the handsomest being picked by the commanders in order of rank; the entire *Iliad,* it will be remembered, turns on the quarrel of Achilles and Agamemnon over one of these slaves. If a hero is of any importance, Homer also mentions the captive girl with whom he shares his tent and his bed. These girls were also taken back to Greece and brought under the same roof as the wife, as Cassandra was brought by Agamemnon in Aeschylus; the sons begotten of them received a small share of the paternal inheritance and had the full status of freemen. Teucer, for instance, is a natural son of Telamon by one of these slaves and has the right to use his father's name. The legitimate wife was expected to put up with all this, but herself to remain strictly chaste and faithful. In the heroic age a Greek woman is, indeed, more respected than in the period of civilization, but to her husband she is after all nothing but the mother of his legitimate children and heirs, his chief housekeeper and the supervisor of his female slaves, whom he can and does take as concubines if he so fancies. It is the existence of slavery side by side with monogamy, the presence of young, beautiful slaves belonging unreservedly to the *man,* that stamps monogamy from the very beginning with its specific character of monogamy *for the woman only,* but not for the man. And that is the character it still has today. . . .

Girls [in Athens] only learned spinning, weaving, and sewing, and at most a little reading and writing. They lived more or less behind locked doors and had no company except other women. The women's apartments formed a separate part of the house, on the upper floor or at the back, where men, especially strangers, could not easily enter, and to which the women retired when men visited the house. They never went out without being accompanied by a female slave; indoors they were kept under regular guard. . . . In Euripides a woman is called an *oikourema,* a thing (the word is neuter) for looking after the house, and, apart from her business of bearing children, that was all she was for the Athenian—his chief female domestic servant. The man had his athletics and his public business, from which women were barred; in addition, he often had female slaves at his disposal and during the most flourishing days of Athens an extensive system of prostitution which the state at least favored. It was precisely through this system of prostitution that the only Greek women of personality were able to develop, and to acquire that intellectual and artistic culture by which they stand out as high above the general level of classical womanhood as the Spartan women by their qualities of character. But that a woman had to be a *hetaira* * before she could be a woman is the worst condemnation of the Athenian family.

This Athenian family became in time the accepted model for domestic relations, not only among the Ionians, but to an increasing extent among all the Greeks of the mainland and colonies also. But, in spite of locks and guards, Greek

* A courtesan, usually a slave.—Ed.

women found plenty of opportunity for deceiving their husbands. . . .

This is the origin of monogamy as far as we can trace it back among the most civilized and highly developed people of antiquity. It was not in any way the fruit of individual sex-love, with which it had nothing whatever to do; marriages remained as before marriages of convenience. It was the first form of the family to be based, not on natural, but on economic conditions—on the victory of private property over primitive, natural communal property. The Greeks themselves put the matter quite frankly: the sole exclusive aims of monogamous marriage were to make the man supreme in the family, and to propagate, as the future heirs to his wealth, children indisputably his own. Otherwise, marriage was a burden, a duty which had to be performed, whether one liked it or not, to gods, state, and one's ancestors. In Athens the law exacted from the man not only marriage but also the performance of a minimum of so-called conjugal duties.

Thus when monogamous marriage first makes its appearance in history, it is not as the reconciliation of man and woman, still less as the highest form of such a reconciliation. Quite the contrary. Monogamous marriage comes on the scene as the subjugation of the one sex by the other; it announces a struggle between the sexes unknown throughout the whole previous prehistoric period. In an old unpublished manuscript, written by Marx and myself in 1846, I find the words: "The first division of labor is that between man and woman for the propagation of children." And today I can add: The first class opposition that appears in history coincides with the development of the antagonism between man and woman in monogamous marriage, and the first class oppression coincides with that of the female sex by the male. Monogamous marriage was a great historical step forward; nevertheless, together with slavery and private wealth, it opens the period that has lasted until today in which every step forward is also relatively a step backward, in which prosperity and development for some is won through the misery and frustration of others. It is the cellular form of civilized society, in which the nature of the oppositions and contradictions fully active in that society can be already studied.

The old comparative freedom of sexual intercourse by no means disappeared with the victory of pairing marriage or even of monogamous marriage. . . . *co-existent with monogomous marriage,* . . . sexual intercourse between men and unmarried women outside marriage, . . . as we know, flourishes in the most varied forms throughout the whole period of civilization and develops more and more into open prostitution. . . . Actually not merely tolerated, but gaily practiced, by the ruling classes particularly, it is condemned in words. But in reality this condemnation never falls on the men concerned, but only on the women; they are despised and outcast, in order that the unconditional supremacy of men over the female sex may be once more proclaimed as a fundamental law of society.

But a second contradiction thus develops within monogamous marriage itself. At the side of the husband who embellishes his existence with hetaerism stands the neglected wife. And one cannot have one side of this contradiction without the other, any more than a man has a whole apple in his hand after eating half. But that seems to have been the husbands' notion, until their wives taught them better. With monogamous marriage, two constant social types, unknown hitherto, make their appearance on the scene—the wife's attendant lover and the cuckold husband. The husbands had won the victory over the wives, but the vanquished magnanimously provided the crown. Together with monogamous marriage and hetaerism, adultery became an unavoidable social institution—denounced, severely penalized, but impossible to suppress. At best, the certain paternity of the children rested on moral conviction as before, and to solve the insoluble contradiction the *Code Napoleon,* Art. 312, decreed: *"L'enfant conçu pendant le mariage a pour père le mari,"* the father of a child conceived during marriage is—the husband. Such is the final result of three thousand years of monogamous marriage.

Thus, wherever the monogamous family remains true to its historical origin and clearly reveals the antagonism between the man and the woman expressed in the man's exclusive supremacy, it exhibits in miniature the same oppositions and contradictions as those in which society has been moving, without power to resolve or overcome them, ever since it split into classes at the beginning of civilization. . . .

However, monogamous marriage did not by any means appear always and everywhere in the classically harsh form it took among the Greeks. Among the Romans, who, as future world-conquerors, had a larger, if a less fine, vision than the Greeks, women were freer and more respected. A Roman considered that his power of life and death over his wife sufficiently guaranteed her conjugal fidelity. Here, moreover, the wife equally with the husband could dissolve the marriage at will. But the greatest progress in the development of individual marriage certainly came with the entry of the Germans into history, and for the reason that the Germans—on account of their poverty, very probably —were still at a stage where monogamy seems not yet to have become perfectly distinct from pairing marriage. . . . women were greatly respected among the Germans, and also influential in public affairs, which is in direct contradiction to the supremacy of men in monogamy. . . . The new monogamy, which now developed from the mingling of peoples amid the ruins of the Roman world, clothed the supremacy of the men in milder forms and gave women a position which, outwardly at any rate, was much more free and respected than it had ever been in classical antiquity. Only now were the conditions realized in which through monogamy—within it, parallel to it, or in opposition to it, as the case might be—the greatest moral advance we owe to it could be achieved: modern individual sex-love, which had hitherto been unknown to the entire world. . . .

But if monogamy was the only one of all the known forms of the family through which modern sex-love could develop, that does not mean that within monogamy modern sexual love developed exclusively or even chiefly as the love of husband and wife for each other. That was precluded by the very nature of strictly monogamous marriage under the rule of the man. Among all historically active classes—that is, among all ruling classes—matrimony remained what it had been since the pairing marriage, a matter of convenience which was arranged by the parents. The first historical form of sexual love as passion, a passion recognized as natural to all human beings (at least if they belonged to the ruling classes), and as the highest form of the sexual impulse— and that is what constitutes its specific character—this first form of individual sexual love, the chivalrous love of the middle ages, was by no means conjugal. Quite the contrary. In its classic form among the Provençals, it heads straight for adultery, and the poets of love celebrated adultery. The flower of Provençal love poetry are the Albas (*aubades,* songs of dawn). They describe in glowing colors how the knight lies in bed beside his love—the wife of another man —while outside stands the watchman who calls to him as soon as the first gray of dawn (*alba*) appears, so that he can get away unobserved; the parting scene then forms the climax of the poem. The northern French and also the worthy Germans adopted this kind of poetry together with the corresponding fashion of chivalrous love; old Wolfram of Eschenbach has left us three wonderfully beautiful songs of dawn on this same improper subject, which I like better than his three long heroic poems.

Nowadays there are two ways of concluding a bourgeois marriage. In Catholic countries the parents, as before, procure a suitable wife for their young bourgeois son, and the consequence is, of course, the fullest development of the contradiction inherent in monogamy: the husband abandons himself to hetaerism and the wife to adultery. Probably the only reason why the Catholic Church abolished divorce was because it had convinced itself that there is no more a cure for adultery than there is for death. In Protestant countries, on the other hand, the rule is that the son of a bourgeois family is allowed to choose a wife from his own class with more or less freedom; hence there may be a certain element of love in the marriage, as, indeed, in accordance with Protestant hypocrisy, is always assumed, for decency's sake. Here the husband's hetaerism is a more sleepy kind of business, and adultery by the wife is less the rule. But since, in every kind of marriage, people remain what they were before, and since the bourgeois of Protestant countries are mostly philistines, all that this Protestant monogamy achieves, taking the average of the best cases, is a conjugal partnership of leaden boredom, known as "domestic bliss." . . .

In both cases, however, the marriage is conditioned by the class position of the parties and is to that extent always a marriage of convenience. In both cases this marriage of convenience turns often enough into crassest prostitution— sometimes of both partners, but far more commonly of the women, who only differs from the ordinary courtesan in that she does not let out her body on piece-work as a wage-worker, but sells it once and for all into slavery. And of all marriages of convenience Fourier's words hold true: "As in grammar two negatives make an affirmative, so in matrimonial morality two prostitutions pass for a virtue." Sex-love in the relationship with a woman becomes, and can only become, the real rule among the oppressed classes, which means today among the proletariat—whether this relation is officially sanctioned or not. But here all the foundations of typical monogamy are cleared away. Here there is no property, for the preservation and inheritance of which monogamy and male supremacy were established; hence there is no incentive to make this male supremacy effective. What is more, there are no means of making it so. Bourgeois law, which protects this supremacy, exists only for the possessing class and their dealings with the proletarians. The law costs money and, on account of the worker's poverty, it has no validity for his relation to his wife. Here quite other personal and social conditions decide. And now that large-scale industry has taken the wife out of the home onto the labor market and into the factory, and made her often the bread-winner of the family, no basis for any kind of male supremacy is left in the proletarian household—except, perhaps, for something of the brutality towards women that has spread since the introduction of monogamy. The proletarian family is therefore no longer monogamous in the strict sense, even where there is passionate love and firmest loyalty on both sides, and maybe all the blessings of religious and civil authority. Here, therefore, the eternal attendants of monogamy, hetaerism and adultery, play only an almost vanishing part. The wife has in fact regained the right to dissolve the marriage, and if two people cannot get on with one another, they prefer to separate. In short, proletarian marriage is monogamous in the etymological sense of the word, but not at all in its historical sense.

Our jurists, of course, find that progress in legislation is leaving women with no further ground of complaint. Modern civilized systems of law increasingly acknowledge, first, that for a marriage to be legal, it must be a contract freely entered into by both partners, and, secondly, that also in the married state both partners must stand on a common footing of equal rights and duties. If both these demands are consistently carried out, say the jurists, women have all they can ask.

This typically legalist method of argument is exactly the same as that which the radical republican bourgeois uses to put the proletarian in his place. The labor contract is to be freely entered into by both partners. But it is considered to have been freely entered into as soon as the law makes both parties equal on *paper*. The power conferred on the one party by the difference of class position, the pressure thereby brought to bear on the other party—the real economic position of both—that is not the law's business. Again, for the duration of the labor contract both parties are to have equal rights, in so far as one or the other does not expressly surrender them. That economic relations compel the worker to surrender even the last semblance of equal rights—here again, that is no concern of the law.

In regard to marriage, the law, even the most advanced, is fully satisfied as soon as the partners have formally recorded that they are entering into the marriage of their own free consent. What goes on in real life behind the juridical scenes, how this free consent comes about—that is not the business of the law and the jurist. And yet the most elementary comparative jurisprudence should show the jurist what this free consent really amounts to. In the countries where an obligatory share of the paternal inheritance is secured to the children by law and they cannot therefore be disinherited—in Germany, in the countries with French law and elsewhere—the children are obliged to obtain their parents' consent to their marriage. In the countries with English law, where parental consent to a marriage is not legally required, the parents on their side have full freedom in the testamentary disposal of their property and can disinherit their children at their pleasure. It is obvious that, in spite and precisely because of this fact, freedom of marriage among the classes with something to inherit is in reality not a whit greater in England and America than it is in France and Germany.

As regards the legal equality of husband and wife in marriage, the position is no better. The legal inequality of the two partners, bequeathed to us from earlier social conditions, is not the cause but the effect of the economic oppression of the woman. In the old communistic household, which comprised many couples and their children, the task entrusted to the women of managing the household was as much a public and socially necessary industry as the procuring of food by the men. With the patriarchal family, and still more with the single monogamous family, a change came. Household management lost its public character. It no longer concerned society. It became a *private service*; the wife became the head servant, excluded from all participation in social production. Not until the coming of modern large-scale industry was the road to social production opened to her again—and then only to the proletarian wife. But it was opened in such a manner that, if she carries out her duties in the private service of her family, she remains excluded from public production and unable to earn; and if she wants to take part in public production and earn independently, she cannot carry out family duties. And the wife's position in the factory is the position of women in all branches of business, right up to medicine and the law. The modern individual family is founded on the open or concealed domestic slavery of the wife, and modern society is a mass composed of these individual families as its molecules.

In the great majority of cases today, at least in the possessing classes, the husband is obliged to earn a living and support his family, and that in itself gives him a position of supremacy, without any need for special legal titles and privileges. Within the family he is the bourgeois and the wife represents the proletariat. In the industrial world, the specific character of the economic oppression burdening the proletariat is visible in all its sharpness only when all special legal privileges of the capitalist class have been abolished and complete legal equality of both classes established. The democratic republic does not do away with the opposition of the two classes; on the contrary, it provides the clear field on which the fight can be fought out. And in the same way, the peculiar character of the supremacy of the husband over the wife in the modern family, the necessity of creating real social equality between them, and the way to do it, will only be seen in the clear light of day when both possess legally complete equality of rights. Then it will be plain that the first condition for the liberation of the wife is to bring the whole female sex back into public industry, and that this in turn demands the abolition of the monogamous family as the economic unit of society. . . .

We are now approaching a social revolution in which the economic foundations of monogamy as they have existed hitherto will disappear just as surely as those of its complement—prostitution. Monogamy arose from the concentration of considerable wealth in the hands of a single individual—a man—and from the need to bequeath this wealth to the children of that man and of no other. For this purpose, the monogamy of the woman was required, not that of the man, so this monogamy of the woman did not in any way interfere with open or concealed polygamy on the part of the man. But by transforming by far the greater portion, at any rate, of permanent, heritable wealth—the means of production—into social property, the coming social revolution will reduce to a minimum all this anxiety about bequeathing and inheriting. Having arisen from economic causes, will monogamy then disappear when these causes disappear?

One might answer, not without reason: far from disappearing, it will, on the contrary, be realized completely. For with the transformation of the means of production into social property there will disappear also wage-labor, the proletariat, and therefore the necessity for a certain—statistically calculable—number of women to surrender themselves for money. Prostitution disappears; monogamy, instead of collapsing, at last becomes a reality—also for men.

In any case, therefore, the position of men will be very much altered. But the position of women, of *all* women, also undergoes significant change. With the transfer of the means of production into common ownership, the single family ceases to be the economic unit of society. Private housekeeping is transformed into a social industry. The care and education of the children becomes a public affair; society looks after all children alike, whether they are legitimate or not. This removes all the anxiety about the "consequences," which today is the most essential social—moral as well as economic—factor that prevents a girl from giving herself completely to the man she loves. Will not that suffice to bring about the gradual growth of unconstrained sexual intercourse and with it a more tolerant public opinion in regard to a maiden's honor and a woman's shame? And, finally, have we not seen that in the modern world monogamy and prostitution are indeed contradictions, but inseparable contradictions, poles of the same state of society? Can prostitution disappear without dragging monogamy with it into the abyss?

Here a new element comes into play, an element which, at the time when monogamy was developing, existed at most in germ: individual sex-love. . . .

[T]he rising bourgeoisie, especially in Protestant countries, where existing conditions had been most severely shaken, increasingly recognized freedom of contract also in marriage, and carried it into effect. . . . Marriage remained class marriage, but within the class the partners were conceded a certain degree of freedom of choice. And on paper, in ethical theory and in poetic description, nothing was more immutably established than that every marriage is immoral which does not rest on mutual sexual love and really free agreement of husband and wife. In short, the love marriage was proclaimed as a human right, and indeed not only as a *droit de l'homme,* one of the rights of man, but also, for once in a way, as *droit de la femme,* one of the rights of woman.

This human right, however, differed in one respect from

all other so-called human rights. While the latter, in practice, remain restricted to the ruling class (the bourgeoisie),
and are directly or indirectly curtailed for the oppressed
class (the proletariat), in the case of the former the irony of
history plays another of its tricks. The ruling class remains
dominated by the familiar economic influences and therefore only in exceptional cases does it provide instances of
really freely contracted marriages, while among the oppressed class, as we have seen, these marriages are the rule.

Full freedom of marriage can therefore only be generally
established when the abolition of capitalist production and
of the property relations created by it has removed all the
accompanying economic considerations which still exert
such a powerful influence on the choice of a marriage partner. For then there is no other motive left except mutual
inclination.

And as sexual love is by its nature exclusive—although
at present this exclusiveness is fully realized only in the
woman—the marriage based on sexual love is by its nature
individual marriage. . . . If now the economic considerations
also disappear which made women put up with the habitual
infidelity of their husbands—concern for their own means
of existence and still more for their children's future—then,
according to all previous experience, the equality of woman
thereby achieved will tend infinitely more to make men
really monogamous than to make women polyandrous.

But what will quite certainly disappear from monogamy
are all the features stamped upon it through its origin in
property relations; these are, in the first place, supremacy of
the man, and, secondly, indissolubility. The supremacy of
the man in marriage is the simple consequence of his economic supremacy, and with the abolition of the latter will
disappear of itself. The indissolubility of marriage is partly
a consequence of the economic situation in which monogamy arose, partly tradition from the period when the con-

nection between this economic situation and monogamy was not yet fully understood and was carried to extremes under a religious form. . . .

What we can now conjecture about the way in which sexual relations will be ordered after the impending overthrow of capitalist production is mainly of a negative character, limited for the most part to what will disappear. But what will there be new? That will be answered when a new generation has grown up: a generation of men who never in their lives have known what it is to buy a woman's surrender with money or any other social instrument of power; a generation of women who have never known what it is to give themselves to a man from any other considerations than real love, or to refuse to give themselves to their lover from fear of the economic consequences. When these people are in the world, they will care precious little what anybody today thinks they ought to do; they will make their own practice and their corresponding public opinion about the practice of each individual—and that will be the end of it.

August Bebel

Woman and Socialism

❦

August Bebel (1840–1913) was a prominent German Marxist, a founder of the German Social Democratic party and a member of the Reichstag. As a practical political leader, Bebel was greatly interested in the relationship of the organized woman's movement to the international socialist movement. Like Engels, Bebel believed that the complete emancipation of women would be possible only under socialism.

He asserted that class antagonisms among women were somewhat mitigated by the fact that *all* women share certain common interests. Thus, women of opposing classes, though "they march in separate armies . . . may strike a united blow" in the fight for equal rights.

But Bebel made clear that ultimately the class struggle was paramount. Alliances of bourgeois and proletarian women for limited gains within the present social order were transcended by the "duty of the proletarian woman to join the men of her class" in transforming capitalistic society to socialism.

Woman and Socialism was published in 1885 and was extremely popular throughout Western Europe and the United States. The body of the work deals with woman in the past, the present and the future. The extensive use of numerical charts and other statistical data has caused the book to become seriously outdated. However, the following reading, from the "Introduction," presents the Marxist attitude toward the "bourgeois" feminist movement.

We are living in an age of great social transformations that are steadily progressing. In all strata of society we perceive an unsettled state of mind and an increasing restlessness, denoting a marked tendency toward profound and radical changes. Many questions have arisen and are being discussed with growing interest in ever widening circles. One of the most important of these questions and one that is constantly coming into greater prominence, is the *woman question*.

The woman question deals with the position that woman should hold in our social organism, and seeks to determine how she can best develop her powers and her abilities, in order to become a useful member of human society, endowed with equal rights and serving society according to her best capacity. From our point of view this question coincides with that other question: In what manner should society be organized to abolish oppression, exploitation, misery and need, and to bring about the physical and mental welfare of individuals and of society as a whole? To us then, the woman question is only one phase of the general social question that at present occupies all intelligent minds; its final solution can only be attained by removing social extremes and the evils which are a result of such extremes.

Nevertheless, the woman question demands our special consideration. What the position of woman has been in ancient society, what her position is to-day and what it will be in the coming social order, are questions that deeply concern at least one half of humanity. Indeed, in Europe they concern a majority of organized society, because women constitute a majority of the population. Moreover, the prevailing conceptions concerning the development of woman's social position during successive stages of history are so faulty, that enlightenment on this subject has become a necessity. Ignorance concerning the position of woman, chiefly accounts for the prejudice that the woman's movement has to contend with among all classes of people, by no means least among the women themselves. Many even venture to assert that there is no woman question at all, since woman's position has always been the same and will remain the same in the future, because nature has destined her to be a wife and a mother and to confine her activities to the home. Everything that is beyond the four narrow walls of her home and is not closely connected with her domestic duties, is not supposed to concern her.

In the woman question then we find two contending parties, just as in the labor question, which relates to the position of the workingman in human society. Those who wish to maintain everything as it is, are quick to relegate woman to her so-called "natural profession," believing that they have thereby settled the whole matter. They do not recognize that millions of women are not placed in a position enabling them to fulfill their natural function of wifehood and motherhood. . . . They furthermore do not recognize that to millions of other women their "natural profession" is a failure, because to them marriage has become a yoke and a condition of slavery, and they are obliged to drag on their lives in misery and despair. But these wiseacres are no more concerned by these facts than by the fact that in various trades and professions millions of women are exploited far beyond their strength, and must slave away their lives for a meagre subsistence. They remain deaf and blind to these disagreeable truths, as they remain deaf and blind to the misery of the proletariat, consoling themselves and others by the false assertion that it has always been thus and will always continue to be so. That woman is entitled, as well as man, to enjoy all the achievements of civilization, to lighten her burdens, to improve her condition, and to develop all her physical and mental qualities, they refuse to admit. When, furthermore, told that woman—to enjoy full physical and mental freedom—should also be economically independent, should no longer depend for subsistence upon the good will and favor of the other sex, the limit of their patience will be reached. Indignantly they will pour forth a bitter [i]ndictment of the "madness of the age" and its "crazy attempts at emancipation." These are the old ladies of both sexes who cannot overcome the narrow circle of their prejudices. They are the human owls that dwell wherever darkness prevails, and cry out in terror whenever a ray of light is cast into their agreeable gloom.

Others do not remain quite as blind to the eloquent facts. They confess that at no time woman's position has been so unsatisfactory in comparison to general social progress, as it is at present. They recognize that it is necessary to investigate how the condition of the self-supporting woman can be improved; but in the case of married women they believe the social problem to be solved. They favor the admission of unmarried women only into a limited number of trades and professions. Others again are more advanced and insist that competition between the sexes should not be limited to the inferior trades and professions, but should be extended to all higher branches of learning and the arts and sciences as well. They demand equal educational opportunities and that women should be admitted to all institutions of learning, including the universities. They also favor the appointment of women to government positions, pointing out the results already achieved by women in such positions, especially in the United States. A few are even coming forward to demand equal political rights for women. Woman, they argue, is a human being and a member of organized society as well as man, and the very fact that men have until now framed and administered the laws to suit their own purposes and to hold woman in subjugation, proves the necessity of woman's participation in public affairs.

It is noteworthy that all these various endeavors do not go beyond the scope of the present social order. The question is not propounded whether any of these proposed reforms will accomplish a decisive and essential improvement in the condition of women. According to the conceptions of

bourgeois, or capitalistic society, the civic equality of men
and women is deemed an ultimate solution of the woman
question. People are either unconscious of the fact, or deceive themselves in regard to it, that the admission of women
to trades and industries is already practically accomplished
and is being strongly favored by the ruling classes in their
own interest. But under prevailing conditions woman's invasion of industry has the detrimental effect of increasing
competition on the labor market, and the result is a reduction in wages for both male and female workers. It is clear
then, that this cannot be a satisfactory solution.

Men who favor these endeavors of women within the
scope of present society, as well as the bourgeois women
who are active in the movement, consider complete civic
equality of women the ultimate goal. These men and women
then differ radically from those who, in their narrow-
mindedness, oppose the movement. They differ radically
from those men who are actuated by petty motives of selfishness and fear of competition, and therefore try to prevent
women from obtaining higher education and from gaining
admission to the better paid professions. But there is no
difference of class between them, such as exists between the
worker and the capitalist.

If the bourgeois suffragists would achieve their aim and
would bring about equal rights for men and women, they
would still fail to abolish that sex slavery which marriage,
in its present form, is to countless numbers of women; they
would fail to abolish prostitution; they would fail to abolish
the economic dependence of wives. To the great majority of
women it also remains a matter of indifference whether a
few thousand members of their sex, belonging to the more
favored classes of society, obtain higher learning and enter
some learned profession, or hold a public office. The general
condition of the sex as a whole is not altered thereby.

The female sex as such has a double yoke to bear. Firstly,
women suffer as a result of their social dependence upon

men, and the inferior position allotted to them in society; formal equality before the law alleviates this condition, but does not remedy it. Secondly, women suffer as a result of their economic dependence, which is the lot of women in general, and especially of the proletarian women, as it is of the proletarian men.

We see, then, that all women, regardless of their social position, represent that sex which during the evolution of society has been oppressed and wronged by the other sex, and therefore it is to the common interest of all women to remove their disabilities by changing the laws and institutions of the present state and social order. But a great majority of women is furthermore deeply and personally concerned in a complete reorganization of the present state and social order which has for its purpose the abolition of wage-slavery, which at present weighs most heavily upon the women of the proletariat, as also the abolition of sex-slavery, which is closely connected with our industrial conditions and our system of private ownership.

The women who are active in the bourgeois suffrage movement, do not recognize the necessity of so complete a transformation. Influenced by their privileged social position, they consider the more radical aims of the proletarian woman's movement dangerous doctrines that must be opposed. The class antagonism that exists between the capitalist and working class and that is increasing with the growth of industrial problems, also clearly manifests itself then within the woman's movement. Still these sister-women, though antagonistic to each other on class lines, have a great many more points in common than the men engaged in the class struggle, and though they march in separate armies they may strike a united blow. This is true in regard to all endeavors pertaining to equal rights of woman under the present social order; that is, her right to enter any trade or profession adapted to her strength and ability, and her right to civic and political equality. These are, as we shall see, very important and very far-reaching aims. Besides striving for these aims, it is in the particular interest of proletarian women to work hand in hand with proletarian men for such measures and institutions that tend to protect the working woman from physical and mental degeneration, and to preserve her health and strength for a normal fulfillment of her maternal functions. Furthermore, it is the duty of the proletarian woman to join the men of her class in the struggle for a thorough-going transformation of society, to bring about an order that by its social institutions will enable both sexes to enjoy complete economic and intellectual independence.

Our goal then is, not only to achieve equality of men and women under the present social order, which constitutes the sole aim of the bourgeois woman's movement, but to go far beyond this, and to remove all barriers that make one human being dependent upon another, which includes the dependence of one sex upon the other. *This* solution of the woman question is identical with the solution of the social question. They who seek a complete solution of the woman question must, therefore, join hands with those who have inscribed upon their banner the solution of the social question in the interest of all mankind—the Socialists.

The Socialist Party is the only one that has made the full equality of women, their liberation from every form of dependence and oppression, an integral part of its program; not for reasons of propaganda, but from necessity. *For there can be no liberation of mankind without social independence and equality of the sexes.*

Thorstein Veblen

The Theory of the Leisure Class

Thorstein Veblen (1857–1929) was born on a Minnesota farm, of Norwegian parents. He studied the lives of his fellow Americans as though he were a visitor among them from another world and described their folkways with mordant accuracy. In analyzing the role of women in the economy, Veblen employed two curious economic concepts: conspicuous leisure and conspicuous consumption.

Leisure, in Veblen's idiosyncratic language, referred to any non-productive use of time; one may therefore be at leisure without in any sense being idle. Veblen saw that most middle- and upper-class women in modern industrial society were excluded from remunerative social labor and that their busy rounds of household activities were for the most part of a ceremonial rather than a useful nature—that is, they were really leisure activities.

It was the duty of women, said Veblen, to perform this leisure conspicuously so as to prove to the world that the male head of the household was able to support a person whose existence was entirely dedicated to his comfort, his home and the pursuit of pleasure. Women of this class were also expected to consume quantities of goods, without respect to need, simply to advertise the abilities of the man as provider.

Veblen's further insight was that the woman had to perform these services of conspicuous consumption and leisure vicariously for the man. She was an "unfree servant" whose own desires and whose own impulses to self-expression, purposeful activity and pride in workmanship had to be suppressed.

The following excerpts from Veblen's best-known work, *The Theory of the Leisure Class,* first published in 1899, indicate the way he applied these concepts of consumption and leisure to such social commonplaces as standards of feminine beauty; women's clothing; the "work" of housewives; and the underlying motives of the nineteenth-century woman's movement.

CONSPICUOUS LEISURE

[T]he term "leisure," as here used, does not connote indolence or quiescence. What it connotes is non-productive consumption of time. . . .

In all grades and walks of life, and at any stage of the economic development, the leisure of the lady and of the lackey differs from the leisure of the gentleman in his own right in that it is an occupation of an ostensibly laborious kind. It takes the form, in large measure, of a painstaking attention to the service of the master, or to the maintenance and elaboration of the household paraphernalia; so that it is leisure only in the sense that little or no productive work is performed by this class, not in the sense that all appearance of labor is avoided by them. The duties performed by the lady, or by the household or domestic servants, are frequently arduous enough, and they are also frequently directed to ends which are considered extremely necessary to the comfort of the entire household. So far as these services conduce to the physical efficiency or comfort of the master or the rest of the household, they are to be accounted productive work. Only the residue of employment left after deduction of this effective work is to be classed as a performance of leisure.

But much of the services classed as household cares in modern everyday life, and many of the "utilities" required for a comfortable existence by civilized man, are of a ceremonial character. They are, therefore, properly to be classed as a performance of leisure in the sense in which the term is here used. . . . and when performed by others than the economically free and self-directing head of the establishment, they are to be classed as vicarious leisure.

The vicarious leisure performed by housewives and menials, under the head of household cares, may frequently develop into drudgery, especially where the competition for reputability is close and strenuous. This is frequently the case in modern life. Where this happens, the domestic service which comprises the duties of this servant class might aptly be designated as wasted effort, rather than as vicarious leisure. But the latter term has the advantage of indicating the line of derivation of these domestic offices, as well as of neatly suggesting the substantial economic ground of their utility; for these occupations are chiefly useful as a method of imputing pecuniary reputability to the master or to the household on the ground that a given amount of time and effort is conspicuously wasted in that behalf.

In this way, then, there arises a subsidiary or derivative leisure class, whose office is the performance of a vicarious leisure for the behoof of the reputability of the primary or legitimate leisure class. This vicarious leisure class is distinguished from the leisure class proper by a characteristic feature of its habitual mode of life. The leisure of the master class is, at least ostensibly, an indulgence of a proclivity for the avoidance of labor and is presumed to enhance the master's own well-being and fulness of life; but the leisure of the servant class exempt from productive labor is in some sort a performance exacted from them, and is not normally or primarily directed to their own comfort. . . . The like is often true of the wife throughout the protracted economic stage during which she is still primarily a servant—that is to say, so long as the household with a male head remains in force. In order to satisfy the requirements of the leisure-class scheme of life, the servant should show not only an attitude of subservience, but also the effects of special training and practice in subservience. The servant or wife should not only perform certain offices and show a servile disposition, but it is quite as imperative that they should show an acquired facility in the tactics of subservience—a trained conformity to the canons of effectual and conspicuous subservience. Even today it is this aptitude and acquired skill in the formal manifestation of the servile relation that constitutes the chief element of utility in our highly paid servants, as well as one of the chief ornaments of the well-bred housewife.

CONSPICUOUS CONSUMPTION

Conspicuous consumption of valuable goods is a means of reputability to the gentleman of leisure. As wealth accumulates on his hands, his own unaided effort will not avail to sufficiently put his opulence in evidence by this method . . . . In the higher grades of society a large volume of both . . . [conspicuous consumption and leisure] is required; and here the wife is of course still assisted in the work by a more or less numerous corps of menials. But as we descend the scale, the point is presently reached where the duties of vicarious leisure and consumption devolve upon the wife alone. In the communities of the Western culture, this point is at present found among the lower middle class.

And here occurs a curious inversion. It is a fact of common observation that in this lower middle class there is no pretense of leisure on the part of the head of the household. Through force of circumstances it has fallen into disuse. But the middle-class wife still carries on the business of vicarious leisure, for the good name of the household and its master. In descending the social scale in any modern industrial community, the primary fact—the conspicuous leisure of the master of the household—disappears at a relatively high point. The head of the middle-class household has been reduced by economic circumstances to turn his hand to gaining a livelihood. . . . It is by no means an uncommon spectacle to find a man applying himself to work with the utmost assiduity, in order that his wife may in due form ren-

der for him that degree of vicarious leisure which the common sense of the time demands.

The leisure rendered by the wife in such cases is, of
course, not a simple manifestation of idleness or indolence.
It almost invariably occurs disguised under some form of
work or household duties or social amenities, which prove
on analysis to serve little or no ulterior end beyond showing
that she does not and need not occupy herself with anything
that is gainful or that is of substantial use. As has already
been noticed . . ., the greater part of the customary round of
domestic cares to which the middle-class housewife gives
her time and effort is of this character. Not that the results
of her attention to household matters, of a decorative and
mundificatory character, are not pleasing to the sense of
men trained in middle-class proprieties; but the taste to
which these effects of household adornment and tidiness
appeal is a taste which has been formed under the selective
guidance of a canon of propriety that demands just these
evidences of wasted effort. The effects are pleasing to us
chiefly because we have been taught to find them pleasing.
There goes into these domestic duties much solicitude for a
proper combination of form and color, and for other ends
that are to be classed as aesthetic in the proper sense of the
term; and it is not denied that effects having some substantial aesthetic value are sometimes attained. Pretty much all
that is here insisted on is that, as regards these amenities of
life, the housewife's efforts are under the guidance of traditions that have been shaped by the law of conspicuously
wasteful expenditure of time and substance. If beauty or
comfort is achieved,—and it is a more or less fortuitous
circumstance if they are,—they must be achieved by means
and methods that commend themselves to the great economic law of wasted effort. The more reputable, "present-
able" portion of middle-class household paraphernalia are,
on the one hand, items of conspicuous consumption, and on

the other hand, apparatus for putting in evidence the vicarious leisure rendered by the housewife.

The requirement of vicarious consumption at the hands of the wife continues in force even at a lower point in the pecuniary scale than the requirement of vicarious leisure. At a point below which little if any pretense of wasted effort, in ceremonial cleanness and the like, is observable, and where there is assuredly no conscious attempt at ostensible leisure, decency still requires the wife to consume some goods conspicuously for the reputability of the household and its head. So that, as the latter-day outcome of this evotion of an archaic institution, the wife, who was at the outset the drudge and chattel of the man, both in fact and in theory,—the producer of goods for him to consume,—has become the ceremonial consumer of goods which he produces. But she still quite unmistakably remains his chattel in theory; for the habitual rendering of vicarious leisure and consumption is the abiding mark of the unfree servant.

This vicarious consumption practiced by the household of the middle and lower classes can not be counted as a direct expression of the leisure-class scheme of life, since the household of this pecuniary grade does not belong within the leisure class. It is rather that the leisure-class scheme of life here comes to an expression at the second remove. . . .

The basis on which good repute in any highly organized industrial community ultimately rests is pecuniary strength; and the means of showing pecuniary strength, and so of gaining or retaining a good name, are leisure and a conspicuous consumption of goods. Accordingly, both of these methods are in vogue as far down the scale as it remains possible; and in the lower strata in which the two methods are employed, both offices are in great part delegated to the wife and children of the household. Lower still, where any degree of leisure, even ostensible, has become impracticable for the wife, the conspicuous consumption of goods remains and is carried on by the wife and children. . . . Very much of squalor and discomfort will be endured before the last trinket or the last pretense of pecuniary decency is put away.

PECUNIARY CANONS OF TASTE

It is more or less a rule that in communities which are at the stage of economic development at which women are valued by the upper class for their service, the ideal of female beauty is a robust, large-limbed woman. The ground of appreciation is the physique, while the conformation of the face is of secondary weight only. A well-known instance of this ideal of the early predatory culture is that of the maidens of the Homeric poems.

This ideal suffers a change in the succeeding development, when, in the conventional scheme, the office of the high-class wife comes to be a vicarious leisure simply. The ideal then includes the characteristics which are supposed to result from or to go with a life of leisure consistently enforced. The ideal accepted under these circumstances may be gathered from descriptions of beautiful women by poets and writers of the chivalric times. In the conventional scheme of those days ladies of high degree were conceived to be in perpetual tutelage, and to be scrupulously exempt from all useful work. The resulting chivalric or romantic ideal of beauty takes cognizance chiefly of the face, and dwells on its delicacy, and on the delicacy of the hands and feet, the slender figure, and especially the slender waist. In the pictured representations of the women of that time, and in modern romantic imitators of the chivalric thought and feeling, the waist is attenuated to a degree that implies extreme debility. The same ideal is still extant among a considerable portion of the population of modern industrial communities; but it is to be said that it has retained its hold most tenaciously in those modern communities which are least advanced in point of economic and civil development. . . .

In modern communities which have reached the higher
levels of industrial development, the upper leisure class has
accumulated so great a mass of wealth as to place its women
above all imputation of vulgarly productive labor. Here the
status of women as vicarious consumers is beginning to lose
its place in the affections of the body of the people; and as a
consequence the ideal of feminine beauty is beginning to
change back again from the infirmly delicate, translucent,
and hazardously slender, to a woman of the archaic type
that does not disown her hands and feet, nor, indeed, the
other gross material facts of her person. In the course of
economic development the ideal of beauty among the
peoples of the Western culture has shifted from the woman
of physical presence to the lady, and it is beginning to shift
back again to the woman; and all in obedience to the changing conditions of pecuniary emulation. The exigencies of
emulation at one time required lusty slaves; at another time
they required a conspicuous performance of vicarious leisure
and consequently an obvious disability; but the situation is
now beginning to outgrow this last requirement, since, under
the higher efficiency of modern industry, leisure in women
is possible so far down the scale of reputability that it will
no longer serve as a definitive mark of the highest pecuniary
grade.

Apart from this general control exercised by the norm of
conspicuous waste over the ideal of feminine beauty, there are
one or two details which merit specific mention as showing
how it may exercise an extreme constraint in detail over
men's sense of beauty in women. It has already been noticed
that at the stages of economic evolution at which conspicuous leisure is much regarded as a means of good repute, the
ideal requires delicate and diminutive hands and feet and a
slender waist. These features, together with the other, related
faults of structure that commonly go with them, go to show
that the person so affected is incapable of useful effort and
must therefore be supported in idleness by her owner. She is

useless and expensive, and she is consequently valuable as evidence of pecuniary strength. It results that at this cultural stage women take thought to alter their persons, so as to conform more nearly to the requirements of the instructed taste of the time; and under the guidance of the canon of pecuniary decency, the men find the resulting artificially induced pathological features attractive. So, for instance, the constricted waist which has had so wide and persistent a vogue in the communities of the Western culture, and so also the deformed foot of the Chinese. Both of these are mutilations of unquestioned repulsiveness to the untrained sense. It requires habituation to become reconciled to them. Yet there is no room to question their attractiveness to men into whose scheme of life they fit as honorific items sanctioned by the requirements of pecuniary reputability.

DRESS AS AN EXPRESSION OF THE PECUNIARY CULTURE

Elegant dress serves its purpose of elegance not only in that it is expensive, but also because it is the insignia of leisure. It not only shows that the wearer is able to consume a relatively large value, but it argues at the same time that he consumes without producing.

The dress of women goes even farther than that of men in the way of demonstrating the wearer's abstinence from productive employment. . . . The substantial reason for our tenacious attachment to the skirt is just this: it is expensive and it hampers the wearer at every turn and incapacitates her for all useful exertion. The like is true of the feminine custom of wearing the hair excessively long. . . .

It may broadly be set down that the womanliness of woman's apparel resolves itself, in point of substantial fact, into the more effective hindrance to useful exertion offered by the garments. . . .

As has been seen in the discussion of woman's status under the heads of Vicarious Leisure and Vicarious Consumption, it has in the course of economic development become

the office of the woman to consume vicariously for the head
of the household; and her apparel is contrived with this object in view. It has come about that obviously productive
labor is in a peculiar degree derogatory to respectable
women, and therefore special pains should be taken in the
construction of women's dress, to impress upon the beholder
the fact (often indeed a fiction) that the wearer does not
and can not habitually engage in useful work. Propriety requires respectable women to abstain more consistently from
useful effort and to make more of a show of leisure than the
men of the same social classes. It grates painfully on our
nerves to contemplate the necessity of any well-bred
woman's earning a livelihood by useful work. It is not
"woman's sphere." Her sphere is within the household,
which she should "beautify," and of which she should be
the "chief ornament." The male head of the household is
not currently spoken of as its ornament. This feature taken
in conjunction with the other fact that propriety requires
more unremitting attention to expensive display in the dress
and other paraphernalia of women, goes to enforce the view
already implied in what has gone before. By virtue of its descent from a patriarchal past, our social system makes it the
woman's function in an especial degree to put in evidence
her household's ability to pay. According to the modern
civilised scheme of life, the good name of the household to
which she belongs should be the special care of the woman;
and the system of honorific expenditure and conspicuous
leisure by which this good name is chiefly sustained is therefore the woman's sphere. In the ideal scheme, as it tends to
realise itself in the life of the higher pecuniary classes, this
attention to conspicuous waste of substance and effort
should normally be the sole economic function of the
woman. . . . So much so that the women have been required
not only to afford evidence of a life of leisure, but even to
disable themselves for useful activity.

It is at this point that the dress of men falls short of that of women, and for a sufficient reason. Conspicuous waste and conspicuous leisure are reputable because they are evidence of pecuniary strength; pecuniary strength is reputable or honorific because, in the last analysis, it argues success and superior force; therefore the evidence of waste and leisure put forth by any individual in his own behalf cannot consistently take such a form or be carried to such a pitch as to argue incapacity or marked discomfort on his part; as the exhibition would in that case show not superior force, but inferiority, and so defeat its own purpose. So, then, wherever wasteful expenditure and the show of abstention from effort is normally, or on an average, carried to the extent of showing obvious discomfort or voluntarily induced physical disability, there the immediate inference is that the individual in question does not perform this wasteful expenditure and undergo this disability for her own personal gain in pecuniary repute, but in behalf of some one else to whom she stands in a relation of economic dependence; a relation which in the last analysis must, in economic theory, reduce itself to a relation of servitude.

To apply this generalization to women's dress, and put the matter in concrete terms: the high heel, the skirt, the impracticable bonnet, the corset, and the general disregard of the wearer's comfort which is an obvious feature of all civilised women's apparel, are so many items of evidence to the effect that in the modern civilised scheme of life the woman is still, in theory, the economic dependent of the man,—that, perhaps in a highly idealised sense, she still is the man's chattel. The homely reason for all this conspicuous leisure and attire on the part of women lies in the fact that they are servants to whom, in the differentiation of economic functions, has been delegated the office of putting in evidence their master's ability to pay.

There is a marked similarity in these respects between the apparel of women and that of domestic servants, especially liveried servants. In both there is a very elaborate show of unnecessary expensiveness, and in both cases there is also a notable disregard of the physical comfort of the wearer. But the attire of the lady goes further in its elaborate insistence on the idleness, if not on the physical infirmity of the wearer, than does that of the domestic. And this is as it should be; for in theory, according to the ideal scheme of the pecuniary culture, the lady of the house is the chief menial of the household.

SURVIVALS OF THE NON-INVIDIOUS INTEREST

It has been well and repeatedly said by popular writers and speakers who reflect the common sense of intelligent people on questions of social structure and function that the position of woman in any community is the most striking index of the level of culture attained by the community, and it might be added, by any given class in the community. This remark is perhaps truer as regards the stage of economic devolopment than as regards development in any other respect. At the same time the position assigned to the woman in the accepted scheme of life, in any community or under any culture, is in a very great degree an expression of traditions which have been shaped by the circumstances of an earlier phase of development, and which have been but partially adapted to the existing economic circumstances, or to the existing exigencies of temperament and habits of mind by which the women living under this modern economic situation are actuated. . . .

The several phases of the "woman question" have brought out in intelligible form the extent to which the life of women in modern society, and in the polite circles especially, is regulated by a body of common sense formulated under the economic circumstances of an earlier phase of development. It is still felt that woman's life, in its civil, economic, and social bearing, is essentially and normally a vicarious life, the merit or demerit of which is, in the nature of things, to be imputed to some other individual who stands in some relation of ownership or tutelage to the woman. . . .

But in spite of this pervading sense of what is the good and natural place for the woman, there is also perceptible an incipient development of sentiment to the effect that this whole arrangement of tutelage and vicarious life and imputation of merit and demerit is somehow a mistake. Or, at least, that even if it may be a natural growth and a good arrangement in its time and place, and in spite of its patent aesthetic value, still it does not adequately serve the more everyday ends of life in a modern industrial community. Even that large and substantial body of well-bred, upper and middle-class women to whose dispassionate, matronly sense of the traditional proprieties this relation of status commends itself as fundamentally and eternally right,—even these, whose attitude is conservative, commonly find some slight discrepancy in detail between things as they are and as they should be in this respect. But that less manageable body of modern women who, by force of youth, education, or temperament, are in some degree out of touch with the traditions of status received from the barbarian culture, and in whom there is, perhaps, an undue reversion to the impulse of self-expression and workmanship,—these are touched with a sense of grievance too vivid to leave them at rest.

In this "New-Woman" movement,—as these blind and incoherent efforts to rehabilitate the woman's pre-glacial standing have been named,—there are at least two elements discernible, both of which are of an economic character. These two elements or motives are expressed by the double watch-word, "Emancipation" and "Work." Each of these words is recognized to stand for something in the way of a wide-spread sense of grievance. The prevalence of the sentiment is recognized even by people who do not see that there is any real ground for a grievance in the situation as it stands to-day. It is among the women of the well-to-do classes, in the communities which are farthest advanced in industrial development, that this sense of a grievance to be redressed is most alive and finds most frequent expression. That is to say, in other words, there is a demand, more or less serious, for emancipation from all relation of status, tutelage, or vicarious life; and the revulsion asserts itself especially among the class of women upon whom the scheme of life handed down from the regime of status imposes with least mitigation a vicarious life, and in those communities whose economic development has departed farthest from the circumstances to which this traditional scheme is adapted. The demand comes from that portion of womankind which is excluded by the canons of good repute from all effectual work, and which is closely reserved for a life of leisure and conspicuous consumption.

More than one critic of this new-woman movement has misapprehended its motive. The case of the American "new woman" has lately been summed up with some warmth by a popular observer of social phenomena: "She is petted by her husband, the most devoted and hard-working of husbands in the world. . . . She is the superior of her husband in education and in almost every respect. She is surrounded by the most numerous and delicate attentions. Yet she is not satisfied. . . . The Anglo-Saxon 'new woman' is the most ridiculous production of modern times, and destined to be the most ghastly failure of the century." Apart from the deprecation—perhaps well placed—which is contained in this presentment, it adds nothing but obscurity to the woman question. The grievance of the new woman is made up of those things which this typical characterisation of the movement urges as reasons why she should be content. She is petted, and is permitted, or even required, to consume largely and conspicuously—vicariously for her husband or other natural guardian. She is exempted, or debarred, from vulgarly useful employment—in order to perform leisure vicariously for the good repute of her natural (pecuniary) guardian. These offices are the conventional marks of the un-free, at the same time that they are incompatible with the human impulse to purposeful activity. . . .

So long as the woman's place is consistently that of a drudge, she is, in the average of cases, fairly contented with her lot. She not only has something tangible and purposeful to do, but she has also no time or thought to spare for a rebellious assertion of such human propensity to self-direction as she has inherited. And after the stage of universal female drudgery is passed, and a vicarious leisure without strenuous application becomes the accredited employment of the women of the well-to-do classes, the prescriptive force of the canon of pecuniary decency, which requires the observance of ceremonial futility on their part, will long preserve high-minded women from any sentimental leaning to self-direction and a "sphere of usefulness." This is especially true during the earlier phases of the pecuniary culture, while the leisure of the leisure class is still in great measure a predatory activity, an active assertion of mastery in which there is enough of tangible purpose of an invidious kind to admit of its being taken seriously as an employment to which one may without shame put one's hand. This condition of things has obviously lasted well down into the present in some communities. It continues to hold to a different extent for different individuals, varying with the vividness of the sense of status and with the feebleness of the impulse to workmanship with which the individual is endowed. But where the economic structure of the community has so far outgrown the scheme of life based on status that the relation of personal subservience is no longer felt to be the sole "natural" human relation; there the ancient habit of purposeful activity will begin to assert itself in the less conformable individuals against the more recent, relatively superficial, relatively ephemeral habits and views which the predatory and the pecuniary culture have contributed to our scheme of life. . . .

In a sense, then, the new-woman movement marks a reversion to a more generic type of human character, or to a less differentiated expression of human nature. . . . It may even be said that in the modern industrial communities the average, dispassionate sense of men says that the ideal character is a character which makes for peace, good-will, and economic efficiency, rather than for a life of self-seeking, force, fraud, and mastery.

V

TWENTIETH-
CENTURY THEMES

Charlotte Perkins Gilman

Women and Economics

Charlotte Perkins Gilman (1860–1935) preferred to be known as a "sociologist" rather than as a "feminist." Her interest in female suffrage as an issue and her connection with the organized suffrage movement were peripheral. However, she spoke extensively for women's groups around the United States and was a highly prolific writer on subjects relating to the emancipation of women.

Charlotte Gilman viewed economic dependence as the main barrier in the way of progress for the female sex. She felt that women should work outside their homes—as they were then already beginning to do in greater and greater numbers—not only to fulfill their "social responsibility as individuals" but to achieve fuller "development of other faculties . . . besides those of sex."

Gilman herself managed to become self-supporting at a very early age. But when she assumed the traditional role of the nineteenth-century wife after her marriage, she suffered an emotional breakdown characterized by depression, fatigue and a sense of despair. Not until she separated permanently from her husband was she able to recover. In her writings, however, she did not oppose marriage per se but only what she described as that "unlovely yoke," that "dreary misery" that was the concomitant of marriage when a woman was economically dependent on her husband.

As a (non-Marxist) socialist, Gilman advocated socialization of housework: professional housecleaners; communal kitchens and dining rooms; day nurseries for children. Debunking the Victorian concept of the hallowed and sacred hearth, Gilman declared that most homes in truth were inefficient, unsanitary, and lacking in companionship or repose.

Women and Economics, which appeared in 1898, was the book that established Charlotte Perkins Gilman's reputation. The following excerpts are from Chapter I, which deals with the housewife's low economic status, and Chapter XI, which is concerned primarily with woman's sex-defined job as selector and preparer of food.

The male human being is thousands of years in advance of the female in economic status. Speaking collectively, men produce and distribute wealth; and women receive it at their hands. As men hunt, fish, keep cattle, or raise corn, so do women eat game, fish, beef, or corn. As men go down to the sea in ships, and bring coffee and spices and silks and gems from far away, so do women partake of the coffee and spices and silks and gems the men bring.

The economic status of the human race in any nation, at any time, is governed mainly by the activities of the male: the female obtains her share in the racial advance only through him.

Studied individually, the facts are even more plainly visible, more open and familiar. From the day laborer to the millionnaire, the wife's worn dress or flashing jewels, her low roof or her lordly one, her weary feet or her rich equipage,—these speak of the economic ability of the husband. The comfort, the luxury, the necessities of life itself, which the woman receives, are obtained by the husband, and given her by him. And, when the woman, left alone with no man to "support" her, tries to meet her own economic necessities, the difficulties which confront her prove conclusively what the general economic status of the woman is. None can deny these patent facts,—that the economic status of women generally depends upon that of men generally, and that the economic status of women individually depends upon that of men individually, those men to whom they are related. But we are instantly confronted by the commonly received opinion that, although it must be admitted that men make and distribute the wealth of the world, yet women earn their share of it as wives. This assumes either that the husband is in the position of employer and the wife as employee, or that marriage is a "partnership," and the wife an equal factor with the husband in producing wealth.

Economic independence is a relative condition at best. In the broadest sense, all living things are economically dependent upon others,—the animals upon the vegetables, and man upon both. In a narrower sense, all social life is economically interdependent, man producing collectively what he could by no possibility produce separately. But, in the closest interpretation, individual economic independence among human beings means that the individual pays for what he gets, works for what he gets, gives to the other an equivalent for what the other gives him. I depend on the shoemaker for shoes, and the tailor for coats; but, if I give the shoemaker and the tailor enough of my own labor as a house-builder to pay for the shoes and coats they give me, I retain my personal independence. I have not taken of their product, and given nothing of mine. As long as what I get is obtained by what I give, I am economically independent.

Women consume economic goods. What economic product do they give in exchange for what they consume? The claim that marriage is a partnership, in which the two persons married produce wealth which neither of them, separately, could produce, will not bear examination. A man happy and comfortable can produce more than one unhappy and uncomfortable, but this is as true of a father or son as of a husband. To take from a man any of the conditions which make him happy and strong is to cripple his industry, generally speaking. But those relatives who make him happy are not therefore his business partners, and entitled to share his income.

Grateful return for happiness conferred is not the method

of exchange in a partnership. The comfort a man takes with his wife is not in the nature of a business partnership, nor are her frugality and industry. A housekeeper, in her place, might be as frugal, as industrious, but would not therefore be a partner. Man and wife are partners truly in their mutual obligation to their children,—their common love, duty, and service. But a manufacturer who marries, or a doctor, or a lawyer, does not take a partner in his business, when he takes a partner in parenthood, unless his wife is also a manufacturer, a doctor, or a lawyer. In his business, she cannot even advise wisely without training and experience. To love her husband, the composer, does not enable her to compose; and the loss of a man's wife, though it may break his heart, does not cripple his business, unless his mind is affected by grief. She is in no sense a business partner, unless she contributes capital or experience or labor, as a man would in like relation. Most men would hesitate very seriously before entering a business partnership with any woman, wife or not.

If the wife is not, then, truly a business partner, in what way does she earn from her husband the food, clothing, and shelter she receives at his hands? By house service, it will be instantly replied. This is the general misty idea upon the subject,—that women earn all they get, and more, by house service. Here we come to a very practical and definite economic ground. Although not producers of wealth, women serve in the final processes of preparation and distribution. Their labor in the household has a genuine economic value.

For a certain percentage of persons to serve other persons, in order that the ones so served may produce more, is a contribution not to be overlooked. The labor of women in the house, certainly, enables men to produce more wealth than they otherwise could; and in this way women are economic factors in society. But so are horses. The labor of horses enables men to produce more wealth than they otherwise could. The horse is an economic factor in society. But the horse is not economically independent, nor is the woman. If a man plus a valet can perform more useful service than he could minus a valet, then the valet is performing useful service. But, if the valet is the property of the man, is obliged to perform this service, and is not paid for it, he is not economically independent.

The labor which the wife performs in the household is given as part of her functional duty, not as employment. The wife of the poor man, who works hard in a small house, doing all the work for the family, or the wife of the rich man, who wisely and gracefully manages a large house and administers its functions, each is entitled to fair pay for services rendered.

To take this ground and hold it honestly, wives, as earners through domestic service, are entitled to the wages of cooks, housemaids, nursemaids, seamstresses, or housekeepers, and to no more. This would of course reduce the spending money of the wives of the rich, and put it out of the power of the poor man to "support" a wife at all, unless, indeed, the poor man faced the situation fully, paid his wife her wages as house servant, and then she and he combined their funds in the support of their children. He would be keeping a servant: she would be helping keep the family. But nowhere on earth would there be "a rich woman" by these means. Even the highest class of private housekeeper, useful as her services are, does not accumulate a fortune. She does not buy diamonds and sables and keep a carriage. Things like these are not earned by house service.

But the salient fact in this discussion is that, whatever the economic value of the domestic industry of women is, they do not get it. The women who do the most work get the least money, and the women who have the most money do the least work. Their labor is neither given nor taken as a factor in economic exchange. It is held to be their duty as women to do this work; and their economic status bears no relation to their domestic labors, unless an inverse one. Moreover, if they were thus fairly paid,—given what they earned, and no more,—all women working in this way would be reduced to the economic status of the house servant. Few women—or men either—care to face this condition. The ground that women earn their living by domestic labor is instantly forsaken, and we are told that they obtain their livelihood as mothers. This is a peculiar position. We speak of it commonly enough, and often with deep feeling, but without due analysis.

In treating of an economic exchange, asking what return in goods or labor women make for the goods and labor given them,—either to the race collectively or to their husbands individually,—what payment women make for their clothes and shoes and furniture and food and shelter, we are told that the duties and services of the mother entitle her to support.

If this is so, if motherhood is an exchangeable commodity given by women in payment for clothes and food, then we must of course find some relation between the quantity or quality of the motherhood and the quantity and quality of the pay. This being true, then the women who are not mothers have no economic status at all; and the economic status of those who are must be shown to be relative to their motherhood. This is obviously absurd. The childless wife has as much money as the mother of many,—more; for the children of the latter consume what would otherwise be hers; and the inefficient mother is no less provided for than the efficient one. Visibly, and upon the face of it, women are not maintained in economic prosperity proportioned to their motherhood. Motherhood bears no relation to their economic status. . . .

Driven off these alleged grounds of women's economic independence; shown that women, as a class, neither produce nor distribute wealth; that women, as individuals, labor mainly as house servants, are not paid as such, and would not be satisfied with such an economic status if they were so paid; that wives are not business partners or co-producers of wealth with their husbands, unless they actually practise the same profession; that they are not salaried as mothers, and that it would be unspeakably degrading if they were,— what remains to those who deny that women are supported by men? This (and a most amusing position it is),—that the function of maternity unfits a woman for economic production, and, therefore, it is right that she should be supported by her husband. . . .

Is this the condition of human motherhood? Does the human mother, by her motherhood, thereby lose control of brain and body, lose power and skill and desire for any other work? Do we see before us the human race, with all its females segregated entirely to the uses of motherhood, consecrated, set apart, specially developed, spending every power of their nature on the service of their children?

We do not. We see the human mother worked far harder than a mare, laboring her life long in the service, not of her children only, but of men; husbands, brothers, fathers, whatever male relatives she has; for mother and sister also; for the church a little, if she is allowed; for society, if she is able; for charity and education and reform,—working in many ways that are not the ways of motherhood.

It is not motherhood that keeps the housewife on her feet from dawn till dark; it is house service, not child service. Women work longer and harder than most men, and not solely in maternal duties. . . .

In spite of her supposed segregation to maternal duties, the human female, the world over, works at extra-maternal duties for hours enough to provide her with an independent living, and then is denied independence on the ground that motherhood prevents her working!

If this ground were tenable, we should find a world full of women who never lifted a finger save in the service of their children, and of men who did *all* the work besides, and waited on the women whom motherhood prevented from waiting on themselves. The ground is not tenable. A human female, healthy, sound, has twenty-five years of life before she is a mother, and should have twenty-five years more after the period of such maternal service as is expected of her has been given. The duties of grandmotherhood are surely not alleged as preventing economic independence.

The working power of the mother has always been a prominent factor in human life. She is the worker *par excellence,* but her work is not such as to affect her economic status. Her living, all that she gets,—food, clothing, ornaments, amusements, luxuries,—these bear no relation to her power to produce wealth, to her services in the house, or to her motherhood. These things bear relation only to the man she marries, the man she depends on,—to how much he has and how much he is willing to give her. The women whose splendid extravagance dazzles the world, whose economic goods are the greatest, are often neither houseworkers nor mothers, but simply the women who hold most power over the men who have the most money. The female of genus homo is economically dependent on the male. He is her food supply. . . .

As a natural consequence of our division of labor on sex-lines, giving to woman the home and to man the world in which to work, we have come to have a dense prejudice in favor of the essential womanliness of the home duties, as opposed to the essential manliness of every other kind of work. We have assumed that the preparation and serving of food and the removal of dirt, the nutritive and excretive processes of the family, are feminine functions; and we have also assumed that these processes must go on in what we call the home, which is the external expression of the family. In the home the human individual is fed, cleaned, warmed, and generally cared for, while not engaged in working in the world.

Human nutrition is a long process. There's many a ship 'twixt the cup and the lip, to paraphrase an old proverb.

Food is produced by the human race collectively,—not by individuals for their own consumption, but by interrelated groups of individuals, all over the world, for the world's consumption. This collectively produced food circulates over the earth's surface through elaborate processes of transportation, exchange, and preparation, before it reaches the mouths of the consumers; and the final processes of selection and preparation are in the hands of woman. She is the final purchaser: she is the final handler in that process of human nutrition known as cooking, which is a sort of extra-organic digestion proven advantageous to our species. This department of human digestion has become a sex-function, supposed to pertain to women by nature. . . .

This great function of human nutrition is confounded with the sex-relation, and is considered a sex-function: it is in the helpless hands of that amiable but abortive agent, the economically dependent women; and the essential incapacity of such an agent is not hard to show. In her position as private house-steward she is the last purchaser of the food of the world, and here we reach the governing factor in our incredible adulteration of food products. . . .

The dealer who sells to a hundred poor women can and does sell a much lower quality of food than he who sells an equal amount to one purchaser. Therefore, the home, as a food agency, holds an essentially and permanently unfavorable position as a purchaser; and it is thereby the principal factor in maintaining the low standard of food products against which we struggle with the cumbrous machinery of legislation.

Most housekeepers will innocently prove their ignorance of these matters by denying that the standard of food products is so low. Let such offended ladies but examine the statutes and ordinances of their own cities,—of any civilized city,—and see how the bread, the milk, the meat, the fruit, are under a steady legislative inspection which endeavors to protect the ignorance and helplessness of the individual purchaser. . . .

As it is, woman brings to her selection from the world's food only the empirical experience gained by practising upon her helpless family, and this during the very time when her growing children need the wise care which she is only able to give them in later years. This experience, with its pitiful limitation and its practical check by the personal taste and pecuniary standing of the family, is lost where it was found. Each mother slowly acquires some knowledge of her business by practising it upon the lives and health of her family and by observing its effect on the survivors; and each daughter begins again as ignorant as her mother was before her. This "rule of thumb" is not transmissible. It is not a genuine education such as all important work demands, but a slow animal process of soaking up experience,—hopelessly ineffectual in protecting the health of society. As the ultimate selecting agent in feeding humanity, the private housewife fails, and this not by reason of any lack of effort on her part, but by the essential defect of her position as individual purchaser. Only organization can oppose such evils as the wholesale adulteration of food; and woman, the house-servant, belongs to the lowest grade of unorganized labor.

Leaving the selection of food, and examining its preparation, one would naturally suppose that the segregation of an entire sex to the fulfilment of this function would insure most remarkable results. It has, but they are not so favorable as might be expected. The art and science of cooking involve a large and thorough knowledge of nutritive value and of the laws of physiology and hygiene. As a science, it verges on preventive medicine. As an art, it is capable of noble expression within its natural bounds. As it stands among us to-day, it is so far from being a science and akin to preventive medicine, that it is the lowest of amateur handicrafts and a prolific source of disease; and, as an art, it has developed under the peculiar stimulus of its position as a sex-function into a voluptuous profusion as false as it is evil. Our innocent proverb, "The way to a man's heart is through his stomach," is a painfully plain comment on the way in which we have come to deprave our bodies and degrade our souls at the table.

On the side of knowledge it is permanently impossible that half the world, acting as amateur cooks for the other half, can attain any high degree of scientific accuracy or technical skill. The development of any human labor requires specialization, and specialization is forbidden to our cook-by-nature system. What progress we have made in the science of cooking has been made through the study and experience of professional men cooks and chemists, not through the Sisyphean labors of our endless generations of isolated women, each beginning again where her mother began before her.

Here, of course, will arise a pained outcry along the "mother's doughnuts" line. . . . The fact that we like a thing does not prove it to be right. A Missouri child may regard his mother's saleratus [baking soda] biscuit with fond desire, but that does not alter their effect upon his spirits or his complexion. Cooking is a matter of law, not the harmless play of fancy. Architecture might be more sportive and varied if every man built his own house, but it would not be the art and science that we have made it; and, while every woman prepares food for her own family, cooking can never rise beyond the level of the amateur's work.

But, low as is the status of cooking as a science, as an art it is lower. Since the wife-cook's main industry is to please, —that being her chief means of getting what she wants or of expressing affection,—she early learned to cater to the palate instead of faithfully studying and meeting the needs of the stomach. For uncounted generations the grown man and the growing child have been subject to the constant efforts of her who cooked from affection, not from knowledge, —who cooked to please. This is one of the widest pathways of evil that has ever been opened. In every field of life it is an evil to put the incident before the object, the means before the end; and here it has produced that familiar result whereby we live to eat instead of eating to live.

This attitude of the woman has developed the rambling excess called "fancy cookery,"—a thing as far removed from true artistic development as a swinging ice-pitcher from a Greek vase. Through this has come the limitless unhealthy folly of high living, in which human labor and time and skill are wasted in producing what is neither pure food nor pure pleasure, but an artificial performance, to be appreciated only by the virtuoso. Lower living could hardly be imagined than that which results from this unnatural race between artifice and appetite, in which body and soul are both corrupted.

In the man, the subject of all this dining-room devotion, has been developed and maintained that cultivated interest in his personal tastes and their gratification. . . .

Our general notion is that we have lifted and ennobled our eating and drinking by combining them with love. On the contrary, we have lowered and degraded our love by combining it with eating and drinking; and, what is more, we have lowered these habits also. Some progress has been made, socially; but this unhappy mingling of sex-interest and self-interest with normal appetites, this Cupid-in-the-kitchen arrangement, has gravely impeded that progress. Professional cooking has taught us much. Commerce and manufacture have added to our range of supplies. Science has shown us what we need, and how and when we need it. But the affectionate labor of wife and mother is little touched by these advances. If she goes to the cooking school, it is to learn how to make the rich delicacies that will please rather than to study the nutritive value of food in order to guard the health of the household. From the constantly enlarging stores opened to her through man's activities she chooses widely, to make "a variety" that shall kindle appetite, knowing nothing of the combination best for physical needs. As to science, chemistry, hygiene,—they are but names to her.

"John likes it so." "Willie won't eat it so." "Your father never could bear cabbage." She must consider what he likes, not only because she loves to please him or because she profits by pleasing him, but because he pays for the dinner, and she is a private servant.

Is it not time that the way to a man's heart through his stomach should be relinquished for some higher avenue? The stomach should be left to its natural uses, not made a thoroughfare for stranger passions and purposes; and the heart should be approached through higher channels. We need a new picture of our overworked blind god,—fat, greasy, pampered with sweetmeats by the poor worshippers long forced to pay their devotion through such degraded means.

No, the human race is not well nourished by making the process of feeding it a sex-function. The selection and preparation of food should be in the hands of trained experts. And woman should stand beside man as the comrade of his soul, not the servant of his body.

This will require large changes in our method of living. To feed the world by expert service, bringing to that great function the skill and experience of the trained specialist, the power of science, and the beauty of art, is impossible in the sexuo-economic relation. While we treat cooking as a sex-function common to all women and eating as a family function not otherwise rightly accomplished, we can develop no farther. We are spending much earnest study and hard labor to-day on the problem of teaching and training women in the art of cooking, both the wife and the servant; for, with our usual habit of considering voluntary individual conduct as the cause of conditions, we seek to modify conditions by changing individual conduct.

What we must recognize is that, while the conditions remain, the conduct cannot be altered. Any trade or profession, the development of which depended upon the labor of isolated individuals, assisted only by hired servants more ignorant than themselves, would remain at a similarly low level. . . .

There was a time when kings and lords retained their private poets to praise and entertain them; but the poet is not truly great until he sings for the world. So the art of cooking can never be lifted to its true place as a human need and a social function by private service. Such an arrangement of our lives and of our houses as will allow cooking to become a profession is the only way in which to free this great art from its present limitations. It should be a reputable, well-paid profession, wherein those women or those men who were adapted to this form of labor could become cooks, as they would become composers or carpenters. Natural distinctions would be developed between the mere craftsman and the artist; and we should have large, new avenues of lucrative and honorable industry, and a new basis for human health and happiness.

This does not involve what is known as "co-operation." Co-operation in the usual sense, is the union of families for the better performance of their supposed functions. The process fails because the principle is wrong. Cooking and cleaning are not family functions. We do not have a family mouth, a family stomach, a family face to be washed. Individuals require to be fed and cleaned from birth to death, quite irrespective of their family relations. The orphan, the bachelor, the childless widower, have as much need of these nutritive and excretive processes as any patriarchal parent. Eating is an individual function. Cooking is a social function. Neither is in the faintest degree a family function. That we have found it convenient in early stages of civilization to do our cooking at home proves no more than the allied fact that we have also found it convenient in such stages to do our weaving and spinning at home, our soap and candle making, our butchering and pickling, our baking and washing.

As society develops, its functions specialize; and the reason why this great race-function of cooking has been so retarded in its natural growth is that the economic dependence of women has kept them back from their share in human progress. When women stand free as economic agents, they will lift and free their arrested functions, to the much better fulfilment of their duties as wives and mothers and to the vast improvement in health and happiness of the human race. . . .

If there should be built and opened in any of our large cities today a commodious and well-served apartment house for professional women with families, it would be filled at once. The apartments would be without kitchens; but there would be a kitchen belonging to the house from which meals could be served to the families in their rooms or in a common dining-room, as preferred. It would be a home where the cleaning was done by efficient workers, not hired separately by the families, but engaged by the manager of the establishment; and a roof-garden, day nursery, and kindergarten, under well-trained professional nurses and teachers, would insure proper care of the children. The demand for such provision is increasing daily, and must soon be met, not by a boarding-house or a lodging-house, a hotel, a restaurant, or any makeshift patching together of these; but by a permanent provision for the needs of women and children, of family privacy with collective advantage. This must be offered on a business basis to prove a substantial business success; and it will so prove, for it is a growing social need.

There are hundreds of thousands of women in New York City alone who are wage-earners, and who also have families; and the number increases. This is true not only among the poor and unskilled, but more and more among business women, professional women, scientific, artistic, literary women. Our school-teachers, who form a numerous class, are not entirely without relatives. To board does not satisfy the needs of a human soul. These women want homes, but they do not want the clumsy tangle of rudimentary industries that are supposed to accompany the home. The strain under which such women labor is no longer necessary. The privacy of the home could be as well maintained in such a building as described as in any house in a block, any room, flat, or apartment, under present methods. The food would be better, and would cost less; and this would be true of the service and of all common necessities.

In suburban homes this purpose could be accomplished much better by a grouping of adjacent houses, each distinct and having its own yard, but all kitchenless, and connected by covered ways with the eating-house. No detailed prophecy can be made of the precise forms which would ultimately prove most useful and pleasant; but the growing social need is for the specializing of the industries practised in the home and for the proper mechanical provision for them.

The cleaning required in each house would be much reduced by the removal of the two chief elements of household dirt,—grease and ashes. . . .

There are several professions involved in our clumsy method of housekeeping. A good cook is not necessarily a good manager, nor a good manager an accurate and thorough cleaner, nor a good cleaner a wise purchaser. Under the free development of these branches a woman could choose her position, train for it, and become a most valuable functionary in her special branch, all the while living in her own home; that is, she would live in it as a man lives in his home, spending certain hours of the day at work and others at home.

This division of the labor of housekeeping would require the service of fewer women for fewer hours a day. Where now twenty women in twenty homes work all the time, and insufficiently accomplish their varied duties, the same work in the hands of specialists could be done in less time by fewer people; and the others would be left free to do other work for which they were better fitted, thus increasing the productive power of the world. Attempts at cooperation so far have endeavored to lessen the existing labors of women without recognizing their need for other occupation, and this is one reason for their repeated failure. . . .

Many women would continue to prefer the very kinds of work which they are doing now, in the new and higher methods of execution. Even cleaning, rightly understood and practised, is a useful, and therefore honorable, profession. It has been amusing heretofore to see how this least desirable of labors has been so innocently held to be woman's natural duty. It is woman, the dainty, the beautiful, the beloved wife and revered mother, who has by common consent been expected to do the chamber-work and scullery work of the world. All that is basest and foulest she in the last instance must handle and remove. Grease, ashes, dust, foul linen, and sooty ironware,—among these her days must pass. As we socialize our functions, this passes from her hands into those of man. The city's cleaning is his work. And even in our houses the professional cleaner is more and more frequently a man.

The organization of household industries will simplify and centralize its cleaning processes, allowing of many mechanical conveniences and the application of scientific skill and thoroughness. We shall be cleaner than we ever were before. There will be less work to do, and far better means of doing it. The daily needs of a well-plumbed house could be met easily by each individual in his or her own room or by one who liked to do such work; and the labor less frequently required would be furnished by an expert, who would clean one home after another with the swift skill of training and experience. The home would cease to be to us a workshop or a museum, and would become far more the personal expression of its occupants—the place of peace and rest, of love and privacy—than it can be in its present condition of arrested industrial development. And woman will fill her place in those industries with far better results than are now provided by her ceaseless struggles, her conscientious devotion, her pathetic ignorance and inefficiency.

Emily James Putnam

The Lady

❧

Emily James Putnam (1865–1944) took advantage of the greater freedom to learn and to work that had been won by her feminist predecessors. She was a member of the first graduating class of Bryn Mawr College and took postgraduate studies at the British school for women at Cambridge, Girton College. She was a classics scholar, specializing in ancient Greek.

At the age of twenty-nine she became the first dean of the recently established Barnard College in New York City. In 1910 her study of *The Lady* was published. Putnam's book analyzes the position of the upper-class woman in society, beginning with the woman in early Greek culture and closing with "The Lady of the Slave States." Regarding the latter, Putnam says that a "special piquancy is lent to the spectacle of the lady as mistress of slaves by a knowledge of her history" of subjugation by man. She concludes that the lady is an outmoded and "somewhat dangerous" social type.

The following is from the book's Introduction.

The lady is proverbial for her skill in eluding definition, and it is far from the intention of the writer to profess to say what she is in essence. For the purpose of the present discussion she may be described merely as the female of the favoured social class. The sketches in this volume aim to suggest in outline the theories that various typical societies have entertained of the lady; to note the changing ideals that she has from time to time proposed to herself; to show in some measure what her daily life has been like, what sort of education she has had, what sort of man she has preferred to marry; in short, what manner of terms she has contrived to make with the very special conditions of her existence. Such an attempt, like every other inquiry into the history of European ideas, must begin with an examination of the Greeks. The lover of Greek literature knows it to be full of the portraits of strong and graceful women who were also great ladies. On the other hand the student of Greek history is aware that during the great period of the bloom of Athens the women of the upper classes were in eclipse. . . .

The difference between the feminism of the Greek in literature, art and social science, and his anti-feminist practice cannot be explained away, but a near view of some of its aspects throws light both forward and backward upon the history of the lady. At Rome she becomes thoroughly intelligible to us. The society in which she lived there is very similar in essentials to that of our own day. We see the Roman lady helping to evolve a manner of life so familiar now that it is difficult to think it began so relatively late in the history of Europe and is not the way people have always lived. But if it is hard to realise the novelty in Roman times of a free, luxurious, mixed society in a great centre, it is even harder to picture its eclipse. The dark age put the lady back where Homer knew her; instead of a social creature she became again a lonely one, supported by the strong hand, kept safe from her enemies behind thick walls, and, as the price of safety, having but few friends. We have glimpses in Greek tradition of the lady in insurrection, refusing the restraint of the patriarchal family. In the dark age the insurgent Germanic lady makes her appearance, and by the oddest of paradoxes finds freedom in the cloister. The lady abbess is in some sort the descendant of the amazon.

The dying-out of violence and the consequent increase of comfort in private life, brought the lady once more into the

stream of human intercourse. The movement called the
Renaissance valued her as the most precious object of art,
the chosen vessel of that visible beauty which men deemed
divine. As conventional social life was organised in the
sixteenth, the seventeenth and the eighteenth centuries, the
lady's position became one of very great strength, reaching
its climax in the career of the salonière. The great social
changes that began to prevail at the end of the eighteenth
century had a corresponding effect on the status of the lady
and their work is not yet complete. In the United States
during the two generations preceding the war for the union,
the Slave States furnished the background for perhaps the
last example the world will see on a large scale of the feudal
lady. But the typical lady everywhere tends to the feudal
habit of mind. In contemporary society she is an archaism,
and can hardly understand herself unless she knows her own
history.

Every discussion of the status of woman is complicated
by the existence of the lady. She overshadows the rest of her
sex. The gentleman has never been an analogous phenomenon, for even in countries and times where he has occupied
the centre of the stage he has done so chiefly by virtue of his
qualities as a man. A line of gentlemen always implies a
man as its origin, and cannot indeed perpetuate itself for
long without at least occasional lapses into manhood. Moreover the gentleman, in the worst sense of the term, is nu-
merically negligible. The lady, on the other hand, has until
lately very nearly covered the surface of womanhood. She
even occurs in great numbers in societies where the gentleman is an exception; and in societies like the feudal where
ladies and gentlemen are usually found in pairs, she soars
so far above her mate in the development of the qualities
they have in common that he sinks back relatively into the
plane of ordinary humanity. She is immediately recognised by everyone when any social spectrum is analysed.
She is an anomaly to which the western nations of this planet

have grown accustomed but which would require a great deal of explanation before a Martian could understand her. Economically she is supported by the toil of others; but while this is equally true of other classes of society, the oddity in her case consists in the acquiescence of those most concerned. The lady herself feels no uneasiness in her equivocal situation, and the toilers who support her do so with enthusiasm. She is not a producer; in most communities productive labour is by consent unladylike. On the other hand she is the heaviest of consumers, and theorists have not been wanting to maintain that the more she spends the better off society is. In aristocratic societies she is required for dynastic reasons to produce offspring, but in democratic societies even this demand is often waived. Under the law she is a privileged character. If it is difficult to hang a gentleman-murderer, it is virtually impossible to hang a lady. Plays like The Doll's House and The Thief show how clearly the lady-forger or burglar should be differentiated from other criminals. Socially she is in general the product and the beneficiary of monogamy; under this system her prestige is created by the existence of great numbers of less happy competitors who present to her the same hopeless problem as the stoker on the liner presents to the saloon-passenger. If the traveller is imaginative, the stoker is a burden on his mind. But after all, how are saloon-passengers to exist if the stoker does not? Similarly the lady reasons about her sisters five decks below. There have been times when the primary social requirement has apparently been waived; it seems difficult, for instance, so to classify the lady as to exclude Aspasia and Louise de la Vallière.* Nevertheless the true lady is in theory either a virgin or a lawful wife. Religion has given the lady perhaps her strongest hold. Historically it is the source of much of her prestige, and it has at times helped her to break her tabu and

* Aspasia was the mistress of Pericles; Louise de la Vallière was one of the mistresses of Louis XIV.—Ed.

revert to womanhood. Her roots are nourished by its good soil and its bad. Enthusiasm, mysticism, renunciation, find her ready. On the other hand the anti-social forces of religion are embodied in her; she can renounce the world more easily than she can identify herself with it. A lady may become a nun in the strictest and poorest order without altering her view of life, without the moral convulsion, the destruction of false ideas, the birth of character that would be the preliminary steps toward becoming an efficient stenographer. Sentimentally the lady has established herself as the criterion of a community's civilisation. Very dear to her is the observance that hedges her about. In some subtle way it is so bound up with her self-respect and with her respect for the man who maintains it, that life would hardly be sweet to her without it. When it is flatly put to her that she cannot become a human being and yet retain her privileges as a non-combatant, she often enough decides for etiquette.

The product of many cross-impulses, exempt apparently in many cases from the action of economic law, of natural law and of the law of the land, the lady is almost the only picturesque survival in a social order which tends less and less to tolerate the exceptional. Her history is distinct from that of woman though sometimes advancing by means of it, as a railway may help itself from one point to another by leasing an independent line. At all striking periods of social development her status has its significance. In the age-long war between men and women, she is a hostage in the enemy's camp. Her fortunes do not rise and fall with those of women but with those of men. . . .

It would be interesting to note if we could the stages by which, through the accumulation of property and through the man's aesthetic development and his snobbish impulses acting in harmony, he came to feel that it was more desirable to have an idle than a working wife. The idle wife ranked with the ornamentally wrought weapon and with the splendid offering to the gods as a measure of the man's power to waste, and therefore his superiority over other men. Her idleness did not come all at once. One by one the more arduous tasks were dropped that made her less constant or less agreeable in unremitting personal attendance on her lord. The work that remained was generally such as could be performed within the house. Here we find her when history dawns, a complete lady, presiding over inferior wives and slaves, performing work herself, for the spirit of workmanship is ineradicable within her, but tending to produce by preference the useless for the sake of its social and economic significance. As is the case with any other object of art, her uselessness is her use.

It follows from the lady's history that she is to-day, when freed from many of the old restrictions and possessed of a social and financial power undreamed of by her originators, a somewhat dangerous element of society. Her training and experience when not antisocial have been unsocial. Women in general have lived an individualistic life. As soon as the division of early labour sent the man out to fight and kept the woman in the house, the process began which taught men to act in concert while women still acted singly. The man's great adventure of warfare was undertaken shoulder to shoulder with his fellows, while the rumble of the tam-tam thrilled his nerves with the collective motive of the group. The woman's great adventure of maternity had to be faced in cold blood by each woman for herself. The man's exploit resulted in loot to be divided in some manner recognised as equitable, thus teaching him a further lesson in social life. The woman's exploit resulted in placing in her arms a little extension of her ego for which she was fiercely ready to defy every social law. Maternity is on the face of it an unsocial experience. The selfishness that a woman has learned to stifle or to dissemble where she alone is concerned, blooms freely and unashamed on behalf of her offspring. The world at large, which may have made some appeal to the sympathies of the disinterested woman, becomes to the mother chiefly a source of contagious disease and objectionable language. The man's fighting instinct can be readily utilised in the form of sports and games to develop in boys the sense of solidarity; the little girl's doll serves no such social end. The women of the working-classes have been saved by their work itself, which has finally carried them out of the house where it kept them so long. In the shop and the factory they have learned what the nursery can never teach. But the lady has had no social training whatever; the noticeable weakness of her play at bridge is the tendency to work for her own hand. Being surrounded by soft observance she has not so much as learned the art of temperate debate. With an excellent heart and the best intentions but with her inevitable limitations, the lady seems about to undertake the championship of a view of society to which her very existence is uncongenial.

As the gentleman decays, the lady survives as the strongest evidence of his former predominance. Where he set her, there she stays. One after another the fabrics that supported her have tottered, but she remains, adapting herself to each new set of circumstances as it arises. It is possible that an advancing social sentiment will extinguish her altogether, but she can never be forgotten.

Senate Report—History of
Women in Industry in
the United States

❦

By the first decade of the twentieth century, feminist social critics had been pointing out for some time that woman's oppression was rooted in her economic dependence. A paying job outside the home was seen as the answer to a wide variety of problems faced by the female sex. However, for approximately two-thirds of all women who worked in 1900, the reality of employment was not financial independence and personal fulfillment, but grueling hours at substandard wages in either domestic service or factory sweatshops.

A vastly increased post-Civil War American industrial capacity resulted in a greatly augmented need for low-paid unskilled labor. This need was met partly through employment of immigrant men and women and partly through increased entry of American women into the work force. By the turn of the century, 20.6 percent of women in the United States over the age of sixteen were employed.

Economic panics and depressions occurred in about twenty-five of the forty years between 1870 and 1910. The attendant unemployment and poverty—unalleviated by any job benefits or governmental welfare measures—deepened the conditions of misery and squalor in the growing urban slums. Dedicated women such as Jane Addams, Lillian Wald and Mary McDowell founded settlement houses in the slums of New York and Chicago to try to help the workingwoman and her family improve their lives.

Since most workingwomen were not members of trade unions, some middle-class feminists stepped into the breach. Consumer Leagues were formed to publicize retail and manufacturing establishments where workingwomen were maltreated. And in

1903 the Women's Trade Union League was established through which middle-class women struggled along with their laboring sisters to better working conditions. The League supported strikes in which large numbers of women were involved in New York, Chicago, Massachusetts mill towns, and elsewhere, with a variety of helpful and essential services (providing bail for strikers who were arrested; organizing picket lines; running relief kitchens and welfare activities).

Little was known about the history, occupations, numbers and other vital statistics of female workers. The joint pressure of many interested individuals and organizations resulted finally in the authorization by Congress of a thorough investigation of the condition of workingwomen and children. The resulting report, on *Women and Child Wage-Earners in the United States,* which took four years to research and prepare (between 1908 and 1911) and filled nineteen volumes, laid the groundwork for the establishment in 1920 of the Women's Bureau of the United States Department of Labor. The Bureau was entrusted with the formulation of "standards and policies for promoting the welfare of wage-earning women . . . and advancing their opportunities for profitable employment."

The author of Volume IX of the report, *History of Women in Industry in the United States,* Helen L. Sumner, imbued the facts with a feminist perspective and sided implicitly with the goal of occupational equality for women. The following is reprinted from Sumner's first chapter, "Introduction and Summary."

The history of women in industry in the United States is the story of a great industrial readjustment, which has not only carried woman's work from the home to the factory, but has changed its economic character from unpaid production for home consumption to gainful employment in the manufacture of articles for sale. Women have always worked, and their work has probably always been quite as important a factor in the total economy of society as it is to-day. But during the nineteenth century a transformation occurred in their economic position and in the character and conditions of their work. Their unpaid services have been transformed into paid services, their work has been removed from the home to the factory and workshop, their range of possible employment has been increased and at the same time their monopoly of their traditional occupations has been destroyed. The individuality of their work has been lost in a standardized product.

The story of woman's work in gainful employments is a story of constant changes or shiftings of work and workshop, accompanied by long hours, low wages, insanitary conditions, overwork, and the want on the part of the woman of training, skill, and vital interest in her work. It is a story of monotonous machine labor, of division and subdivision of tasks until the woman, like the traditional tailor who is called the ninth part of a man, is merely a fraction, and that rarely as much even as a tenth part, of an artisan. It is a story, moreover, of underbidding, of strike breaking, of the lowering of standards for men breadwinners.

In certain industries and certain localities women's unions have raised the standard of wages. The opening of industrial schools and business colleges, too, though affecting almost exclusively the occupations entered by the daughters of middle-class families who have only recently begun to pass from home work to the industrial field, has at least enabled these few girls to keep from further swelling the vast numbers of the unskilled. The evil of long hours and in certain cases other conditions which lead to overstrain, such as the constant standing of saleswomen, have been made the subject of legislation. The decrease of strain due to shorter hours has, however, been in part nullified by increased speed of machinery and other devices designed to obtain the greatest possible amount of labor from each woman. Nevertheless, the history of woman's work in this country shows that legislation has been the only force which has improved the working conditions of any large number of women wage-earners. Aside from the little improvement that has been effected in the lot of working women, the most surprising fact brought out in this study is the long period of time through which large numbers of women have worked under conditions which have involved not only great hardships to themselves but shocking waste to the community.

CHANGES IN OCCUPATIONS OF WOMEN.

The transfer of women from nonwage-earning home work to gainful occupations is evident to the most superficial observer, and it is well known that most of this transfer has been effected since the beginning of the nineteenth century. In 1870 it was found that 14.7 per cent of the female population 16 years of age and over were breadwinners, and by 1900 the percentage was 20.6 per cent. During the period for which statistics exist, moreover, the movement toward the increased employment of women in gainful pursuits was clear and distinct in all sections of the country and was even more marked among the native-born than among the foreign-born. It must be borne in mind, however, that even in colonial days there were many women who worked for wages, especially at spinning, weaving, the sewing trades, and domestic service. Many women, too, carried on business on their own account in the textile and sewing trades and also in such industries as the making of blackberry brandy. The wage labor of women is as old as the country itself and has merely increased in importance. The amount, however, of unremunerated home work performed by women must still be considerably larger than the amount of gainful labor, for even in 1900 only about one-fifth of the women 16 years of age and over were breadwinners.

Along with the decrease in the importance of unremunerated home labor and the increase in the importance of wage labor has gone a considerable amount of shifting of occupations. Under the old domestic system the work of the woman was to spin, to do a large part of the weaving, to sew, to knit; in general, to make most of the clothing worn by the family, to embroider tapestry in the days and regions where there was time for art, to cook, to brew ale and wine, to clean, and to perform the other duties of the domestic servant. These things women have always done. But machines have now come in to aid in all these industries—machines which in some cases have brought in their train men operatives and in other cases have enormously increased the productive power of the individual and have made it necessary for many women, who under the old régime, like Priscilla, would have calmly sat by the window spinning, to hunt other work. One kind of spinning is now done by men only. Men tailors make every year thousands of women's suits. Men dressmakers and even milliners are common. Men make our bread and brew our ale and do much of the work of the steam laundry where our clothes are washed. Recently, too, men have learned to clean our houses by the vacuum process.

Before the introduction of spinning machinery and the sewing machine the supply of female labor appears never to have been excessive. But the spinning jenny threw out of employment thousands of "spinsters," who were obliged to resort to sewing as the only other occupation to which they were in any way trained. This accounts for the terrible pressure in the clothing trades during the early decades of the nineteenth century. Later on, before any readjustment of women's work had been effected, the sewing machine was introduced, which enormously increased the pressure of competition among women workers. Shortly after the substitution of machinery for the spinning wheel the women of certain localities in Massachusetts found an outlet in binding shoes—an opportunity opened to them by the division of labor and by the development of the ready-made trade. But when the sewing machine was introduced this field, at least for a time, was again contracted. Under this pressure, combined with the rapid development of wholesale industry and division of labor, women have been pressed into

other industries, almost invariably in the first instance into
the least skilled and most poorly paid occupations. This
has gone on until there is now scarcely an industry which
does not employ women. Thus woman's sphere has expanded, and its former boundaries can now be determined
only by observing the degree of popular condemnation
which follows their employment in particular industries.

Attitude of the Public Toward the Employment of Women.

The attitude of the public toward the employment of
women has, indeed, made their progress into gainful occupations slow and difficult, and has greatly aggravated the
adjustment pains which the industrial revolution has forced
upon woman as compared with those of man, whose traditional sphere is bounded only by the humanly possible. This
attitude has, moreover, been an important factor in deter-
mining the woman's choice of occupations. . . .

Causes of the Entrance of Women into Industry.

Machinery, combined with division of labor and the substitution of water, steam, and electric power for human
muscles, has certainly made it possible to employ the unskilled labor of women in occupations formerly carried on
wholly by men. Machinery, however, has as yet affected
only slightly the broad lines of division between woman's
work and man's work. And especially upon its first introduction the sex of the employees is rarely at once changed
to any considerable extent. Thus when spinning machinery
was first introduced women and children were employed to
operate it. Later women became the power-loom weavers.
The sewing machine, too, has always been operated largely
by women. On the other hand, most of the machinery of the
iron and steel industry is operated by men. . . .

Division of labor, indeed, which has always accompanied
and frequently preceded machinery, is probably even more

responsible than the latter for the introduction of women into new occupations. The most striking single tendency in manufacturing industries has been toward the division and the subdivision of processes, thereby making possible the use of woman's work, as well as of unskilled man's work, in larger proportion to that of skilled operatives. A more recent tendency toward the combination of several machines into one has even been checked, in some cases, because a competent machinist would have to be hired. Unless the advantage of the complicated mechanism is very great, in many industries simpler machinery, which can be easily run by women, is preferred.

As a result, both of machinery and of division of labor, the actual occupations of women, within industries, do not differ so widely as do the occupations of men within the same industries. It frequently happens, indeed, that the work of a woman in one industry is almost precisely the same as that of another woman in an entirely different industry.

Other historical forces have brought about changes in the occupations of women. Often, especially in the printing trades and in cigar making, women have been introduced as strike breakers. On the other hand trade unions have in some places been strong enough to prevent the introduction of women in industries to which they were well adapted. Usually, however, this has been only for a short period.

The scarcity of labor supply in particular places or at particular times has often been responsible for the use of women's work. Thus during the early years of the Republic the employment of women in manufacturing industries was doubtless greatly accelerated by the scarcity and high price of other labor. This, too, was doubtless largely responsible for the fact that, in the early years of the cotton industry, a larger proportion of women was employed in the cotton mills of Massachusetts and New Hampshire than in those of Rhode Island, New Jersey, and Pennsylvania. One of the remedies frequently suggested in the thirties and forties for the evils under which working women suffered was that "the excess of spinsters" should be transported to the places where "there is a deficiency of women."

The Civil War was another force which not only drove into gainful occupations a large number of women, but compelled many changes in their employments. In 1869 it was estimated that there were 25,000 working women in Boston who had been forced by the war to earn their living. The war, too, caused a large number of cotton factories to shut down, and thousands of women thus thrown out of employment were obliged to seek other occupations.

Similar to war in its influence, and in some ways more direful, has been the influence of industrial depressions. The industrial depression which began in 1837, for example, temporarily destroyed the newly-arisen wholesale clothing manufacture, and caused untold hardships to the tailoresses and seamstresses of New York and Philadelphia. These women turned, naturally, to any occupation in which it was possible for them to engage. Industrial depressions, too, like war, have taken away from thousands of women the support of the men upon whom they were dependent and have forced them to snatch at any occupation which promised them a pittance.

EXPANSION OF WOMAN'S SPHERE.

As a result of these factors and forces and in many cases of others less general in their operation, woman's sphere of employment has been greatly expanded during the past hundred years. . . .

When, however, the occupations in which women are engaged are considered with reference to the relative number of women employed in each, at different periods, it is evident that the vast majority of working women have remained within the limits of their traditional field. . . . in every census year considerably more than half of all the women employed in manufacturing industries have been in the first two groups, textile and clothing industries. These industries . . . have as houshold industries been theirs from time immemorial. But women have been driven, by the industrial forces already in part analyzed, into many occupations formerly considered as belonging exclusively to man's sphere. . . .

It is evident that, on the whole, there has been a certain expansion of woman's sphere—a decrease in the proportion employed in certain traditional occupations, such as "servants and waitresses," "seamstresses," and "textile workers," but an increase in the proportion employed in most other industries, many of them not originally considered as within woman's domain. There has been, for instance, an increase in the proportion of women engaged as "bookkeepers and accountants," as "saleswomen," as "stenographers and typewriters," and in "other manufacturing and mechanical pursuits," and this movement has affected, roughly speaking, all elements, according to nativity or conjugal condition, of the population of working women. . . .

HOME AND FACTORY WORK.

In general, it may be said that during the past century the amount of home work of women for pay has steadily decreased and the amount of factory work has steadily increased. . . . Home workers have become sweat-shop workers and sweat-shop workers are gradually becoming factory workers. So long ago as now to be almost forgotten a similar transformation took place in the textile industries. Indeed, this is the general tendency of the employment of both men and women in manufacturing industries. Independent domestic production has practically become a thing of the past. But the history of woman's work shows that their wage labor under the domestic system has often been under worse conditions than their wage labor under the factory system. The hours of home workers have been longer, their wages lower, and the sanitary conditions surrounding them more unwholesome than has generally been the case with factory workers. The movement away from home work can hardly, then, be regretted.

GENERAL CONDITIONS OF LIFE AND LABOR.

The conditions under which the working women of this country have toiled have long made them the object of commiseration. Mathew Carey devoted a large part of the last years of his life, from 1828 to 1839, to agitation in their behalf. Again and again he pointed out in newspaper articles, pamphlets, and speeches that the wages of working women in New York, Philadelphia, Baltimore and Boston were utterly insufficient for their support; that their food and lodging were miserably poor and unwholesome; and that the hours they were obliged to work were almost beyond human endurance. . . .

In 1845 an investigation of "female labor" in New York, used as the basis of a series of articles in the New York Tribune, developed "a most deplorable degree of servitude, privation, and misery among this helpless and dependent class of people," including "hundreds and thousands" of shoe binders, type rubbers, artificial-flower makers, match-box makers, straw braiders, etc., who "drudge away, heart-broken, in want, disease, and wretchedness." . . .

Again in 1869 the working women of Boston, in a petition to the Massachusetts legislature . . . asserted that they were insufficiently paid, scantily clothed, poorly fed, and badly lodged, that their physical health, if not already undermined by long hours and bad conditions of work, was rapidly becoming so, and that their moral natures were being undermined by lack of proper society and by their inability to attend church on account of the want of proper clothing and the necessity, being constantly occupied throughout the week, "to bring up the arrears of our household duties by working on the Lord's Day."

Hours of Labor.

Hours, however, except for home workers, have been reduced by legislation. In the early part of the nineteenth century from 12 to 13 hours a day was common, and it is safe to say that 12 hours was about the average day's work in factories. Gradually, through legislation, these hours have been reduced to perhaps nearer 10 a day. The change, too, from home to factory labor has tended to reduce hours, for women home workers have always lived up to the old adage that "woman's work is never done."

Wages and Unemployment.

The low wages paid to women and the inequality of men's and women's wages have always been the chief causes of complaint. . . .

The average wages paid to women in New York in 1863, taking all the trades together, were said to have been about $2 a week and in many instances only 20 cents a day, while the hours ranged from 11 to 16 a day. The price of board, which before the war had been about $1.50 a week, had been raised by 1864 to from $2.50 to $3.

During the war period, indeed, . . . the wages of women increased less, on the whole, than the wages of men, while their cost of living increased out of all proportion to their wages. This fact was recognized, at least, by the labor papers of that period. "While the wages of workingmen have been increased more than 100 per cent," said the Daily Evening Voice, in commenting upon the report for 1864 of the New York Working Women's Protective Union, "and complaint is still made that this is not sufficient to cover the increased cost of food and fuel, the average rate of wages for female labor has not been raised more than 20 per cent since the war was inaugurated; and yet the poor widow is obliged to pay as much for a loaf of bread or a pail of coal as the woman who has a husband or a stalwart son to assist her.

In many trades the rate of wages has been lowered during the year, until it has become a mere pittance, while in other occupations the prices paid to females are generally insufficient to maintain them comfortably." . . .

One of the causes of complaint of the organized working women of Boston in 1869 was "the present fragmentary nature, the insufficiency, and great precariousness of the poor working women's labors," which "render it impossible for them to procure the common necessaries of existence, or make any provision for sickness and old age." . . .

History teaches that working women have suffered fully as much and perhaps more than workingmen from unemployment. Especially is this true in the sewing trades, nearly all of which are seasonal in character. Domestic servants, who have always been in great demand, have long had employment agencies to aid them in their search for work, but little aid has been given the women engaged in manufacturing industries, except by wholly or partially charitable societies, which have given them work, often at starvation prices. The Working Women's Protective Association of New York, it is true, during the three years ending in April, 1868, obtained employment for 3,222 young women, and during the year 1870 is said to have procured employment for about 2,000. But in 1869 the applications for employment were given as 16,625 and the places filled as only 3,318. While these figures may not be strictly accurate, there can be no doubt that there was in these years an enormous amount of unemployment among women workers.

In the sewing trades, since the early part of the nineteenth century, the proportion of workers who have been without steady employment has always been large. Piecework and a fluctuating demand for labor, combined with a constant oversupply, have been largely responsible. Even in other trades, however, women, partly because of their lack of training and skill, have continually suffered from unemployment. In 1890, according to the census figures, 12.7

per cent, and in 1900, 23.3 per cent of all the females engaged in gainful occupations were unemployed during some portion of the census year. . . .

That working women should receive the same pay as men for the same work has long been the desire of trade-unionists. Though not expressly stated, it was implied in the resolution of the National Trades' Union in 1835, which complained that "the extreme low prices given for female labor, afford scarcely sufficient to satisfy the necessary wants of life, and create a destructive competition with the male laborer." . . . A generation later the National Labor Union, moreover, repeatedly passed resolutions expressing sympathy for the "sewing women and daughters of toil," urging them to unite in trade-unions, and demanding for them "equal pay for equal work." . . .

Again in 1868 the president of the National Labor Union, in his opening address to the congress, referred to "the extent to which female labor is introduced into many trades" as "a serious question," and stated that "the effect of introducing female labor is to undermine prices, that character of labor being usually employed, unjustly to the women, at a lower rate than is paid for male labor on the same kind of work." . . .

Scope and Sources of the Report.

In this report on the history of women in industry, wage-earning occupations alone are considered. The unremunerated home work of women, . . . is necessarily neglected. Women engaged in professions, in independent business, and in agriculture, too, are considered only in relation to the wage-earning women in industry. . . .

The character and conditions of woman's work within recent years have been fully described in reports, books, magazines, and newspapers which can be easily obtained, but the history of the formative period of woman's work has long been buried away in rare old books and papers, many of them until recently unknown even to close students of the labor question. The history of the wage labor of woman during and shortly after this formative period, moreover, is not only comparatively unknown, but furnishes the only positive basis for any historical interpretation of women in industry.

Anna Garlin Spencer

Woman's Share in Social Culture

❧

Anna Garlin Spencer (1851–1931) was one of a number of American professional women—like Emily Putnam, Charlotte Gilman and Helen L. Sumner—who participated in that brief flowering of feminist social analysis which took place in the late nineteenth and early twentieth centuries. Spencer pursued a variety of careers as a public school teacher, a journalist, a minister and a college professor (she lectured in social science at Columbia's Teachers College and at the University of Wisconsin, and was Professor of Sociology and Ethics at Meadville Theological School). As a feminist, she was identified with the established woman's suffrage organization, and was a frequent speaker at National American conventions.

Anna Spencer's most important work, *Woman's Share in Social Culture,* displayed her wide intellectual range. In it, she outlined the contributions of women from primitive to modern times in the evolution of civilization and their role (at the time of her writing) in industry, education, the arts and other aspects of national life.

The book also expressed her disagreement with Charlotte Gilman's suggestion that the domestic responsibilities of women be taken over by professional specialists. Spencer believed this idea was not "economically practical or socially useful"; she defended the home and family and emphasized their central importance to the personality development and socialization of the child.

In the selection below, Anna Spencer addressed herself to the vocational problems faced by the woman of talent in the larger world outside the home. She elucidated the many obstacles imposed by male-dominated cultures in all ages that have prevented gifted women from realizing their potential for achievement.

The following excerpt from *Woman's Share in Social Culture* —published in 1912—is from Chapter III, "The Drama of the Woman of Genius."

The failure of women to produce genius of the first rank in most of the supreme forms of human effort has been used to block the way of all women of talent and ambition for intellectual achievement in a manner that would be amusingly absurd were it not so monstrously unjust and socially harmful. A few ambitious girls in the middle of the nineteenth century in Boston, the Athens of America, want to go to High School. The Board of Education answers them, in effect: Produce a Michael Angelo or a Plato and you shall have a chance to learn a bit of mathematics, history and literature. A few women of marked inclination toward the healing art want a chance to study in a medical school and learn facts and methods in a hospital. Go to! the managing officials in substance reply: Where is your great surgeon; what supreme contribution has any woman ever made to our science? A group of earnest students beg admission to college and show good preparation gained by hard struggle with adverse conditions. You can't come in, the trustees respond, until you produce a Shakespeare or a Milton. The demand that women shall show the highest fruit of specialized talent and widest range of learning before they have had the general opportunity for a common-school education is hardly worthy of the sex that prides itself upon its logic. In point of fact no one, neither the man who denies woman a proper human soul nor the woman who claims "superiority" for her sex, can have any actual basis for accurate answer to the question, Can a woman become a genius of the first class? Nobody can know unless women in general shall have equal opportunity with men in education, in vocational choice, and in social welcome of their best intellectual work for a number of generations. So far women have suffered so many disabilities in the circumstances of their lives, in their lack of training, in what Buckle calls "that preposterous system called their education," in their segregation from all the higher intellectual comradeship, in the personal and family and social hindrances to their mental growth and expression, that not even women themselves, still less men, can have an adequate idea of their possibilities of achievement. Nothing therefore is more foolish than to try to decide *a priori* the limits of a woman's capacity. What we do know is this, that there have been women of talent, and even of genius reaching near to the upper circles of the elect; and we know also that these women of marked talent have appeared whenever and wherever women have had opportunities of higher education and have been held in esteem by men as intellectual companions as well as wives and manual workers. The connection between these two facts is obvious. . . .

At this point it is well to remind ourselves not only how few are the men of supreme genius, but also how few have been fortunate enough in their biographies to get their names on the chief lists of the second rank. Not all "inglorious Miltons" were "mute." Many sang sweetly to their contemporaries, but lacked voice to echo down the ages. Doubtless many quite equal to Dr. Johnson, yet lacking his Boswell, received only a fine print recognition in a biographical dictionary. Women, far more than men, it is reasonable to suppose, have suffered hasty eclipse for want of adequate mention in the permanent records.* Sappho has been sadly overworked as an instance of feminine genius; yet to be called "the poetess" as Homer was "the poet" in Greece, nearly five hundred years before our era, was not only proof

* The change of name at marriage has tended toward confusion and loss in the record of women's work.—A. G. S.

of her own greatness, but also that there must have been many smaller poetesses to win her that distinction. The ancient world must also have produced numbers of women-philosophers of ability to have made a place for Hypatia at the head of a School; and her powers, which won her a martyrdom for truth equal in dignity to that of Socrates, must have had their rooting in the rich soil of the higher education of women. Indeed, we hear of over thirty "lady philosophers" and students of the most advanced learning in the School Pythagoras. Again that Pulcheria, of whom Gibbon says, "She alone of all the descendants of the great Theodosius appears to have inherited any share of his manly spirit and abilities," could not have been the only woman of her time and her court to show intellectual achievements as well as noble statesmanship. And that Paula, friend of Jerome, descendant of the Gracchi, and one of the richest women of antiquity, who chose simplicity and frugality for herself, using her wealth for education and charity, could not have carried into effect such noble forms of self-sacrifice had she not lived in a time and place in which women had control over their purses and their lives. Superlative genius, although usually quite unexpected in appearance, always arises out of a group of secondary great ones, and these in turn out of a crowd of the merely talented. Following this general law, when the Lady reached her heyday of supremacy in the thirteenth to the sixteenth century, her class gave to the world many women of marked intellectual power and of special gifts in many lines. . . .

Budding genius in the Lady-class naturally developed along the lines of least resistance to the habits and conventions of the age and station of the exceptional woman. Writing, scholarship in all the learning of the period, teaching, public lecturing, preaching (then thought entirely suitable for the great lady who could do it well), leadership in church affairs and contribution to the higher statesmanship of royal houses and princely courts—these were her achievements. . . . we remember Casandre Fidèle who wrote equally well in the languages of Homer, Virgil and Dante and who, it is said, "by her graces embellished even theology." She gave public lessons at Padua, sustained these in public debate, and had also "many agreeable talents such as music." She could not have stood alone, although probably none of the learned ladies of her town were her equals; and surely to but few women of any age has it been given, as it was to her, to prove that higher education is not inimical to a woman's health, by living more than one hundred years! As to the women preachers of that time, we may be sure that the Spanish Isabella who often spoke in the great church of Barcelona, "converting even the Jews by her eloquence," must have had humble followers who were the pride of their smaller congregations.

This was the period of extravagant praise for gifted women, as in Venice, where in 1555, Signora Jeanne d'Aragon had constructed for her a "Temple of Praise" for her wit, her learning and her eloquence, to which the greatest writers of her time contributed in all the principal languages of the world. . . .

A celebrated Venetian lady, Modesta di Pozzo di Forzi, in 1593 maintained the superiority of her sex in no uncertain words. Her biographer in giving an account of the "great success of her book" shrewdly remarks that "unfortunately for her that which perhaps assisted in that success was that men could praise her without fear, since she died just as the work appeared." He also confesses that "men always see with pleasure these sorts of works by women; for pride, which calculates everything, makes men regard as a proof of their advantage the efforts which are made to combat them." In the seventeenth century another Venetian lady went so far as to entitle her book, *The Nobleness and Excellence of Women and the Defects and Imperfections of Men*. It is said that she too had "the success that beauty gives to wit." Marguerite, Queen of Navarre, undertook in a letter to prove the superiority of her sex; while Mlle. de Gournay contented herself with simply claiming equality. . . .

The whole discussion seems to have been a sort of play-battle, doubtless taken seriously by few, if any. It was the prelude to a more serious struggle for democratic rights in government, in education, and in industry which wrought itself out first by and for men, and in which for a long season all claims of women to justice and consideration were forgotten.

Carlyle * reminds us that while the French Revolution was smouldering toward conflagration the "paper people" (those at ease in their own circumstances from having already profited by class privilege) were playing with radical ideas that were later to make rallying cries in the bloody struggle. It was a time, he says, when "Philosophism sat joyful in her glittering saloons, the dinner guest of Opulence grown ingenuous, the very nobles proud to sit by her, and Preaching, lifted up over all Bastiles, a coming millennium." So in the times when womanhood in general suffered all unspeakable outrage and misery, this little comedy of mock homage, which yet had in it some notes of true reverence, was played out on the stage of polite society.

There were hard days coming, days when the rights of man were to embroil the world in conflict; days when the common life was to surge up to the drawing room and rudely break up the dinners of Opulence; days when the Lady was lost sight of and the stern times called even for the woman of genius to bury herself in the primal labors of her sex, that so the home might be kept and the children saved alive and the grain harvested while men held their hands at the throat of Despotism, until all the common folk were counted as people. When the time came for a genuine movement for equality of education and opportunity for

* Thomas Carlyle, *The French Revolution.*—A. G. S.

women, it was the great middle class, not the nobility, that led in the sober struggle; and it was martyrdom, not "success," that came first.

Victor Hugo says: "The eighteenth century was man's century; the nineteenth is woman's." In that man's century of revolution against class privilege, the lowest level of "female education" seems to have been reached in our Anglo-Saxon civilization. In our own country, in the early days, the vigor of mind as well as of body of both men and women went of necessity into the pioneer building of our mighty States. . . . Although in Massachusetts as early as 1636 the General Court established Harvard College, and in 1644 ordered the several towns to make sure that "Evry family alow one peck of corne or 12d. in money or other commodity to be sent in to ye Treasurer for the colledge at Cambridge," and in 1683 voted that "Every towne consisting of more than five hundred families shall set up and maintain scholes to instruct youth as the law directs," no girls were thought of in this connection. The provision of "free schools," "schools for the people," etc., left the girls entirely out of the count. Hartford, Connecticut, indeed, in 1771, began to allow girls to learn "reading, spelling, writing" and sometimes "to add"; but not until the close of the eighteenth century did the majority of towns of New England make provision, even in a meagre manner, for the education of girls.

At first all the Common Schools for girls were held between April and October, when the boys were at work on the farms; and as late as 1792 Newburyport most reluctantly allowed girls over nine years of age "instruction in grammar and reading during the summer months for an hour and a half after the dismission of the boys." This opportunity was extended in 1804 to a provision for "girls' schools," "to be kept for six months in the year from six to eight o'clock in the morning and on Thursday afternoons," when the boys, presumably, were not using the school rooms! As late as

1788 the town of Northampton, Massachusetts, voted "not to be at any expense for schooling girls," and only yielded, after an appeal to the courts by the tax paying fathers of the girls, a small chance to learn in the summer months. Up to 1828 girls did not go to public schools in Rhode Island; and not until 1852 was the "Girls' High School" securely established in Boston itself, and not until 1878 the "Girls' Latin School" of that city to prepare for college.

As Abigail Adams wrote in 1817, when over seventy years of age, speaking of the opportunities of women in her day: "The only chance for much intellectual improvement in the female sex, was to be found in the families of the educated class and in occasional intercourse with the learned." To this should be added the partiality of men teachers to some bright girls, which gave an exceptional training to a favored few. . . . To . . . happy accidents of personal favoritism toward exceptional girls must be added the earliest contributions to co-education made by the religious sects, the Moravians who founded in Bethlehem, Pennsylvania, in 1749, the first private institution in America which admitted girls to higher educational opportunities than the elementary school; and the Friends, who established in 1697 the Penn Charter School in Philadelphia which made provision for the education of "all Children and Servants, Male and Female, the rich to be instructed at reasonable rates and the poor to be maintained and schooled for nothing"; although in this provision the boys were provided with a more extended course of study than the girls.

These reminders of the period before the days of the Ladies' Academies for the well-to-do, of which Mrs. Willard's was the most ambitious, and of Mary Lyon's school in which the poorer girls could earn a part of their living by housework, cannot be omitted from consideration of the intellectual output of women in the United States.* Oberlin,

* Emma Willard's Troy Female Seminary was established in 1821; Mary Lyon founded Mount Holyoke in 1837.—Ed.

with its "Female Department" and its offers of education to black as well as white, the Cincinnati Wesleyan Woman's College and Ripon and Antioch Colleges, were object-lessons long more observed than followed. The establishment of Normal Schools gave the first great democratic opportunity in education to women in America; and, characteristically in the history of women's higher education, this opportunity was given women not for themselves as human beings entitled to intellectual development, but as women who could give the State a larger and cheaper supply of teachers for the free public schools. . . . In spite of their poverty in education, however, the women of the eighteenth and first half of the nineteenth centuries made some good showing in letters; and their struggles for professional training and opportunity, especially in the field of medicine, show an heroic temper as well as a persistent purpose second to no class of men in a similar effort to obtain rights and chances in the larger life. . . .

All this, however, does not reach the deepest considerations involved in taking account of the intellectual contribution of women to art, science, philosophy and affairs. Whatever may be the reasons in nature for the lower level of women along these lines of man's greatest achievement, there are the gravest reasons in circumstance for the comparatively meagre showing. In addition to the handicap of lack of education, a handicap which no exceptional success of the self-made man or woman can offset for the majority of the talented, there is a no less important deprivation which all women have suffered in the past and most women now suffer. This deprivation is that of the informal but highly stimulating training which the good fellowship of their chosen guild of study and of service gives to men, but which is denied for the most part even to professional women. For example, women have been in the medical profession for a considerable time, and have obtained high distinction in it. They have won just recognition from many influential doctors of the other sex. Yet they can hardly be said to have entered the inner circle of their clan. They may stop to dinner at medical conventions, it is true, provided they make no fuss about smoking and do not mind being in the minority; but there are few men, even in that enlightened group, who can so sink sex-consciousness in professional comradeship as either to give or get the full social value that might be gained from a mixed company of like vocation. The women lawyers and members of the clergy are in even smaller minority, and hence suffer still more from that embarrassment of "the exception" which prevents easy and familiar association. In the teaching profession, where the relative numbers of the sexes are reversed, there is often more adequate professional intercourse; but the woman college professor, or college president, is still that one among many whose reception into her special class, even if courteous and friendly, is too formal and occasional for real guild fellowship.

To this negative deprivation must be added the positive opposition of men to the entrance of women into that professional life and work from which the genius arises as the rare flower from a vast field. The whole course of evolution in industry, and in the achievements of higher education and exceptional talent, has shown man's invariable tendency to shut women out when their activities have reached a highly specialized period of growth. . . . This monopolistic tendency of men is shown most clearly in the history of the learned professions. Women were seldom, if ever, priests but they participated in religious services when religion was a family affair. When a priestly caste arose and became the symbol of peculiar authority, only men entered its ranks. Woman can reënter her natural place as religious leader only through the Theological Schools and Ordination, and these have been forbidden her until very recently and are now seldom open to her in full measure.

A striking illustration of this process of sex-exclusion

following the perfecting of standards in training is shown in recent years in the United States in the action of the Methodist Episcopal Church. This religious body, of which Susanna Wesley has been called "the real founder" and Barbara Heck the first and most effective teacher in the United States, had for all its earlier propaganda the services of lay-preachers, later called "licensed exhorters," among whom were many gifted women whose "call" was well attested by the crowds that thronged to hear them. When, however, through an effort to raise all the standards of leadership in the Methodist Church to the plane of an "educated ministry," this lay service was crippled and finally abolished, women were shut out of the Methodist ministry altogether; thus losing to this Church many brilliant and devout preachers.

Again, women developed law and its application to life in the germs of family rule and tribal custom quite as much as did men; but when statutes took the place of tradition, and courts superseded personal judgeship, and when a special class of lawyers was needed to define and administer laws, which grew more difficult to understand with growing complexity of social relationship, men alone entered that profession. Women can now become members of that class only by graduating from law-schools and being "admitted to the bar," and only very recently have they been allowed these privileges. The prophetess Deborah, who was a "judge in Israel," was not the only woman to embody the ancient authority of woman in formal fashion; and Aspasia pleading causes in the Athenian forum and Hortensia appearing before the Roman Senate against unjust taxes do not stand alone in history as familiar with and influencing legislation. The rudimentary law of the ancient Germans, especially, took care to "represent every woman at the court of the suzerain, in judicial acts and debates." The Court of Maryland in January, 1648, ordered that Mistress Brent be received as Lord Baltimore's attorney; although when she asked, on that account, for "Voyce and vote in the General Assembly," she was refused. These exceptions do not disprove but give point to that general rule of development of law that in the ratio of its perfecting as a separate profession women were excluded from its training and its practice. When Arabella Mansfield of Iowa was admitted to the bar in 1869 she was a pioneer in the road all women must now travel to reënter any stronghold of the law.

This process of differentiating and perfecting intellectual labor, the process in which at most acute periods of specialization and advance, women were wholly shut out of their own ancient work, finds its most complete and its most dramatic illustration in the history of the medical profession. Some phases of the healing art have always been connected in primitive society with the priestly office and, hence, in the hands of men. Three great branches, however, were always, in all forms of social organization of which we have knowledge, in the hands exclusively of women, namely, midwifery, the treatment of diseases of women so far as those were cared for at all, and the diseases of children. . . . The result of this sex-segregation in the care of the sick in these important branches has been that women doctors, unschooled but often not unskilled, have served all the past of human experience in childbirth, in child-care, and in the special illnesses of women. This has been true in our own, as well as in older civilizations up to the 18th century. In our own country, in colonial times, only women ushered into a bleak New England the potential citizens of the new world. We read of Mrs. Wiat, who died in 1705 at the age of 94 years, having assisted as midwife at the birth of more than 1,100 children.* And in Rehoboth, one of the oldest communities in Massachusetts, the Town Meeting itself "called" from England "Dr. Sam Fuller and his mother," he to practice medicine and she "as midwife to answer to the town's necessity, which was great." Busied with other matters, the

* Mary Putnam Jacobi, M.D., in *Women in Medicine*—A. G. S.

Colonies paid little attention to medical science until the
war of the American Revolution betrayed the awful results
of ignorance in the slaughter of soldiers by preventable
disease. When the healing art began to become a true science and took great strides toward better training and
facilities of practice for the student, attention was at once
drawn to the need for better service in the fields wholly
occupied by women. The opening and improvement of the
medical schools, however, was a new opportunity for men
alone and the new demand for more scientific care of women
in childbirth and for higher medical service to childhood
and for the women suffering from special diseases, resulted
in the greatest of innovations, namely, the assumption by
men of the office of midwife and their entrance into the
most intimate relationships with women patients. Dr. James
Lloyd, after two years' study in England, began to practice
"obstetrics" (the new name that disguised in some degree
the daring change in medical practice) in Boston, in 1762.
Dr. Shippen, similarly trained abroad, took up the same
practice in Philadelphia and added lectures upon the subject. Thus began in our own country the elevation of this
important branch of the healing art to a professional standard and the consequent exclusion of women from their
immortal rights in the sickroom. It was a poor recognition
of the debt the race owed to the mother-sex, both as suffering the pangs of childbirth and as helping to assuage them
and in caring for the infants and children of all time! After
men entered upon the task of perfecting the medical profession, and incidentally shutting women out of it, it did not
take long, however, for the thoughtful to see the propriety
of allowing women those advantages of training which
would put them back again into their rightful place on the
higher plane of science now demanded. What gave sharp
point to this feeling was the common opposition to men
engaging in these ancient prerogatives of women. This was
at first as intense and as bitter as the later opposition to the

entrance of women into the co-educational medical schools. Dr. Samuel Gregory, who founded, in Boston, Mass., in 1848, the first medical training school for women,—a poor affair but a prophecy of better things,—wrote a pamphlet which was widely circulated, entitled "Man-midwifery Exposed and Corrected; or the Employment of men to attend women in child-birth shown to be a modern Innovation, Unnecessary, Unnatural and Injurious to the physical Welfare of the Community, and Pernicious in its influence on Professional and Public Morality." Dr. Gregory brought forward in support of the claims of his new School of Medicine with its meagre opportunities for study, that it would enable the "surplus female population," numbering already in 1849 at least "20,000 in New England," to prepare for a "useful, honorable and remunerative occupation as midwives"; and as they "could afford to give their services at a much cheaper rate than men, five dollars instead of fifteen dollars" would be all the poor would have to pay in confinement cases. It may well be imagined that this prospect of being undersold by women, in a field of medical practice which men were suddenly finding very remunerative, added fuel to the flame of opposition by men doctors to any form of medical education for women. . . . The first women who tried to secure training in medical schools in order to re-ënter those branches of the healing art from which they had so recently been driven, and on the higher plane of science now properly demanded, endured such hardships as made them veritable martyrs. In 1847 Harriot K. Hunt knocked at the door of Harvard Medical School to be persistently refused admission. In 1849 Elizabeth Blackwell graduated from Geneva Medical School, having secured instruction as a special favor, and began her great career; devoted equally to securing the best possible medical training for women, and to elevating to higher standards than had as yet been attained by men the whole area of medical training. Among the heroic figures of these early days are to be found many married women whose husbands, often themselves physicians, helped them to obtain their training. . . . The attitude of the men of the medical profession generally, however, was one of the utmost hostility, showing every form of monopolistic selfishness and injustice. England, which had led the United States in all medical advance, gave belated attention to the needs of women. Not until 1872 was the Medical department of the London University opened to women, and when they were declared eligible for its medical degree many indignant men-graduates of the institution protested that their "property rights had been invaded by this action"; that for women to be able legally to practise medicine "lowered the value of their own diplomas, and, therefore, the University had violated its contract with men by allowing women to share its privileges." * All this was without reference to the intellectual standing or practical efficiency of the women graduates. The mere fact of women entering the profession meant, in the minds of these protestants, degradation to the men already in it! Earlier than this, in 1859, the Medical Society of the County of Philadelphia passed "resolutions of excommunication" against every physician who should "teach in a medical school for women" and every one who should "consult with a woman physician or with a man teaching a woman medical student." In Massachusetts after qualified women physicians were given State certificates to practise, the Massachusetts Medical Society forbade them membership, thus refusing to admit the legality of diplomas already sanctioned by the highest authority.** The facts that women medical students, like those of the other sex, required clinic teaching and hospital training for proper preparation, and that, since hospital opportunities could not be adequately duplicated, women must be taught with men in this field,

* Dr. Putnam Jacobi, *History of Women in Medicine*—A. G. S.
** Admitted, 1879—A. G. S.

gave the pioneer women medical students a peculiar discipline of hardship. . . . Nevertheless, the women did reënter their ancient profession of healing after a brief exclusion. So far from permanently lowering the standards of training newly established, their chief pioneer leader, Elizabeth Blackwell, was instrumental in inaugurating modern preventive medicine, by the establishment in the New York Medical College for Women, opened in 1865, of the first chair of Hygiene ever set apart in a medical college in the United States. In 1882 this pioneer medical college for women set forth the bravest and truest of philosophies respecting women's work in the following words: "We call upon all those who believe in the higher education of women to help set the highest possible standards for their medical education; and we call upon those who do not believe in such higher education to help in making such requirements as shall turn aside the incompetent;—not by any exercise of arbitrary power, but by a demonstration of incapacity, which is the only logical, manly reason for refusing to allow women to pursue an honorable calling in an honorable way." . . .

Dr. Mary Putnam Jacobi, first woman to be admitted to the Paris School of Medicine and winner of its second prize at graduation. . . . summed up in vivid and truthful manner not only for her own profession but, inferentially, for all the higher intellectual pursuits of women, the just basis of judgment of feminine powers. "When," she says, "a century shall have elapsed after general higher education has become diffused among women; after generations have had increased opportunities for inheritance of trained intellectual aptitudes; after the work of establishing, in the face of resolute opposition, the right to privileged work, in addition to the drudgeries imposed by necessity, shall have ceased to preoccupy the energies of women; after selfish monopolies of privilege and advantage shall have been broken down; after the rights and capacities of women as individuals shall have received thorough, serious and practical recognition; a century after this" we may fitly judge of the natural capacity of women for that intellectual leadership out of which genius must spring.

In addition to these handicaps must be named the well-known but scarcely adequately measured interruptions to both study and self-expression which the women of talent and specialized power have always experienced. Anyone can see that to write *Uncle Tom's Cabin* on the knee in the kitchen, with constant calls to cooking and other details of housework to punctuate the paragraphs, was a more difficult achievement than to write it at leisure in a quiet room. And when her biographer says of an Italian woman poet, "during some years her Muse was intermitted," we do not wonder at the fact when he casually mentions her ten children. No record, however, can even name the women of talent who were so submerged by child-bearing and its duties, and by "general housework," that they had to leave their poems and stories all unwritten. Moreover, the obstacles to intellectual development and achievement which marriage and maternity interpose (and which are so important that they demand a separate study) are not the only ones that must be noted. It is not alone the fact that women have generally had to spend most of their strength in caring for others that has handicapped them in individual effort; but also that they have almost universally had to care wholly for themselves. Women even now have the burden of the care of their belongings, their dress, their home life of whatever sort it may be, and the social duties of the smaller world, even if doing great things in individual work. A successful woman preacher was once asked "what special obstacles have you met as a woman in the ministry?" "Not one," she answered, "except the lack of a minister's wife." When we read of Charles Darwin's wife not only relieving him from financial cares but seeing that he had his breakfast in his room, with "nothing to disturb the freshness of his morning," we do not find the explanation of Darwin's genius, but we do see how he was helped to express it. . . .

Added to all this, the woman of talent and of special gifts has had until very lately, and in most countries has still, to go against the massed social pressure of her time in order to devote herself to any particular intellectual task. The expectation of society has long pushed men toward some special work; the expectation of society has until recently been wholly against women's choosing any vocation beside their functional service in the family. . . . No book has yet been written in praise of a woman who let her husband and children starve or suffer while she invented even the most useful things, or wrote books, or expressed herself in art, or evolved philosophic systems. On the contrary, the mildest approach on the part of a wife and mother, or even of a daughter or sister, to that intense interest in self-expression which has always characterized genius has been met with social disapproval and until very recent times with ostracism fit only for the criminal. Hence her inner impulsion has needed to be strong indeed to make any woman devote herself to ideas. . . .

The universal social pressure upon women to be all alike, and do all the same things, and to be content with identical restrictions, has resulted not only in terrible suffering in the lives of exceptional women, but also in the loss of unmeasured feminine values in special gifts. The Drama of the Woman of Genius has been too often a tragedy of misshapen and perverted power.

Carrie Chapman Catt

The World Movement for Woman Suffrage 1904 to 1911: Is Woman Suffrage Progressing?

❧

Carrie Chapman Catt (1859–1947) was a Midwestern educator and newspaperwoman, active in local state suffrage activities. Susan B. Anthony recognized her abilities and brought her into the national organization in 1890. Catt was Anthony's hand-picked successor when the eighty-year-old leader stepped down from the presidency of the National American Woman Suffrage Association ten years later. Catt served as president from 1900 to 1904 and again from 1915 to 1920, when the goal was finally achieved.

In her single-minded devotion to winning the fight for woman suffrage, Carrie Chapman Catt was pragmatic rather than ideological. From the start, she displayed an amazing ability to inspire loyalty in her co-workers; yet at the same time she never allowed personalities to stand in the way of the needs of the cause. Thus, as early as 1896 she sided with the majority of National American convention delegates when a resolution was passed disclaiming any connection between the Association and Elizabeth Cady Stanton's recently published book, the *Woman's Bible*. Although Anthony was personally somewhat critical of Stanton's impious exegesis, she was furious at Catt for backing the convention's resolution. "When this platform is too narrow for all to stand on," Anthony declared, "I shall not be on it."

During Catt's tenure as president, the platform of the organization was broad enough to hold *only* those whose presence she deemed helpful to the winning of suffrage. Thus, Southern white supremacist women and well-to-do Northern liberals were accommodated within the National American Association; radicals, black women and immigrant working-class women in any but token numbers were not. Also excluded were militant feminists. The organization Catt fashioned later became the League of Women Voters.

As for strategy, Catt believed that the "woman's hour" was finally at hand, and could be grasped through legal democratic means. To put unremitting pressure on those who had the power to bring about passage of a federal female suffrage amendment, she devised many different forms of agitation. Sometimes mass action was utilized—millions of American women participated in the suffrage campaign after 1915—and sometimes high-level persuasion techniques were involved, such as the extensive congressional lobbying that was carried on.

In the eleven years between her two presidential terms, Catt was by no means idle. Her brilliant organizational talents were exercised in setting up an International Woman Suffrage Alliance. The speech below was delivered in Stockholm in 1911. It demonstrates her overriding optimism in the eventual victory of the cause and in the power of female suffrage to bring about "woman's full liberty."

In a debate upon the Woman Suffrage Bill in the Swedish Parliament, a few weeks ago, a University Professor said, in a tone of eloquent finality: "The Woman Suffrage movement has reached and passed its climax; the suffrage wave is now rapidly receding." To those who heard the tone of voice and saw the manner with which he spoke, there was no room for doubt that he believed what he said. . . .

Long centuries before the birth of Darwin an old-time Hindoo wrote: "I stand on a river's bank. I know not from whence the waters come or whither they go. So deep and silent is its current that I know not whether it flows north or south; all is a mystery to me; but when I climb yon summit the river becomes a silver thread weaving its length in and out among the hills and over the plains. I see it all from its source in yonder mountains to its outlet in yonder sea. There is no more mystery." So these university professors buried in school books, these near-sighted politicians, fail to note the meaning of passing events. To them, the woman movement is an inexplicable mystery, an irritating excrescence upon the harmonious development of society. But to us, standing upon the summit of international union, where we may observe every manifestation of this movement in all parts of the world, there is no mystery. From its source, . . . we clearly trace the course of this movement through the centuries, moving slowly but majestically onward, gathering momentum with each century, each generation; until just before us lies the golden sea of woman's full liberty. Others may theorise about the woman movement but to us has been vouchsafed positive knowledge. Once, this movement represented the scattered and disconnected protests of individual women. In that period women as a whole were blinded by ignorance, because society denied them education; they were compelled to silence, for society forbade them to speak. They struggled against their wrongs singly and alone, for society forbade them to organise; they dwelt in poverty, for the law denied them the control of property and even the collection of wages. Under such conditions of sexual serfdom, what wonder that their cries for justice were stiffled, and that their protests never reached the ears of the men who wrote the history of those times? Happily those days are past; and out of that incoherent and seemingly futile agitation, which extended over many centuries, there has emerged a present-day movement possessing a clear understanding and a definite, positive purpose. . . .

To follow up the advantages already won, there is to-day an army of women, united, patient, invincible. In every land there are trained pens in the hands of women, eloquence and wit on women's lips to defend their common cause. More, there is an allied army of broad-minded, fearless, unyielding men who champion our reform. The powers of opposition, armed as they are with outworn tradition and sickly sentiment *only,* are as certain to surrender to these irresistible forces as is the sun to rise to-morrow.

These are the things *we know.* That others may share the faith that is ours, permit me to repeat a few familiar facts. A call for the first International Conference was issued nine years ago, and it was held in the City of Washington.* At that time the Woman Suffrage agitation had resulted in nationally organised movements in five countries only. In chronological order of organisation these were: The United States, Great Britain, Australia, Norway, the Netherlands. Two years later, in 1904, the organisation of the Alliance was completed in Berlin, and associations in Canada, Germany, Denmark, and Sweden were ready to join. . . . Today, seven years later, however, our Alliance counts 24 auxiliary national associations, and correspondence groups in two additional countries. Are these evidences of a wave rapidly receding? . . .

Those unfamiliar with our work may ask, what does this great body of men and women do? They do everything which human ingenuity can devise and human endurance carry out, to set this big, indifferent world to thinking. I believe more money has been contributed, more workers enlisted, more meetings held, more demonstrations made in Great Britain alone in behalf of Woman Suffrage than in the entire world's movement for man suffrage. Certainly the man suffrage movement never brought forth such originality of campaign methods, such superb organisation, such masterly alertness. Yet it is said in all countries that women do not want to vote. It is to be devoutly hoped that the obstinacy of no other Government will drive women to such waste of time, energy, and money, to such sacrifice and suffering, as has that of Great Britain.

* She is referring here to the first international *suffrage* conference; there had been previous international assemblages devoted to problems of women.—Ed.

Nor are demonstrations and unusual activities confined to Great Britain. Two thousand women swarmed to the Parliament of Canada last winter, thousands flocked to the Legislatures of the various capitals in the United States. A procession of the best womanhood in New York a few weeks ago marched through that city's streets in protest against legislative treatment. Sweden has filled the great Circus building in Stockholm to overflowing. Hungary, Germany, France, "demonstrate," and in my opinion no campaign is moved by more self-sacrificing devotion, more passionate fervour, than that in Bohemia. . . . In our combined countries many thousands upon thousands of meetings are held every year, and millions of pages of leaflets are distributed, carrying our plea for justice into the remotest corners of the globe.

There are doubtless hard encounters ahead, but there are now educated women's brains ready to solve every campaign problem. There are hands willing to undertake every wearisome task; yea, and women's lives ready for any sacrifice. It is because they know the unanswerable logic behind our demands and the irresistible force of our growing army that Suffragists throughout the world repeat in unison those thrilling words of the American leader, Susan B. Anthony, "Failure is impossible." . . .

As all the world knows, an obstinate and recalcitrant Government alone stands between the women of Great Britain and their enfranchisement. A campaign which will always be conspicuous among the world's movements for human rights for its surpassing fervour, sacrifice, and originality has been maintained without a pause. . . . The Government evidently nurses a forlorn hope that by delay it may tire out the workers and destroy the force of the campaign. It little comprehends the virility of the movement. When a just cause reaches its flood-tide, as ours has done in that country, whatever stands in the way must fall before its overwhelming power. Political parties, governments, constitutions must yield to the inevitable or take the consequences of ruin. Which horn of the dilemma the English Government will choose is the only question remaining. Woman Suffrage in Great Britain is inevitable. . . .

Some may ask why we are not now content to wait for the processes of reason and evolution to bring the result we want. Why do we disturb ourselves to hasten progress? I answer, because we refuse to sit idly by while other women endure hideous wrongs. Women have suffered enough of martyrdom through the false position they have been forced to occupy for centuries past. We make our protest now hotly and impatiently, perhaps, for we would bequeath to those who come after us a fair chance in life. Modern economic conditions are pushing hundreds of thousands of women out of their homes into the labour market. Crowded into unskilled employments for want of proper training, they are buffeted about like a cork upon a sea. Everywhere paid less than men for equal work, everywhere discriminated against, they are utterly at the mercy of forces over which they have no control. Law-making bodies, understanding neither women nor the meaning of this woman's invasion of modern industry, are attempting to regulate the wages, the hours, the conditions under which they shall work. Already serious wrong has been done many women because of this ill-advised legislation. Overwhelmed by the odds against them in this struggle for existence, thousands are driven to the streets. There they swell that horrid, unspeakably unclean peril of civilisation, prostitution—augmented by the White Slave Traffic and by the machinations of the male parasites who live upon the earnings of women of vice. . . . We must be merciful, for they are the natural and inevitable consequence of centuries of false reasoning concerning women's place in the world. . . . Upon these women we have no right to turn our backs. Their wrongs are our wrongs. Their existence is part of our problem. They have been created by the very injustices against which we protest.

It is the helpless cry of these lost women who are the victims of centuries of wrong; it is the unspoken plea of thousands of women now standing on the brink of similar ruin; it is the silent appeal of the army of women in all lands who in shops and factories are demanding fair living and working conditions; it is the need to turn the energies of more favoured women to public service; it is the demand for a complete revision of women's legal, social, educational, and industrial status all along the line, which permits us no delay, no hesitation. The belief that we are defending the highest good of the mothers of our race and the ultimate welfare of society makes every sacrifice seem trivial, every duty a pleasure. The pressing need spurs us on, the certainty of victory gives us daily inspiration.

We have come upon a new time, which has brought new and strange problems. Old problems have assumed new significance. In the adjustment of the new order of things we women demand an equal voice; we shall accept nothing less.

Emmeline Pankhurst

I Incite This Meeting to Rebellion

❦

Emmeline Goulden Pankhurst (1858–1928) led the militant English suffragists from 1903 until the outbreak of World War I. She had first become interested in feminist causes at the age of fourteen, when she attended a lecture in her native city of Manchester given by Lydia Becker, the pioneer organizer of the British woman's movement. Pankhurst participated in the final phases of the struggle to secure passage of a Married Women's Property Act in Great Britain (achieved in 1882). She also worked with early suffrage groups.

Finally, discouraged by the inactivity and timidity of established suffrage organizations, Emmeline Pankhurst and some co-workers who were recruiting Manchester factory operatives for the suffrage campaign founded the Women's Social and Political Union in 1903. At first they were relatively few in number and had little money or political influence. How could they bring their fervent desire for political representation before the public? Not until 1905 was a workable strategy devised.

In that year Pankhurst's daughter, Christabel, and an associate, Annie Kenney, attended a Manchester political rally, and from the floor, repeatedly questioned the speaker about his party's policy on the suffrage issue. The two young women were forcibly ejected from the building. In the ensuing uproar, they were arrested and charged with obstruction. Both refused to pay the fines imposed and served prison terms instead.

The incident caused a great sensation in the nation's press and gave the suffrage cause its first big publicity boost in years. Continued disruption of political meetings for the next several years focused increasing attention on the women's demands and brought new vigor to the feminist cause—militant and conservative alike.

When the government evinced no readiness to back female suffrage, the militants gradually heightened their tactics. The government responded with increased violence. Suffragists who were arrested refused to eat; they were force-fed, a process which was both painful and dangerous. In March, 1912, the bitterness and disillusionment of the activist women exploded in a wave of window-smashing. Windows of shops on London's most elegant streets—Bond Street and Regent Street, for example—as well as the windows at 10 Downing Street were assaulted by women wielding hammers. Emmeline Pankhurst and some 150 others were arrested and imprisoned. Within a few months, however, all had to be released because of their precarious states of health due to hunger strikes and forced feeding.

The following speech was delivered at Royal Albert Hall in London on October 17, 1912. It was Emmeline Pankhurst's first public address after getting out of prison and signaled still another intensification in the actions of her followers.

It always seems to me when the anti-suffrage members of the Government criticize militancy in women that it is very like beasts of prey reproaching the gentler animals who turn in desperate resistance when at the point of death. . . . Ladies and gentlemen, the only recklessness the militant suffragists have shown about human life has been about their own lives and not about the lives of others, and I say here and now that it never has been and never will be the policy of the Women's Social and Political Union recklessly to endanger human life. We leave that to the enemy. We leave that to the men in their warfare. It is not the method of women. . . . There is something that governments care far more for than human life, and that is the security of property, and so it is through property that we shall strike the enemy. From henceforward the women who agree with me will say, "We disregard your laws, gentlemen, we set the liberty and the dignity and the welfare of women above all such considerations, and we shall continue this war as we have done in the past; and what sacrifice of property, or what injury to property accrues will not be our fault. It will be the fault of that Government who admits the justice of our demands, but refuses to concede them. . . ."

Be militant each in your own way. Those of you who can express your militancy by going to the House of Commons and refusing to leave without satisfaction, as we did in the early days—do so. . . . Those of you who can express your militancy by joining us in our anti-Government by-election policy—do so. Those of you who can break windows— break them. Those of you who can still further attack the secret idol of property, so as to make the Government realize that property is as greatly endangered by women's suffrage as it was by the Chartists of old—do so.

And my last word is to the Government: I incite this meeting to rebellion! . . . Take me, if you dare, but if you dare I tell you this, . . . you will not keep me in prison.

When Civil War Is Waged
by Women

In April, 1913, Emmeline Pankhurst was convicted of "coun-selling" unknown persons in the setting of a suspicious fire and sentenced to three years of penal servitude. A recently adopted law—known as the "Cat and Mouse Act"—enabled prison of-ficials to temporarily release imprisoned suffragists who were ill from hunger-striking and forced feeding, and then, when they had recovered sufficiently, to rearrest them. Pankhurst herself endured a dozen hunger strikes in 1913; 182 other British women similarly risked their health and lives that year. Finally, Pankhurst was allowed to leave Great Britain. She arrived in the United States in the fall of 1913 on a speaking tour.

At the time her techniques already were being experimented with to a very modest extent in the United States by Lucy Burns and Alice Paul in Washington (both formerly had been activists with the Pankhurst group in England) and by the daughter of Elizabeth Cady Stanton, Harriot Stanton Blatch, in New York. (One of the paths Harriot Blatch had been pursuing was an effort to involve more workingwomen in the suffrage movement.) The suffrage movement as a whole was enjoying the rejuvenating effects of publicity.

By 1917 Pankhurst's tactics were being used more boldly—causing great animosity between militant and moderate Amer-ican suffragists—and there were ninety-seven American women in prison on charges later to be thrown out of court. They re-fused food and were forcibly fed by prison officials.

The following speech was delivered by Emmeline Pankhurst in Hartford, Connecticut, on November 13, 1913.

I am here as a soldier who has temporarily left the field of battle in order to explain—it seems strange it should have to be explained—what civil war is like when civil war is waged by women. I am not only here as a soldier temporarily absent from the field of battle; I am here—and that, I think, is the strangest part of my coming—I am here as a person . . . under sentence of penal servitude in a convict prison. . . .

Now, first of all I want to make you understand the inevitableness of revolution and civil war, even on the part of women, when you reach a certain stage in the development of a community's life. . . .

If an Irish revolutionary had addressed this meeting, and many have addressed meetings all over the United States during the last twenty or thirty years, it would not be necessary for that revolutionary to explain the need of revolution beyond saying that the people of his country were denied—and by people, meaning men—were denied the right of self-government. That would explain the whole situation. If I were a man and I said to you: "I come from a country which professes to have representative institutions and yet denies me, a taxpayer, an inhabitant of the country, representative rights," you would at once understand that that human being, being a man, was justified in the adoption of revolutionary methods to get representative institutions. But since I am a woman it is necessary in the twentieth century to explain why women have adopted revolutionary methods in order to win the rights of citizenship.

You see, in spite of a good deal that we hear about revolutionary methods not being necessary for American women, because American women are so well off, most of the men of the United States quite calmly acquiesce in the fact that half of the community are deprived absolutely of citizen rights, and we women, in trying to make our case clear, always have to make a part of our argument, and urge upon men in our audience the fact—a very simple fact—that women are human beings. It is quite evident you do not all realize we are human beings or it would not be necessary to argue with you that women may, suffering from intolerable injustice, be driven to adopt revolutionary methods. We have, first of all, to convince you we are human beings, and I hope to be able to do that in the course of the evening before I sit down, but before doing that, I want to put a few political arguments before you . . . arguments for the adoption of militant methods in order to win political rights.

A great many of you have been led to believe, from the somewhat meagre accounts you get in the newspapers, that in England there is a strange manifestation taking place, a new form of hysteria being swept across part of the feminist population of those Isles, and this manifestation takes the shape of irresponsible breaking of windows, burning of letters, general inconvenience to respectable, honest business people who want to attend to their business. It is very irrational you say; even if these women had sufficient intelligence to understand what they were doing, and really did want the vote, they have adopted very irrational means for getting the vote. "How are they going to persuade people that they ought to have the vote by breaking their windows?" you say. Now, if you say that, it shows you do not understand the meaning of our revolution at all, and I want to show you that when damage is done to property it is not done in order to convert people to woman suffrage at all. It is a practical political means, the only means we consider open to voteless persons to bring about a political situation, which can only be solved by giving women the vote. . . .

We know what happened when your forefathers decided that they must have representation for taxation, many, many years ago. When they felt they couldn't wait any longer, when they laid all the arguments before an obstinate British government that they could think of, and when their arguments were absolutely disregarded, when every other means had failed, they began by the Tea Party at Boston, and they went on until they had won the independence of the United States of America. . . .

Now, it would take too long to trace the course of militant methods as adopted by women because it is about eight years since the word *militant* was first used to describe what we were doing; it is about eight years since the first militant action was taken by women. It was not militant at all, except that it provoked militancy on the part of those who were opposed to it. . . . in Great Britain it is a custom, a time-honored one, to ask questions of candidates for parliament and ask questions of members of the government. No man was ever put out of a public meeting for asking a question until Votes for Women came onto the political horizon. The first people who were put out of a political meeting for asking questions, were women; they were brutally ill-used; they found themselves in jail before twenty-four hours had expired. But instead of the newspapers . . . putting militancy and the reproach of militancy, if reproach there is, on the people who had assaulted the women, they actually said it was the women who were militant and very much to blame. How different the reasoning is that men adopt when they are discussing the cases of men and those of women. Had they been men who asked the questions, and had those men been brutally ill-used, you would have heard a chorus of reprobation. . . . However, we were called militant for doing that, and we were quite willing to accept the name. . . . We were determined to press this question of the enfranchisement of women to the point where we were no longer to be ignored by the politicians as had been the case for about fifty years, during which time women had patiently used every means open to them to win their political enfranchisement. We found that all the fine phrases about freedom and liberty were entirely for male consumption, and that they did not in any way apply to women. . . .

Now, I am going to pass rapidly over all the incidents that happened after the two first women went to prison for asking questions of Cabinet Ministers, and come right up to the time when our militancy became *real* militancy, when we organized ourselves on an army basis, when we determined, if necessary, to fight for our rights just as our forefathers had fought for their rights. Then people began to say that while they believed they had no criticism of militancy, as militancy, while they thought it was quite justifiable for people to revolt against intolerable injustice, it was absurd and ridiculous for women to attempt it because women could not succeed. After all the most practical criticism of our militancy coming from men has been the argument that it could not succeed. They would say, "We would be with you if you could succeed but it is absurd for women who are the weaker sex, for women who have not got the control of any large interests, for women, who have got very little money, who have peculiar duties as women, which handicaps them extremely—for example, the duty of caring for children—it is absurd for women to think they can ever win their rights by fighting; you had far better give it up and submit because there it is, you have always been subject and you always will be." Well now, that really became the testing time. Then we women determined to show the world, that women, handicapped as women are, can still fight and can still win. . . .

We felt we had to rouse the public to such a point that they would say to the government, you must give women the vote. . . .

You have to make more noise than anybody else, you have to make yourself more obtrusive than anybody else, you have to fill all the papers more than anybody else, in fact you have to be there all the time and see that they do not snow you under, if you are really going to get your reform realized. That is what we women have been doing, and in the course of our desperate struggle we have had to make a great many people very uncomfortable. Now, one woman was arrested on an occasion when a great many windows were broken in London, as a protest against a piece of trickery on the part of the government, which will be incredible in fifty years, when the history of the movement is read. Women broke some windows as a protest; they broke a good many shop-keepers' windows; they broke the windows of shop-keepers where they spent most of their money when they bought their hats and their clothing; they also broke the windows of many of the Clubs, the smart Clubs in Piccadilly. . . . One woman broke the windows of the Guard Club, and when she broke those windows she stood there quietly until the Guard hall porter came out and seized her and held her until the policemen came to take her to prison. A number of the guards came out to see the kind of woman it was who had broken their windows, and they saw there a quiet little woman. She happened to be an actress, a woman who had come into our militant movement because she knew of the difficulties and dangers and temptations of the actress's life, of how badly paid she is, what her private sorrows are and her difficulties, and so she had come into the militant movement to get votes for actresses as quickly as possible, so that through the vote they could secure better conditions. Some of the guards— I think men who had never known what it was to earn a living, who knew nothing of the difficulties of a man's life, let alone the difficulties of a woman's life—came out, and they said: "Why did you break our windows? We have done nothing." She said: "It is because you have done nothing I have broken your windows." . . .

Well then, there were the men of pleasure, or the businessmen who were so busy earning money during the week that all they could think of when the week came to an end was recreation, and the great recreation in England today is playing golf. Everywhere on Saturday you see men streaming away into the country for the weekend to play golf. They so monopolize the golf links that they have made a rule that although the ladies may play golf all the week, the golf links

are entirely reserved for men on Saturday and Sunday. . . .
Well, we attacked the golf links . . . all the beautiful greens
that had taken years to make, had been cut up or destroyed
with an acid or made almost impossible to play upon. . . .

Now then, let me come to the more serious matters and
to some of the more recent happenings. You know when
you have war, many things happen that all of us deplore.
We fought a great war not very long ago, in South Africa.
Women were expected to face with equanimity the loss of
those dearest to them in warfare; . . . they were expected to
pay the war tax exactly like the men for a war about which
the women were never consulted at all. . . .

Within the last few days you have read . . . that some
more empty houses have been burned, that a cactus has
been destroyed and some valuable plants have suffered in
that house, that some pavilion at a pleasure ground has also
been burned. Well, it is quite possible that it has happened.
I knew before I came here that for one whole day tele-
graphic and telephonic communication between Glasgow
and London was entirely suspended. . . . I am not going to
tell you how it was done. I am not going to tell you how the
women got to the mains and cut the wires; but it was done.
It was done, and it was proved to the authorities that weak
women, suffrage women, as we are supposed to be, had
enough ingenuity to create a situation of that kind. . . .

"Put them in prison" they said; "that will stop it." But it
didn't stop it. They put women in prison for long terms of
imprisonment, for making a nuisance of themselves—that
was the expression when they took petitions in their hands
to the door of the House of Commons; and they thought
that by sending them to prison, giving them a day's imprisonment, would cause them to all settle down again and there
would be no further trouble. But it didn't happen so at all:
instead of the women giving it up, more women did it, and
more and more and more women did it until there were three
hundred women at a time, who had not broken a single law,

only "made a nuisance of themselves" as the politicians say. Well then they thought they must go a little farther, and so then they began imposing punishments of a very serious kind. The Judge who sentenced me last May to three years penal servitude for certain speeches in which I had accepted responsibility for acts of violence done by other women, said that if I would say I was sorry, if I would promise not to do it again, that he would revise the sentence. . . . he said he was giving a determinate sentence, a sentence that would convince me that I would have to give up my "evil ways" and would also deter other women from imitating me. But it hadn't that effect at all. So far from it having that effect more and more women have been doing these things that I had incited them to do, and were more determined in doing them; so that the long determinate sentence had no effect in crushing the agitation.

Well then they felt they must do something else, and they began to legislate. . . .* They had to dip back into the middle ages to find a means of repressing women in revolt, and the whole history shows how futile it is. . . .

When they put us in prison at first, simply for taking petitions, we submitted. . . . I am always glad to remind American audiences that two of the first women that came to the conclusion that they would not submit to unjust imprisonment any longer, were two American girls, who are doing some of the most splendid suffrage work in America today. . . . I am always proud to think that Miss Lucy Burns and Miss Alice Paul served their suffrage apprenticeship in the militant ranks in England. . . .

At the present time there are women lying at death's door, recovering enough strength to undergo operations, who have had both systems [repeated "cat and mouse" hunger strikes and forcible feeding] applied to them and have not given in and won't give in, and who will be prepared, as soon as they get up from their sick-beds, to go on as before. There

* She is referring to the "Cat and Mouse Act."—Ed.

are women who are being carried from their sick-beds on stretchers into meetings. . . .

Now, I want to say to you who think women cannot succeed, we have brought the government of England to this position, that it has to face this alternative: either women are to be killed or women are to have the vote. . . . Now that is the outcome of our civil war. . . .

Now whether you approve of us or whether you do not, you must see that we have brought the question of women's suffrage into a position where it is of first rate importance, where it can be ignored no longer. Even the most hardened politician will hesitate to take upon himself directly the responsibility of sacrificing the lives of women of undoubted honor, or undoubted earnestness of purpose. That is the political situation as I lay it before you today.

Bread and Roses

Of the five million women in the United States who were gainfully employed at the turn of the century, very few belonged to labor unions. In general, unions were reluctant to recruit female workers and many barred them from membership. But between 1909 and 1912 tens of thousands of previously unorganized women working in the garment and textile industry sweatshops got together and went on strike. Furthermore, the women stayed out tenaciously for months, despite severe deprivations caused by their loss of wages.

The first of the series of major strikes involving large numbers of women occurred in 1909 among shirtwaist makers in New York, about 20,000 of whom walked out to protest their working conditions. (Some of those participating in the strike were employed by the Triangle Waist Company, in whose crowded unsafe quarters 146 women lost their lives by fire just two years later.) In Chicago, a similar walkout of about 40,000 employees of clothing manufacturing firms took place in 1910. Both the New York and Chicago actions were terminated after about three months without clear-cut union victories. But the organizing of the mass of women workers had begun.

The famous Lawrence, Massachusetts, strike of woolen mill employees erupted in January, 1912. Male and female strikers in Lawrence were militant: machines were smashed and windows in the mills were broken. Before long, the city resembled an armed camp and there were almost daily clashes between the strikers and police, state troopers and armed militiamen. On January 30 a woman striker was killed in street fighting with police.

The principal union on the scene in Lawrence was the socialist Industrial Workers of the World—the Wobblies. Elizabeth Gurley Flynn, then a twenty-one-year-old Wobbly organizer, set up special meetings for female strikers. The women workers had particular grievances. Not only did they work the same hours in the mills as their husbands for less pay, they had to do cooking and cleaning at home, in addition. They wanted to join actively in the strike, although their husbands frequently tried to discourage their participation. Wrote Flynn: "The women wanted to picket. They were strikers as well as wives and were valiant fighters."

With the workers suffering from shortages of food and fuel, living conditions that winter were harsh. A decision was made to send some of the children of Lawrence out of the city. A first group of about 150 was escorted to New York by Margaret Sanger, then chairman of the Women's Committee of the Socialist Party and a nurse. The departure of a subsequent group of children was violently interrupted by police. The ensuing nationwide publicity and outcry put intense pressure on the mill owners and the strike was settled with most of the workers' demands met.

The following poem was written by James Oppenheim. It was inspired by a slogan carried by some women strikers of Lawrence: "We want bread and roses too."

As we come marching, marching, in the beauty of the day,
A million darkened kitchens, a thousand mill lofts gray,
Are touched with all the radiance that a sudden sun
    discloses,
For the people hear us singing, "Bread and Roses,
    Bread and Roses."

As we come marching, marching, we battle too for men,
For they are women's children, and we mother them
    again,
Our lives shall not be sweated from birth until life closes,
Hearts can starve as well as bodies: "Give us Bread and
    give us Roses."

As we come marching, marching, un-numbered women
    dead
Go crying through our singing their ancient song of bread;

Small art and love and beauty their drudging spirits
     knew—
Yes, it is Bread we fight for, but we fight
     For Roses, too.
As we come marching, marching, we bring the greater
     days;
The rising of the women means the rising of the race.
No more the drudge and idler, ten that toil where one
     reposes,
But a sharing of life's glories, Bread and Roses,
     Bread and Roses.

Emma Goldman

The Traffic in Women

Emma Goldman (1869–1940), the rebellious daughter of a
Russian Jewish family, emigrated to the United States while
still in her teens. The Haymarket conspiracy trial and the death
by hanging of four of the defendants were crucial radicalizing
experiences for her. Shortly afterward she divorced the man to
whom she had been briefly and unhappily married and came to
New York a dedicated anarchist revolutionary.

Goldman's anarchism was founded on a passionate belief in
individual freedom. Similarly, as a feminist she was not interested in legal or political "rights" but in the right of women to
live as free and equal human beings. In particular, Goldman
recognized the exploitation of women as sexual objects. She
believed that everyone should be able to choose sexual partners
without sanction of church or state.

Emma Goldman's political and sexual heresies aroused both
fervent admiration and animosity; she was one of the most talked
about women in the United States. She engaged in an active
career as a public speaker, covering such a broad spectrum of
topics as anarchism, the theater, penology, feminism and birth
control. In 1916 she served a fifteen-day prison term for giving
out information on contraceptives. Said a contemporary magazine: "Emma Goldman was sent to prison for advocating that
women need not always keep their mouths shut and their wombs
open."

The two essays that follow were both published by Goldman's
own press, Mother Earth Publishing Association, in 1910. In
The Traffic in Women she connects the exploitation of prostitutes with the exploitation of all women. Everywhere, she says,
the woman must "pay for her right to exist . . . with sex favors."

(Goldman herself once tried to earn money for a revolutionary venture by working as a prostitute—but was unsuccessful.)

Marriage and Love, the second selection below, details Goldman's view that marriage is primarily "an economic arrangement"—and a poor one at that.

Our reformers have suddenly made a great discovery—the white slave traffic. The papers are full of these "unheard-of conditions," and lawmakers are already planning a new set of laws to check the horror.

It is significant that whenever the public mind is to be diverted from a great social wrong, a crusade is inaugurated against indecency, gambling, saloons, etc. And what is the result of such crusades? Gambling is increasing, saloons are doing a lively business through back entrances, prostitution is at its height, and the system of pimps and cadets is but aggravated.

How is it that an institution, known almost to every child, should have been discovered so suddenly? How is it that this evil, known to all sociologists, should now be made such an important issue?

To assume that the recent investigation of the white slave traffic (and, by the way, a very superficial investigation) has discovered anything new, is, to say the least, very foolish. Prostitution has been, and is, a widespread evil, yet mankind goes on its business, perfectly indifferent to the sufferings and distress of the victims of prostitution. As indifferent, indeed, as mankind has remained to our industrial system, or to economic prostitution.

Only when human sorrows are turned into a toy with glaring colors will baby people become interested—for a while at least. The people are a very fickle baby that must have new toys every day. The "righteous" cry against the white slave traffic is such a toy. It serves to amuse the people

for a little while, and it will help to create a few more fat
political jobs—parasites who stalk about the world as in-
spectors, investigators, detectives, and so forth.

What is really the cause of the trade in women? Not
merely white women, but yellow and black women as well.
Exploitation, of course; the merciless Moloch of capitalism
that fattens on underpaid labor, thus driving thousands of
women and girls into prostitution. With Mrs. Warren these
girls feel, "Why waste your life working for a few shillings
a week in a scullery, eighteen hours a day?"

Naturally our reformers say nothing about this cause.
They know it well enough, but it doesn't pay to say anything about it. It is much more profitable to play the Pharisee,
to pretend an outraged morality, than to go to the bottom
of things. . . .

Nowhere is woman treated according to the merit of her
work, but rather as a sex. It is therefore almost inevitable
that she should pay for her right to exist, to keep a position
in whatever line, with sex favors. Thus it is merely a question of degree whether she sells herself to one man, in or
out of marriage, or to many men. Whether our reformers
admit it or not, the economic and social inferiority of
woman is responsible for prostitution.

Just at present our good people are shocked by the dis-
closures that in New York City alone, one out of every ten
women works in a factory, that the average wage received
by women is six dollars per week for forty-eight to sixty
hours of work, and that the majority of female wage workers face many months of idleness which leaves the average
wage about $280 a year. In view of these economic horrors,
is it to be wondered at that prostitution and the white slave
trade have become such dominant factors? . . .

Dr. Alfred Blaschko, in *Prostitution in the Nineteenth
Century,* is even more emphatic in characterising economic
conditions as one of the most vital factors of prostitution.

"Although prostitution has existed in all ages, it was left

to the nineteenth century to develop it into a gigantic social institution. The development of industry with vast masses of people in the competitive market, the growth and congestion of large cities, the insecurity and uncertainty of employment, has given prostitution an impetus never dreamed of at any period in human history."

And again Havelock Ellis, while not so absolute in dealing with the economic cause, is nevertheless compelled to admit that it is indirectly and directly the main cause. Thus he finds that a large percentage of prostitutes is recruited from the servant class, although the latter have less care and greater security. On the other hand, Mr. Ellis does not deny that the daily routine, the drudgery, the monotony of the servant girl's lot, and especially the fact that she may never partake of the companionship and joy of a home, is no mean factor in forcing her to seek recreation and forgetfulness in the gaiety and glimmer of prostitution. In other words, the servant girl, being treated as a drudge, never having the right to herself, and worn out by the caprices of her mistress, can find an outlet, like the factory or shopgirl, only in prostitution.

The most amusing side of the question now before the public is the indignation of our "good, respectable people," especially the various Christian gentlemen, who are always to be found in the front ranks of every crusade. Is it that they are absolutely ignorant of the history of religion, and especially of the Christian religion? Or is it that they hope to blind the present generation to the part played in the past by the Church in relation to prostitution? Whatever their reason, they should be the last to cry out against the unfortunate victims of today, since it is known to every intelligent student that prostitution is of religious origin, maintained and fostered for many centuries, not as a shame but as a virtue, hailed as such by the Gods themselves. . . .

In modern times the Church is a little more careful in that direction. At least she does not openly demand tribute from prostitutes. She finds it much more profitable to go in for real estate, like Trinity Church, for instance, to rent out death traps at an exorbitant price to those who live off and by prostitution.

Much as I should like to, my space will not admit speaking of prostitution in Egypt, Greece, Rome, and during the Middle Ages. The conditions in the latter period are particularly interesting, inasmuch as prostitution was organized into guilds, presided over by a brothel Queen. These guilds employed strikes as a medium of improving their condition and keeping a standard price. Certainly that is more practical a method than the one used by the modern wage slave in society.

It would be one-sided and extremely superficial to maintain that the economic factor is the only cause of prostitution. There are others no less important and vital. That, too, our reformers know, but dare discuss even less than the institution that saps the very life out of both men and women. I refer to the sex question, the very mention of which causes most people moral spasms.

It is a conceded fact that woman is being reared as a sex commodity, and yet she is kept in absolute ignorance of the meaning and importance of sex. Everything dealing with that subject is suppressed, and persons who attempt to bring light into this terrible darkness are persecuted and thrown into prison. Yet it is nevertheless true that so long as a girl is not to know how to take care of herself, not to know the function of the most important part of her life, we need not be surprised if she becomes an easy prey to prostitution, or to any other form of a relationship which degrades her to the position of an object for mere sex gratification.

It is due to this ignorance that the entire life and nature of the girl is thwarted and crippled. We have long ago taken it as a self-evident fact that the boy may follow the call of the wild; that is to say, that the boy may, as soon as his sex nature asserts itself, satisfy that nature; but our moralists are scandalized at the very thought that the nature of a girl should assert itself. To the moralist prostitution does not consist so much in the fact that the woman sells her body, but rather that she sells it out of wedlock. That this is no mere statement is proved by the fact that marriage for monetary considerations is perfectly legitimate, sanctified by law and public opinion, while any other union is condemned and repudiated. Yet a prostitute, if properly defined, means nothing else than "any person for whom sexual relationships are subordinated to gain."

"Those women are prostitutes who sell their bodies for the exercise of the sexual act and make of this a profession." *

In fact, Banger goes further; he maintains that the act of prostitution is "intrinsically equal to that of a man or woman who contracts a marriage for economic reasons."

Of course, marriage is the goal of every girl, but as thousands of girls cannot marry, our stupid social customs condemn them either to a life of celibacy or prostitution. Human nature asserts itself regardless of all laws, nor is there any plausible reason why nature should adapt itself to a perverted conception of morality.

Society considers the sex experiences of a man as attributes of his general development, while similar experiences in the life of a woman are looked upon as a terrible calamity, a loss of honor and of all that is good and noble in a human being. This double standard of morality has played no little part in the creation and perpetuation of prostitution. It involves the keeping of the young in absolute ignorance on sex matters, which alleged "innocence," together with an overwrought and stifled sex nature, helps to bring about a state of affairs that our Puritans are so anxious to avoid or prevent.

Not that the gratification of sex must needs lead to prostitution; it is the cruel, heartless, criminal persecution of

* Banger, *Criminalité et Condition Economique*—E.G.

those who dare divert from the beaten track, which is responsible for it.

Girls, mere children, work in crowded, over-heated rooms ten to twelve hours daily at a machine, which tends to keep them in a constant over-excited sex state. Many of these girls have no home or comforts of any kind; therefore the street or some place of cheap amusement is the only means of forgetting their daily routine. This naturally brings them into close proximity with the other sex. It is hard to say which of the two factors brings the girl's over-sexed condition to a climax, but it is certainly the most natural thing that a climax should result. That is the first step toward prostitution. Nor is the girl to be held responsible for it. On the contrary, it is altogether the fault of society, the fault of our lack of understanding, of our lack of appreciation of life in the making; especially is it the criminal fault of our moralists, who condemn a girl for all eternity, because she has gone from the "path of virtue"; that is, because her first sex experience has taken place without the sanction of the Church.

The girl feels herself a complete outcast, with the doors of home and society closed in her face. Her entire training and tradition is such that the girl herself feels depraved and fallen, and therefore has no ground to stand upon, or any hold that will lift her up, instead of dragging her down. Thus society creates the victims that it afterwards vainly attempts to get rid of. The meanest, most depraved and decrepit man still considers himself too good to take as his wife the woman whose grace he was quite willing to buy, even though he might thereby save her from a life of horror. Nor can she turn to her own sister for help. In her stupidity the latter deems herself too pure and chaste, not realizing that her own position is in many respects even more deplorable than her sister's of the street.

"The wife who married for money, compared with the prostitute," says Havelock Ellis, "is the true scab. She is paid less, gives much more in return in labor and care, and is absolutely bound to her master. The prostitute never signs away the right over her own person, she retains her freedom and personal rights, nor is she always compelled to submit to man's embrace."

Nor does the better-than-thou woman realize the apologist claim of Lecky that "though she may be the supreme type of vice, she is also the most efficient guardian of virtue. But for her, happy homes would be polluted, unnatural and harmful practice would abound."

Moralists are ever ready to sacrifice one-half of the human race for the sake of some miserable institution which they can not outgrow. As a matter of fact, prostitution is no more a safeguard for the purity of the home than rigid laws are a safeguard against prostitution. Fully fifty per cent of married men are patrons of brothels. It is through this virtuous element that the married women—nay, even the children—are infected with venereal diseases. Yet society has not a word of condemnation for the man, while no law is too monstrous to be set in motion against the helpless victim. She is not only preyed upon by those who use her, but she is also absolutely at the mercy of every policeman and miserable detective on the beat, the officials at the station house, the authorities in every prison.

In a recent book by a woman who was for twelve years the mistress of a "house," are to be found the following figures: "The authorities compelled me to pay every month fines between $14.70 to $29.70, the girls would pay from $5.70 to $9.70 to the police." Considering that the writer did her business in a small city, that the amounts she gives do not include extra bribes and fines, one can readily see the tremendous revenue the police department derives from the blood money of its victims, whom it will not even protect. Woe to those who refuse to pay their toll; they would be rounded up like cattle, "if only to make a favorable impression upon the good citizens of the city, or if the powers needed extra money on the side. For the warped mind who believes that a fallen woman is incapable of human emotion it would be impossible to realize the grief, the disgrace, the tears, the wounded pride that was ours every time we were pulled in."

Strange, isn't it, that a woman who has kept a "house" should be able to feel that way? But stranger still that a good Christian world should bleed and fleece such women, and give them nothing in return except obloquy and persecution. Oh, for the charity of a Christian world!

Much stress is laid on white slaves being imported into America. How would America ever retain her virtue if Europe did not help her out? I will not deny that this may be the case in some instances, any more than I will deny that there are emissaries of Germany and other countries luring economic slaves into America; but I absolutely deny that prostitution is recruited to any appreciable extent from Europe. It may be true that the majority of prostitutes of New York City are foreigners, but that is because the majority of the population is foreign. The moment we go to any other American city, to Chicago or the Middle West, we shall find that the number of foreign prostitutes is by far a minority.

Equally exaggerated is the belief that the majority of street girls in this city were engaged in this business before they came to America. Most of the girls speak excellent English, are Americanized in habits and appearance,—a thing absolutely impossible unless they had lived in this country many years. That is, they were driven into prostitution by American conditions, by the thoroughly American custom for excessive display of finery and clothes, which, of course, necessitates money,—money that cannot be earned in shops or factories.

In other words, there is no reason to believe that any set of men would go to the risk and expense of getting foreign products, when American conditions are overflooding the market with thousands of girls. On the other hand, there is sufficient evidence to prove that the export of American girls for the purpose of prostitution is by no means a small factor. . . .

Those who sit in a glass house do wrong to throw stones about them; besides, the American glass house is rather thin, it will break easily, and the interior is anything but a gainly sight. . . .

An educated public opinion, freed from the legal and moral hounding of the prostitute, can alone help to ameliorate present conditions. Wilful shutting of eyes and ignoring of the evil as a social factor of modern life, can but aggravate matters. We must rise above our foolish notions of "better than thou," and learn to recognize in the prostitute a product of social conditions. Such a realization will sweep away the attitude of hypocrisy, and insure a greater understanding and more humane treatment. As to a thorough eradication of prostitution, nothing can accomplish that save a complete transvaluation of all accepted values —especially the moral ones—coupled with the abolition of industrial slavery.

Marriage and Love

Marriage is primarily an economic arrangement, an insurance pact. It differs from the ordinary life insurance agreement only in that it is more binding, more exacting. Its returns are insignificantly small compared with the investments. In taking out an insurance policy one pays for it in dollars and cents, always at liberty to discontinue payments. If, however, woman's premium is a husband, she pays for it with her name, her privacy, her self-respect, her very life, "until death doth part." Moreover, the marriage insurance condemns her to life-long dependency, to parasitism, to complete uselessness, individual as well as social. Man, too, pays his toll, but as his sphere is wider, marriage does not limit him as much as woman. He feels his chains more in an economic sense. . . .

[B]ehind every marriage stands the life-long environment of the two sexes; an environment so different from each other that man and woman must remain strangers. Separated by an insurmountable wall of superstition, custom, and habit, marriage has not the potentiality of developing knowledge of, and respect for, each other, without which every union is doomed to failure.

Henrik Ibsen, the hater of all social shams, was probably the first to realize this great truth. Nora leaves her husband, not—as the stupid critic would have it—because she is tired of her responsibilities or feels the need of woman's rights, but because she has come to know that for eight years she had lived with a stranger and borne him children. Can there be anything more humiliating, more degrading than a lifelong proximity between two strangers? No need for the woman to know anything of the man, save his income. As to the knowledge of the woman—what is there to know except that she has a pleasing appearance? We have not yet outgrown the theologic myth that woman has no soul, that she is a mere appendix to man, made out of his rib just for the convenience of the gentleman who was so strong that he was afraid of his own shadow.

Perchance the poor quality of the material whence woman comes is responsible for her inferiority. At any rate, woman has no soul—what is there to know about her? Besides, the less soul a woman has the greater her asset as a wife, the more readily will she absorb herself in her husband. It is this slavish acquiescence to man's superiority that has kept the marriage institution seemingly intact for so long a period. Now that woman is coming into her own, now that she is actually growing aware of herself as a being outside of the master's grace, the sacred institution of marriage is gradually being undermined, and no amount of sentimental lamentation can stay it.

From infancy, almost, the average girl is told that marriage is her ultimate goal; therefore her training and education must be directed towards that end. Like the mute beast fattened for slaughter, she is prepared for that. Yet, strange to say, she is allowed to know much less about her function as wife and mother than the ordinary artisan of his trade. It is indecent and filthy for a respectable girl to know anything of the marital relation. Oh, for the inconsistency of respectability, that needs the marriage vow to turn something which is filthy into the purest and most sacred arrangement that none dare question or criticize. Yet that is exactly the attitude of the average upholder of marriage. The prospective wife and mother is kept in complete ignorance of her only asset in the competitive field—sex. Thus she enters into life-long relations with a man only to find herself shocked, repelled, outraged beyond measure by the most natural and healthy instinct, sex. It is safe to say that a large percentage of the unhappiness, misery, distress, and physical suffering of matrimony is due to the criminal ignorance in sex matters that is being extolled as a great virtue. Nor is it at all an exaggeration when I say that more than one home has been broken up because of this deplorable fact.

If, however, woman is free and big enough to learn the mystery of sex without the sanction of State or Church, she will stand condemned as utterly unfit to become the wife of a "good" man, his goodness consisting of an empty head and plenty of money. Can there be anything more outrageous than the idea that a healthy, grown woman, full of life and passion, must deny nature's demand, must subdue her most intense craving, undermine her health and break her spirit, must stunt her vision, abstain from the depth and glory of sex experience until a "good" man comes along to take her unto himself as a wife? That is precisely what marriage means. How can such an arrangement end except in failure? This is one, though not the least important, factor of marriage, which differentiates it from love.

Ours is a practical age. The time when Romeo and Juliet risked the wrath of their fathers for love, when Gretchen exposed herself to the gossip of her neighbors for love, is no more. If, on rare occasions, young people allow themselves the luxury of romance, they are taken in care by the elders, drilled and pounded until they become "sensible."

The moral lesson instilled in the girl is not whether the man has aroused her love, but rather is it, "How much?" The important and only God of practical American life: Can the man make a living? Can he support a wife? That is the only thing that justifies marriage. Gradually this saturates every thought of the girl; her dreams are not of moonlight and kisses, of laughter and tears; she dreams of shopping tours and bargain counters. This soul-poverty and sordidness are the elements inherent in the marriage institution. The State and the Church approve of no other ideal, simply because it is the one that necessitates the State and Church control of men and women.

Doubtless there are people who continue to consider love above dollars and cents. Particularly is this true of that class whom economic necessity has forced to become self-supporting. The tremendous change in woman's position, wrought by that mighty factor, is indeed phenomenal when we reflect that it is but a short time since she has entered the industrial arena. Six million women wage workers; six million women, who have the equal right with men to be exploited, to be robbed, to go on strike; aye, to starve even. Anything more, my lord? Yes, six million wage workers in every walk of life, from the highest brain work to the mines and the railroad tracks; yes, even detectives and policemen. Surely the emancipation is complete.

Yet with all that, but a very small number of the vast army of women wage workers look upon work as a permanent issue, in the same light as does man. No matter how decrepit the latter, he has been taught to be independent, self-supporting. Oh, I know that no one is really independent in our economic treadmill; still, the poorest specimen of a man hates to be a parasite; to be known as such, at any rate.

The woman considers her position as worker transitory, to be thrown aside for the first bidder. That is why it is infinitely harder to organize women than men. "Why should I join a union? I am going to get married, to have a home." Has she not been taught from infancy to look upon that as her ultimate calling? She learns soon enough that the home, though not so large a prison as the factory, has more solid doors and bars. It has a keeper so faithful that naught can escape him. The most tragic part, however, is that the home no longer frees her from wage slavery; it only increases her task.

According to the latest statistics submitted before a Committee "on labor and wages, and congestion of population," ten per cent of the wage workers in New York City alone are married, yet they must continue to work at the most poorly paid labor in the world. Add to this horrible aspect the drudgery of housework, and what remains of the protection and glory of the home? As a matter of fact, even the middle-class girl in marriage can not speak of her home, since it is the man who creates her sphere. It is not important whether the husband is a brute or a darling. What I wish to prove is that marriage guarantees woman a home only by the grace of her husband. There she moves about in *his* home, year after year, until her aspect of life and human affairs becomes as flat, narrow, and drab as her surroundings. Small wonder if she becomes a nag, petty, quarrelsome, gossipy, unbearable, thus driving the man from the house. She could not go, if she wanted to; there is no place to go. Besides, a short period of married life, of complete surrender of all faculties, absolutely incapacitates the average woman for the outside world. She becomes reckless in appearance, clumsy in her movements, dependent in her decisions, cowardly in her judgment, a weight and a bore, which most men grow to hate and despise. . . .

The institution of marriage makes a parasite of woman, an absolute dependent. It incapacitates her for life's struggle, annihilates her social consciousness, paralyzes her imagination, and then imposes its gracious protection, which is in reality a snare, a travesty on human character.

If motherhood is the highest fulfillment of woman's nature, what other protection does it need save love and freedom? Marriage but defiles, outrages, and corrupts her fulfillment. Does it not say to woman, Only when you follow me shall you bring forth life? Does it not condemn her to the block, does it not degrade and shame her if she refuses to buy her right to motherhood by selling herself? Does not marriage only sanction motherhood, even though conceived in hatred, in compulsion? Yet, if motherhood be of free choice, of love, of ecstasy, of defiant passion, does it not place a crown of thorns upon an innocent head and carve in letters of blood the hideous epithet, Bastard? Were marriage to contain all the virtues claimed for it, its crimes against motherhood would exclude it forever from the realm of love.

Love, the strongest and deepest element in all life, the harbinger of hope, of joy, of ecstasy; love, the defier of all laws, of all conventions; love, the freest, the most powerful moulder of human destiny; how can such an all-compelling force be synonymous with that poor little State and Church-begotten weed, marriage?

Free love? As if love is anything but free! Man has bought brains, but all the millions in the world have failed to buy love. Man has subdued bodies, but all the power on earth has been unable to subdue love. Man has conquered whole nations, but all his armies could not conquer love. Man has chained and fettered the spirit, but he has been utterly helpless before love. High on a throne, with all the splendor and pomp his gold can command, man is yet poor and desolate, if love passes him by. And if it stays, the poorest hovel is radiant with warmth, with life and color. Thus love has the magic power to make of a beggar a king. Yes, love is free; it can dwell in no other atmosphere. In freedom it gives itself unreservedly, abundantly, completely. All the laws on the statutes, all the courts in the universe, cannot tear it from the soil, once love has taken root. If, however, the soil is sterile, how can marriage make it bear fruit? It is like the last desperate struggle of fleeting life against death.

Love needs no protection; it is its own protection. So long as love begets life no child is deserted, or hungry, or famished for the want of affection. I know this to be true. I know women who became mothers in freedom by the men they loved. Few children in wedlock enjoy the care, the protection, the devotion free motherhood is capable of bestowing. . . .

Some day, some day men and women will rise, they will reach the mountain peak, they will meet big and strong and free, ready to receive, to partake, and to bask in the golden rays of love. What fancy, what imagination, what poetic genius can foresee even approximately the potentialities of such a force in the life of men and women. If the world is ever to give birth to true companionship and oneness, not marriage, but love will be the parent.

Margaret Sanger

Woman and the New Race

❧

Margaret Sanger (1883–1966) dedicated her book, *Woman and the New Race,* to the memory of her mother "who gave birth to eleven living children" and who died at the age of forty-eight. In her work as a public-health nurse, Margaret Sanger witnessed first-hand the disastrous economic and physical effects on poor women and their families of uncontrolled fertility. It became her life's mission to give to every woman the right "to control her own body."

In Europe, Sanger studied the history of birth control and visited clinics in Holland, where doctors and nurses had been dispensing contraceptives since 1881. On her return to the United States in 1915, she launched a massive campaign to break down legal barriers to dissemination of contraceptive information and devices by physicians.

Birth control, to Sanger, was a part—and the most important part—of the struggle to liberate women. As she expressed it, the right to voluntary motherhood was woman's "key to the temple of liberty."

The following selection is excerpted from *Woman and the New Race,* first published in 1920.

The most far-reaching social development of modern times is the revolt of woman against sex servitude. The most important force in the remaking of the world is a free motherhood. . . .

Only in recent years has woman's position as the gentler and weaker half of the human family been emphatically and generally questioned. Men assumed that this was woman's place; woman herself accepted it. It seldom occurred to anyone to ask whether she would go on occupying it forever.

Upon the mere surface of woman's organized protests there were no indications that she was desirous of achieving a fundamental change in her position. She claimed the right of suffrage and legislative regulation of her working hours, and asked that her property rights be equal to those of the man. None of these demands, however, affected directly the most vital factors of her existence. Whether she won her point or failed to win it, she remained a dominated weakling in a society controlled by men.

Woman's acceptance of her inferior status was the more real because it was unconscious. She had chained herself to her place in society and the family through the maternal functions of her nature, and only chains thus strong could have bound her to her lot as a brood animal for the masculine civilizations of the world. In accepting her role as the "weaker and gentler half," she accepted that function. In turn, the acceptance of that function fixed the more firmly her rank as an inferior.

Caught in this "vicious circle," woman has, through her reproductive ability, founded and perpetuated the tyrannies of the Earth. Whether it was the tyranny of a monarchy, an oligarchy or a republic, the one indispensable factor of its existence was, as it is now, hordes of human beings—human beings so plentiful as to be cheap, and so cheap that ignorance was their natural lot. Upon the rock of an unenlightened, submissive maternity have these been founded; upon the product of such a maternity have they flourished. . . .

To-day, however, woman is rising in fundamental revolt. . . . Millions of women are asserting their right to voluntary motherhood. They are determined to decide for themselves whether they shall become mothers, under what conditions and when. This is the fundamental revolt referred to. It is for woman the key to the temple of liberty.

Even as birth control is the means by which woman attains basic freedom, so it is the means by which she must and will uproot the evil she has wrought through her submission. As she has unconsciously and ignorantly brought about social disaster, so must and will she consciously and intelligently *undo* that disaster and create a new and better order. . . .

Two chief obstacles hinder the discharge of this tremendous obligation. The first and the lesser is the legal barrier. Dark-Age laws would still deny to her the knowledge of her reproductive nature. Such knowledge is indispensable to intelligent motherhood and she must achieve it, despite absurd statutes and equally absurd moral canons.

The second and more serious barrier is her own ignorance of the extent and effect of her submission. Until she knows the evil her subjection has wrought to herself, to her progeny and to the world at large, she cannot wipe out that evil. . . .

Most women who belong to the workers' families have no accurate or reliable knowledge of contraceptives, and are, therefore, bringing children into the world so rapidly that they, their families and their class are overwhelmed with numbers. Out of these numbers . . . have grown many of the burdens with which society in general is weighted; out of them have come, also, the want, disease, hard living conditions and general misery of the workers.

The women of this class are the greatest sufferers of all. Not only do they bear the material hardships and deprivations in common with the rest of the family, but in the case of the mother, these are intensified. It is the man and the child who have first call upon the insufficient amount of food. It is the man and the child who get the recreation, if there is any to be had, for the man's hours of labor are usually limited by law or by his labor union.

It is the woman who suffers first from hunger, the woman

whose clothing is least adequate, the woman who must work all hours, even though she is not compelled, as in the case of millions, to go into a factory to add to her husband's scanty income. It is she, too, whose health breaks first and most hopelessly, under the long hours of work, the drain of frequent childbearing, and often almost constant nursing of babies. There are no eight-hour laws to protect the mother against overwork and toil in the home; no laws to protect her against ill health and the diseases of pregnancy and reproduction. In fact there has been almost no thought or consideration given for the protection of the mother in the home of the workingman.

There are no general health statistics to tell the full story of the physical ills suffered by women as a result of too great reproductivity. But we get some light upon conditions through the statistics on maternal mortality, compiled by Dr. Grace L. Meigs, for the Children's Bureau of the United States Department of Labor. These figures do not include the deaths of women suffering from diseases complicated by pregnancy.

"In 1913, in this country at least 15,000 women, it is estimated, died from conditions caused by childbirth; about 7,000 of these died from childbed fever and the remaining 8,000 from diseases now known to be to a great extent preventable or curable," says Dr. Meigs in her summary. "Physicians and statisticians agree that these figures are a *great underestimate*."

Think of it—the needless deaths of 15,000 women a "great underestimate"! Yet even this number means that virtually every hour of the day and night two women die as the result of childbirth in the healthiest and supposedly the most progressive country in the world.

It is apparent that Dr. Meigs leaves out of consideration the many thousands of deaths each year of women who become pregnant while suffering from tuberculosis. . . . Nor were syphilis, various kidney and heart disorders and other diseases, often rendered fatal by pregnancy, taken into account by Dr. Meigs' survey. . . .

From what sort of homes come these deaths from childbirth? Most of them occur in overcrowded dwellings, where food, care, sanitation, nursing and medical attention are inadequate. Where do we find most of the tuberculosis and much of the other disease which is aggravated by pregnancy? In the same sort of home.

The deadly chain of misery is all too plain to anyone who takes the trouble to observe it. A woman of the working class marries and with her husband lives in a degree of comfort upon his earnings. Her household duties are not beyond her strength. Then the children begin to come—one, two, three, four, possibly five or more. The earnings of the husband do not increase as rapidly as the family does. Food, clothing and general comfort in the home grow less as the numbers of the family increase. The woman's work grows heavier, and her strength is less with each child. Possibly—probably—she has to go into a factory to add to her husband's earnings. There she toils, doing her housework at night. Her health goes, and the crowded conditions and lack of necessities in the home help to bring about disease—especially tuberculosis. Under the circumstances, the woman's chances of recovering from each succeeding childbirth grow less. Less too are the chances of the child's surviving. . . .

Women who have a knowledge of contraceptives are not compelled to make the choice between a maternal experience and a marred love life; they are not forced to balance motherhood against social and spiritual activities. Motherhood is for them to choose, as it should be for every woman to choose. Choosing to become mothers, they do not thereby shut themselves away from thorough companionship with their husbands, from friends, from culture, from all those manifold experiences which are necessary to the completeness and the joy of life.

Fit mothers of the race are these, the courted comrades of the men they choose, rather than the "slaves of slaves." For theirs is the magic power—the power of limiting their families to such numbers as will permit them to live full-rounded lives. Such lives are the expression of the feminine spirit which is woman *and all of her*—not merely art, nor professional skill, nor intellect—but all that woman is, or may achieve. . . .

Thousands of well-intentioned people who agree that there are times and conditions under which it is woman's highest duty to avoid having children advocate continence as the one permissible means of birth control. . . .

Loathing, disgust or indifference to the sex relationship nearly always lies behind the advocacy to continence. . . .

Much of the responsibility for this feeling upon the part of many thousands of women must be laid to two thousand years of Christian teaching that all sex expression is unclean. Part of it, too, must be laid to the dominant male's habit of violating the love rights of his mate.

The habit referred to grows out of the assumed and legalized right of the husband to have sexual satisfaction at any time he desires, regardless of the woman's repugnance for it. The law of the state upholds him in this regard. A husband need not support his wife if she refuses to comply with his sexual demands. . . .

When I have had the confidence of women indifferent to physical union, I have found the fault usually lay with the husband. His idea of marriage is too often that of providing a home for a female who would in turn provide for his physical needs, including sexual satisfaction. Such a husband usually excludes such satisfaction from the category of the wife's needs, physical or spiritual.

This man is not concerned with his wife's sex urge, save as it responds to his own at times of his choosing. Man's code has taught woman to be quite ashamed of such desires. Usually she speaks of indifference without regret; often proudly. She seems to regard herself as more chaste and highly endowed in purity than other women who confess to feeling physical attraction toward their husbands. She also secretly considers herself far superior to the husband who makes no concealment of his desire toward her. Nevertheless, because of this desire upon the husband's part, she goes on "pretending" to mutual interest in the relationship. . . .

As a means of birth control, continence is as impracticable for most people as it is undesirable. . . .

Despite the unreliability of some methods and the harmfulness of some others, there *are* methods which are both harmless and certain. This much the woman who is seeking means of limiting her family may be told here. . . .

More and more perfect means of preventing conception will be developed as women insist upon them. Every woman should make it plain to her physician that she expects him to be informed upon this subject. She should refuse to accept evasive answers. An increasing demand upon physicians will inevitably result in laboratory researches and experimentation. Such investigation is indeed already beginning and we may expect great progress in contraceptive methods in the near future. We may also expect more authoritative opinions upon preventive methods and devices. When women confidently and insistently demand them, they will have access to contraceptives which are both certain and harmless. . . .

Sneers and jests at birth control are giving way to a reverent understanding of the needs of woman. They who to-day deny the right of a woman to control her own body speak with the hardihood of invincible ignorance or with the folly of those blind ones who in all ages have opposed the light of progress. . . .

As far back as 1900, I began to inquire of my associates among the nurses what one could tell these worried women who asked constantly: "What can I do?" It is the voice of the elemental urge of woman—it has always been there; and whether we have heeded it or neglected it, we have always heard it. Out of this cry came the birth control movement.

Economic conditions have naturally made this elemental need more plain; sometimes they have lent a more desperate voice to woman's cry for freedom. . . . But the birth control movement as a movement for woman's *basic* freedom was born of that unceasing cry of the socially repressed, spiritually stifled woman who is constantly demanding: "What can I do to avoid more children?". . .

After a year's study in foreign countries for the purpose of supplementing the knowledge gained in my fourteen years as a nurse, I came back to the United States determined to open a clinic. I had decided that there could be no better way of demonstrating to the public the necessity of birth control and the welcome it would receive than by taking the knowledge of contraceptive methods directly to those who most needed it.

A clinic was opened in Brooklyn. There 480 women received information before the police closed the consulting rooms and arrested Ethel Byrne, a registered nurse, Fania Mindell, a translator, and myself.* The purpose of this clinic was to demonstrate to the public the practicability and the necessity of such institutions. All women who came seeking information were workingmen's wives. All had children. No unmarried girls came at all. Men came whose wives had nursing children and could not come. Women came from the farther parts of Long Island, from cities in Massachusetts and Connecticut and even more distant places. Mothers brought their married daughters. Some whose ages were from 25 to 35 looked fifty, but the clinic gave them new hope to face the years ahead. These women

* The first birth control clinic in the United States was opened in 1916 in the Brownsville section of Brooklyn. Ethel Byrne was Margaret Sanger's sister.—Ed.

invariably expressed their love for children, but voiced a common plea for means to avoid others, in order that they might give sufficient care to those already born. . . .

For ten days the two rooms of this clinic were crowded to their utmost. Then came the police. We were hauled off to jail and eventually convicted of a "crime."

Ethel Byrne instituted a hunger strike for eleven days, which attracted attention throughout the nation. It brought to public notice the fact that women were ready to die for the principle of voluntary motherhood. So strong was the sentiment evoked that Governor Whitman pardoned Mrs. Byrne.

No single act of self-sacrifice in the history of the birth-control movement has done more to awaken the conscience of the public or to arouse the courage of women, than did Ethel Byrne's deed of uncompromising resentment at the outrage of jailing women who were attempting to disseminate knowledge which would emancipate the motherhood of America.

Courage like hers and like that of others who have undergone arrest and imprisonment, or who night after night and day after day have faced street crowds to speak or to sell literature—the faith and the untiring labors of still others who have not come into public notice—have given the movement its dauntless character and assure the final victory.

One dismal fact had become clear long before the Brownsville clinic was opened. The medical profession as a whole had ignored the tragic cry of womanhood for relief from forced maternity. The private practitioners, one after another, shook their heads and replied: "It cannot be done. It is against the law," and the same answer came from clinics and public hospitals. . . . One of the chief results of the Brownsville clinic was that of establishing for physicians a [legal] right which they neglected to establish for themselves but which they are bound, in the very nature of things, to exercise to an increasing degree. Similar tests by women in other states would doubtless establish the right elsewhere in America.

We know of some thirty-five arrests of women and men who have dared entrenched prejudice and the law to further the cause of birth control. . . . Each of these arrests brought added publicity. Each became a center of local agitation. Each brought a part of the public, at least, face to face with the issue between the women of America and this barbarous law. . . .

Voluntary motherhood implies a new morality—a vigorous, constructive, liberated morality. That morality will, first of all, prevent the submergence of womanhood into motherhood.

Clara Zetkin

My Recollections of Lenin: An Interview on the Woman Question

♲

Clara Zetkin (1857–1933) was one of the founders of the German Communist Party and for many years led the international Communist woman's movement. Inasmuch as Marxist theory unequivocally supports the complete equality of women, the Communist victory in the October Revolution was regarded by female radicals with intense interest.

Initially, as Lenin described the situation in the Soviet Union to Zetkin in 1920, many excellent legal and social provisions for women were enacted. And a few years after their interview, in 1924, the Comintern called for an end to the family, legalization of abortion and easy divorce.

What happened? In 1936 and 1941 the new divorce and abortion laws were replaced by far more stringent ones, and the family—the goal of abolishing it forgotten—was restored to a position of social esteem.

Today, in the Soviet Union, women obviously enjoy an enormously improved status over that of Czarist days. Nevertheless, although women are a definite majority of the Soviet population, they hold few if any positions in the top government leadership. Moreover, most Russian men by all accounts behave toward their wives just like the men with a "slave-owners point of view" that Lenin deplored in his conversation with Zetkin.

Clara Zetkin recorded her memory of this meeting with the Soviet leader in 1925, the year after Lenin's death.

Comrade Lenin repeatedly discussed with me the problem of women's rights. He obviously attached great importance to the women's movement, which was to him an essential component of the mass movement that in certain circumstances might become decisive. Needless to say he saw full social equality of women as a principle which no Communist could dispute.

We had our first lengthy talk on this subject in the autumn of 1920, in Lenin's big study in the Kremlin. Lenin sat at his desk, which was covered with books and papers, indicating study and work without the "brilliant disorder" associated with genius.

"We must by all means set up a powerful international women's movement on a clear-cut theoretical basis," he began after greeting me. "It is clear that without Marxist theory we cannot have proper practice. Here, too, we Communists need the greatest clarity of principle. . . .

"What inspires your comrades, the proletarian women of Germany? What about their proletarian class-consciousness? Do their interests and activities centre on the political demands of the moment? What is the focal point of their thoughts?

"I have heard strange things about that from Russian and German comrades. I must tell you what I mean. I understand that in Hamburg a gifted Communist woman is bringing out a newspaper for prostitutes, and is trying to organise them for the revolutionary struggle. Now Rosa [Luxemburg], a true Communist, felt and acted like a human being when she wrote an article in defence of prostitutes who have landed in jail for violating a police regulation concerning their sad trade. They are unfortunate double victims of bourgeois society. Victims, first, of its accursed system of property and, secondly, of its accursed moral hypocrisy. There's no doubt about this. Only a coarse-grained and short-sighted person could forget this. To understand this is one thing, but it is quite another thing—how shall I put it?—to organize the prostitutes as a special revolutionary guild contingent and publish a trade union paper for them. Are there really no industrial working women left in Germany who need organising, who need a newspaper, who should be enlisted in your struggle? . . ."

Before I could answer Lenin continued:

"The record of your sins, Clara, is even worse. I have been told that at the evenings arranged for reading and discussion with working women, sex and marriage problems come first. They are said to be the main objects of interest in your political instruction and educational work. I could not believe my ears when I heard that. The first state of proletarian dictatorship is battling with the counter-revolutionaries of the whole world. The situation in Germany itself calls for the greatest unity of all proletarian revolutionary forces, so that they can repel the counter-revolution which is pushing on. But active Communist women are busy discussing sex problems and the forms of marriage. . . ."

I interposed that where private property and the bourgeois social order prevail, questions of sex and marriage gave rise to manifold problems, conflicts and suffering for women of all social classes and strata. As far as women are concerned, the war and its consequences exacerbated the existing conflicts and suffering to the utmost precisely in the sphere of sexual relations. Problems formerly concealed from women were now laid bare. To this was added the atmosphere of incipient revolution. The world of old emotions and thoughts was cracking up. Former social connections were loosening and breaking. The makings of new relations between people were appearing. Interest in the relevant problems was an expression of the need for enlightenment and a new orientation. It was also a reaction against the distortions and hypocrisy of bourgeois society. Knowledge of the modifications of the forms of marriage and family that took place in the course of history, and of their dependence on economics, would serve to rid the minds of working women of their preconceived idea of the eternity of bourgeois society. The critically historical attitude to this had to lead to an unrelenting analysis of bourgeois society, an exposure of its essence and its consequences, including the branding of false sex morality. All roads led to Rome. Every truly Marxist analysis of an important part of the ideological superstructure of society, of an outstanding social phenomenon, had to lead to an analysis of bourgeois society and its foundation, private property. It should lead to the conclusion that "Carthage must be destroyed."

Lenin nodded with a smile.

"There you are! You defend your comrades and your Party like a lawyer. What you say is of course true. But that can at best excuse, not justify, the mistake made in Germany. It remains a mistake. Can you assure me in all sincerity that during those reading and discussion evenings, questions of sex and marriage are dealt with from the point of view of mature, vital historical materialism? . . .

"Besides, and this isn't the least important point, Solomon the Wise said there is a time for everything. I ask you, is this the time to keep working women busy for months at a stretch with such questions as how to love or be loved, how to woo or be wooed? . . . For the German proletariat, the problem of the Soviets, of the Versailles Treaty and its impact on the lives of women, the problem of unemployment, of falling wages, of taxes and many other things remain the order of the day. . . .

"In our country, too, considerable numbers of young people are busy 'revising bourgeois conceptions and morals' in the sex question. And let me add that this involves a considerable section of our best boys and girls, of our truly promising youth. It is as you have just said. In the atmosphere created by the aftermath of war and by the revolution which has begun, old ideological values, finding themselves in a society whose economic foundations are undergoing a

radical change, perish, and lose their restraining force. . . .
All this applies also to the field of sexual relations, marriage,
and the family. The decay, putrescence, and filth of bourgeois marriage with its difficult dissolution, its licence for
the husband and bondage for the wife, and its disgustingly
false sex morality and relations fill the best and most spiritually active of people with the utmost loathing.

"The coercion of bourgeois marriage and bourgeois legislation on the family enhance the evil and aggravate the
conflicts. It is the coercion of 'sacrosanct' property. It sancti-
fies venality, baseness, and dirt. The conventional hypocrisy of 'respectable' bourgeois society takes care of the rest.
People revolt against the prevailing abominations and per-
versions. And at a time when mighty nations are being destroyed, when the former power relations are being
disrupted, when a whole social world is beginning to decline,
the sensations of the individual undergo a rapid change. A
stimulating thirst for different forms of enjoyment easily
acquires an irresistible force. Sexual and marriage reforms
in the bourgeois sense will not do. In the sphere of sexual
relations and marriage, a revolution is approaching—in
keeping with the proletarian revolution. Of course, women
and young people are taking a deep interest in the complex
tangle of problems which have arisen as a result of this.
Both the former and the latter suffer greatly from the present messy state of sex relations. Young people rebel against
them with the vehemence of their years. This is only natural.
Nothing could be falser than to preach monastic self-denial
and the sanctity of the filthy bourgeois morals to young
people. However, it is hardly a good thing that sex, already
strongly felt in the physical sense, should at such a time
assume so much prominence in the psychology of young
people. The consequences are nothing short of fatal. . . .

"Youth's altered attitude to questions of sex is of course
'fundamental,' and based on theory. Many people call it
'revolutionary' and 'communist.' They sincerely believe that

this is so. I am an old man, and I do not like it. I may be a morose ascetic, but quite often this so-called 'new sex life' of young people—and frequently of the adults too—seems to me purely bourgeois and simply an extension of the good old bourgeois brothel. . . ."

Lenin sprang to his feet, slapped the table with his hand and paced up and down the room.

"The revolution calls for concentration and rallying of every nerve by the masses and by the individual. It does not tolerate orgiastic conditions so common among d'Annunzio's decadent heroes and heroines. Promiscuity in sexual matters is bourgeois. It is a sign of degeneration. The proletariat is a rising class. It does not need an intoxicant to stupefy or stimulate it, neither the intoxicant of sexual laxity or of alcohol. . . .

"[You] must emphasise strongly that true emancipation of women is not possible except through communism. You must lay stress on the unbreakable connection between woman's human and social position and the private ownership of the means of production. This will draw a strong, ineradicable line against the bourgeois movement for the 'emancipation of women.' This will also give us a basis for examining the woman question as part of the social, working-class question, and to bind it firmly with the proletarian class struggle and the revolution. The communist women's movement itself must be a mass movement, a part of the general mass movements; and not only of the proletarians, but of all the exploited and oppressed, of all victims of capitalism or of the dominant class. Therein, too, lies the significance of the women's movement for the class struggle of the proletariat and its historic mission, the creation of a communist society. . . .

"Unfortunately, we may still say of many of our comrades, 'Scratch the Communist and a philistine appears.' To be sure, you have to scratch the sensitive spots,—such as their mentality regarding women. Could there be any more

palpable proof than the common sight of a man calmly
watching a woman wear herself out with trivial, monotonous,
strength- and time-consuming work, such as her housework, and watching her spirit shrinking, her mind growing
dull, her heartbeat growing faint, and her will growing
slack? It goes without saying that I am not referring to the
bourgeois ladies who dump all housework and the care for
their children on the hired help. What I say applies to the
vast majority of women, including the wives of workers,
even if these spend the day at the factory and earn money.

"Very few husbands, not even the proletarians, think of
how much they could lighten the burdens and worries of
their wives, or relieve them entirely, if they lent a hand in
this 'women's work.' But no, that would go against the 'privilege and dignity of the husband.' He demands that he have
rest and comfort. The domestic life of the woman is a daily
sacrifice of self to a thousand insignificant trifles. The ancient rights of her husband, her lord and master, survive
unnoticed. Objectively, his slave takes her revenge. Also in
concealed form. Her backwardness and her lack of understanding for her husband's revolutionary ideals act as a
drag on his fighting spirit, on his determination to fight.
They are like tiny worms, gnawing and undermining im-
perceptably, slowly but surely. I know the life of the workers, and not only from books. Our communist work among
the masses of women, and our political work in general,
involves considerable educational work among the men. We
must root out the old slave-owner's point of view, both in
the Party and among the masses. That is one of our political
tasks, a task just as urgently necessary as the formation of a
staff composed of comrades, men and women, with thorough theoretical and practical training for Party work
among working women."

To my question about present-day conditions in Soviet
Russia, Lenin replied:

"The government of the proletarian dictatorship—jointly

with the Communist Party and the trade unions of course —makes every effort to overcome the backward views of men and women and thus uproot the old, non-communist psychology. It goes without saying that men and women are absolutely equal before the law. A sincere desire to give effect to this equality is evident in all spheres. We are enlisting women to work in the economy, the administration, legislation and government. All courses and educational institutions are open to them, so that they can improve their professional and social training. We are organising community kitchens and public dining-rooms, laundries and repair shops, crèches, kindergartens, children's homes and educational institutions of every kind. In brief, we are quite in earnest about carrying out the requirements of our programme to shift the functions of housekeeping and education from the individual household to society. Woman is thus being relieved from her old domestic slavery and all dependence on her husband. She is enabled to give her capabilities and inclinations full play in society. Children are offered better opportunities for their development than at home. We have the most progressive female labour legislation in the world, and it is enforced by authorised representatives of organised labour. We are establishing maternity homes, mother-and-child homes, mothers' health centres, courses for infant and child care, exhibitions of mother and child care, and the like. We are making every effort to provide for needy and unemployed women.

"We know perfectly well that all this is still too little, considering the needs of the working women, and that it is still far from sufficient for their real emancipation. Yet it is an immense stride forward from what there was in tsarist and capitalist Russia. Moreover, it is a lot as compared with the state of affairs where capitalism still holds undivided sway. It is a good start in the right direction, and we shall continue to develop it consistently, and with all available energy, too. You abroad may rest assured. Because with each day that passes it becomes clearer that we cannot make progress without the millions of women. . . ."

Someone had knocked twice in the last ten minutes, but Lenin had continued to speak. Now he opened the door and shouted:

"I'm coming!"

Turning in my direction, he added with a smile:

"You know, Clara, I am going to take advantage of the fact that I was conversing with a woman and will name the notorious female loquacity as the excuse for being late. Although this time it was the man and not the woman who did most of the talking. In general, I must say that you are really a good listener. But it was this that probably prompted me to talk so much."

With this jocular remark Lenin helped me on with my coat.

"You should dress more warmly," he suggested solici-tously. "Moscow is not Stuttgart. You need someone to look after you. Don't catch cold. Good-bye."

He shook my hand firmly.

Virginia Woolf

A Room of One's Own

☙

The English novelist and critic Virginia Woolf (1882–1941) was the author of two explicitly feminist non-fiction works. *Three Guineas,* first published in 1938, explores the connections between three causes which have appealed to her for a financial contribution. (The first is a woman's college building program; the second, a society that promotes employment of professional women; the third, a male-directed peace group.)

A Room of One's Own, published in 1929, is oblique rather than polemical in its arguments. Based on speeches written by Woolf for delivery at the British women's colleges of Girton and Newnham, this book surpasses any feminist writing since Mary Wollstonecraft in artistry and profundity of emotion. Through her flexible and evocative use of language, Woolf conveys the longing, frustration and disabling rage—in all their subtle variations—that are experienced by every woman and by the female creative writer especially. She looks ahead to a time—to be brought to realization by the work of present women and those of the immediate future—when Shakespeare's sister might "find it possible to live and write her poetry."

But, you may say, we asked you to speak about women and fiction—what has that got to do with a room of one's own? I will try to explain. When you asked me to speak about women and fiction I sat down on the banks of a river and began to wonder what the words meant. They might mean

simply a few remarks about Fanny Burney; a few more
about Jane Austen; a tribute to the Brontës and a sketch of
Haworth Parsonage under snow; some witticisms if possible
about Miss Mitford; a respectful allusion to George Eliot;
a reference to Mrs. Gaskell and one would have done. But
at second sight the words seemed not so simple. The title
women and fiction might mean, and you may have meant it
to mean, women and what they are like; or it might mean
women and the fiction that they write; or it might mean
women and the fiction that is written about them; or it might
mean that somehow all three are inextricably mixed together
and you want me to consider them in that light. But when
I began to consider the subject in this last way, which
seemed the most interesting, I soon saw that it had one fatal
drawback. I should never be able to come to a conclusion.
I should never be able to fulfil what is, I understand, the
first duty of a lecturer—to hand you after an hour's dis-
course a nugget of pure truth to wrap up between the pages
of your notebooks and keep on the mantelpiece for ever.
All I could do was to offer you an opinion upon one minor
point—a woman must have money and a room of her own
if she is to write fiction; and that, as you will see, leaves the
great problem of the true nature of woman and the true
nature of fiction unsolved. I have shirked the duty of coming
to a conclusion upon these two questions—women and fiction remain, so far as I am concerned, unsolved problems.
But in order to make some amends I am going to do what
I can to show you how I arrived at this opinion about the
room and the money. I am going to develop in your presence as fully and freely as I can the train of thought which
led me to think this. Perhaps if I lay bare the ideas, the
prejudices, that lie behind this statement you will find that
they have some bearing upon women and some upon fiction.
At any rate, when a subject is highly controversial—and
any question about sex is that—one cannot hope to tell
the truth. One can only show how one came to hold what-

ever opinion one does hold. One can only give one's audience
the chance of drawing their own conclusions as they observe the limitations, the prejudices, the idiosyncrasies of
the speaker. Fiction here is likely to contain more truth than
fact. Therefore I propose, making use of all the liberties and
licences of a novelist, to tell you the story of the two days
that preceded my coming here—how, bowed down by the
weight of the subject which you have laid upon my shoulders, I pondered it, and made it work in and out of my
daily life. . . .

Life for both sexes—and I looked at them [through a
restaurant window while waiting for my lunch to be served],
shouldering their way along the pavement—is arduous, difficult, a perpetual struggle. It calls for gigantic courage and
strength. More than anything, perhaps, creatures of illusion
as we are, it calls for confidence in oneself. Without self-
confidence we are as babes in the cradle. And how can we
generate this imponderable quality, which is yet so invalu-
able, most quickly? By thinking that other people are inferior to oneself. By feeling that one has some innate
superiority—it may be wealth, or rank, a straight nose, or
the portrait of a grandfather by Romney—for there is no
end to the pathetic devices of the human imagination—over
other people. Hence the enormous importance to a patriarch
who has to conquer, who has to rule, of feeling that great
numbers of people, half the human race indeed, are by nature inferior to himself. It must indeed be one of the chief
sources of his power. . . . Women have served all these centuries as looking glasses possessing the magic and delicious
power of reflecting the figure of man at twice its natural
size. Without that power probably the earth would still be
swamp and jungle. The glories of all our wars would be
unknown. We should still be scratching the outlines of deer
on the remains of mutton bones and bartering flints for
sheepskins or whatever simple ornament took our unsophis-
ticated taste. Supermen and Fingers of Destiny would never

have existed. The Czar and the Kaiser would never have worn their crowns or lost them. Whatever may be their use in civilised societies, mirrors are essential to all violent and heroic action. That is why Napoleon and Mussolini both insist so emphatically upon the inferiority of women, for if they were not inferior, they would cease to enlarge. That serves to explain in part the necessity that women so often are to men. And it serves to explain how restless they are under her criticism; how impossible it is for her to say to them this book is bad, this picture is feeble, or whatever it may be, without giving far more pain and rousing far more anger than a man would do who gave the same criticism. For if she begins to tell the truth, the figure in the looking-glass shrinks; his fitness for life is diminished. How is he to go on giving judgment, civilising natives, making laws, writing books, dressing up and speechifying at banquets, unless he can see himself at breakfast and at dinner at least twice the size he really is? So I reflected, crumbling my bread and stirring my coffee and now and again looking at the people in the street. The looking-glass vision is of supreme importance because it charges the vitality; it stimulates the nervous system. Take it away and man may die, like the drug fiend deprived of his cocaine. Under the spell of that illusion, I thought, looking out of the window, half the people on the pavement are striding to work. They put on their hats and coats in the morning under its agreeable rays. They start the day confident, braced, believing themselves desired at Miss Smith's tea party; they say to themselves as they go into the room, I am the superior of half the people here, and it is thus that they speak with that self-confidence, that self-assurance, which have had such profound consequences in public life and lead to such curious notes in the margin of the private mind.

But these contributions to the dangerous and fascinating subject of the psychology of the other sex—it is one, I hope, that you will investigate when you have five hundred a year of your own—were interrupted by the necessity of paying the bill. It came to five shillings and ninepence. I gave the waiter a ten-shilling note and he went to bring me change. There was another ten-shilling note in my purse; I noticed it, because it is a fact that still takes my breath away—the power of my purse to breed ten-shilling notes automatically. I open it and there they are. Society gives me chicken and coffee, bed and lodging, in return for a certain number of pieces of paper which were left me by an aunt, for no other reason than that I share her name.

My aunt, Mary Beton, I must tell you, died by a fall from her horse when she was riding out to take the air in Bombay. The news of my legacy reached me one night about the same time that the act was passed that gave votes to women. A solicitor's letter fell into the post-box and when I opened it I found that she had left me five hundred pounds a year for ever. Of the two—the vote and the money—the money, I own, seemed infinitely the more important. Before that I had made my living by cadging odd jobs from newspapers, by reporting a donkey show here or a wedding there; I had earned a few pounds by addressing envelopes, reading to old ladies, making artificial flowers, teaching the alphabet to small children in a kindergarten. Such were the chief occupations that were open to women before 1918. I need not, I am afraid, describe in any detail the hardness of the work, for you know perhaps women who have done it; nor the difficulty of living on the money when it was earned, for you may have tried. But what still remains with me as a worse infliction than either was the poison of fear and bitterness which those days bred in me. To begin with, always to be doing work that one did not wish to do, and to do it like a slave, flattering and fawning, not always necessarily perhaps, but it seemed necessary and the stakes were too great to run risks; and then the thought of that one gift which it was death to hide—a small one but dear to the possessor—perishing and with it myself, my soul—all this became like a rust eating away the bloom of the spring, destroying the tree at its heart. However, as I say, my aunt died; and whenever I change a ten-shilling note a little of that rust and corrosion is rubbed off; fear and bitterness go. Indeed, I thought, slipping the silver into my purse, it is remarkable, remembering the bitterness of those days, what a change of temper a fixed income will bring about. No force in the world can take from me my five hundred pounds. Food, house and clothing are mine for ever. Therefore not merely do effort and labour cease, but also hatred and bitterness. I need not hate any man; he cannot hurt me. I need not flatter any man; he has nothing to give me. So imperceptibly I found myself adopting a new attitude toward the other half of the human race. It was absurd to blame any class or any sex, as a whole. Great bodies of people are never responsible for what they do. They are driven by instincts which are not within their control. They too, the patriarchs, the professors, had endless difficulties, terrible drawbacks to contend with. Their education had been in some ways as faulty as my own. It had bred in them defects as great. True, they had money and power, but only at the cost of harbouring in their breasts an eagle, a vulture, for ever tearing the liver out and plucking at the lungs—the instinct for possession, the rage for acquisition which drives them to desire other people's fields and goods perpetually; to make frontiers and flags; battleships and poison gas; to offer up their own lives and their children's lives. Walk through the Admiralty Arch (I had reached that monument), or any other avenue given up to trophies and cannon, and reflect upon the kind of glory celebrated there. Or watch in the spring sunshine the stockbroker and the great barrister going indoors to make money and more money and more money when it is a fact that five hundred pounds a year will keep one alive in the sunshine. These are unpleasant instincts to harbour, I reflected. They are bred of the conditions of life; of the lack of civilisation, I thought, looking at the statue of the Duke of Cambridge, and in particular at the feathers in his cocked hat, with a fixity that they have scarcely ever received before. And, as I realised these drawbacks, by degrees fear and bitterness modified themselves into pity and toleration; and then in a year or two, pity and toleration went, and the greatest release of all came, which is freedom to think of things in themselves. That building, for example, do I like it or not? Is that picture beautiful or not? Is that in my opinion a good book or a bad? Indeed my aunt's legacy unveiled the sky to me, and substituted for the large and imposing figure of a gentleman, which Milton recommended for my perpetual adoration, a view of the open sky.

So thinking, so speculating, I found my way back to my house by the river. Lamps were being lit and an indescribable change had come over London since the morning hour. . . .

It was disappointing not to have brought back in the evening some important statement, some authentic fact. Women are poorer than men because—this or that. Perhaps now it would be better to give up seeking for the truth, and receiving on one's head an avalanche of opinion hot as lava, discoloured as dish-water. It would be better to draw the curtains; to shut out distractions; to light the lamp; to narrow the enquiry and to ask the historian, who records not opinions but facts, to describe under what conditions women lived, not throughout the ages, but in England, say in the time of Elizabeth.

For it is a perennial puzzle why no woman wrote a word of that extraordinary literature when every other man, it seemed, was capable of song or sonnet. What were the conditions in which women lived, I asked myself; for fiction, imaginative work that is, is not dropped like a pebble upon the ground, as science may be; fiction is like a spider's web, attached ever so lightly perhaps, but still attached to life at all four corners. Often the attachment is scarcely perceptible; Shakespeare's plays, for instance, seem to hang there complete by themselves. But when the web is pulled askew, hooked up at the edge, torn in the middle, one remembers that these webs are not spun in midair by incorporeal creatures, but are the work of suffering human beings, and are attached to grossly material things, like health and money and the houses we live in. . . .

Here am I asking why women did not write poetry in the Elizabethan age, and I am not sure how they were educated; whether they were taught to write; whether they had sitting-rooms to themselves; how many women had children before they were twenty-one; what, in short, they did from eight in the morning till eight at night. They had no money evidently; according to [the historian] Professor Trevelyan they were married whether they liked it or not before they were out of the nursery, at fifteen or sixteen very likely. It would have been extremely odd, even upon this showing, had one of them suddenly written the plays of Shakespeare, I concluded, and I thought of that old gentleman, who is dead now, but was a bishop, I think, who declared that it was impossible for any woman, past, present, or to come, to have the genius of Shakespeare. He wrote to the papers about it. He also told a lady who applied to him for information that cats do not as a matter of fact go to heaven, though they have, he added, souls of a sort. How much thinking those old gentlemen used to save one! How the borders of ignorance shrank back at their approach! Cats do not go to heaven. Women cannot write the plays of Shakespeare.

Be that as it way, I could not help thinking, as I looked at the works of Shakespeare on the shelf, that the bishop was right at least in this; it would have been impossible, completely and entirely, for any woman to have written the plays of Shakespeare in the age of Shakespeare. Let me imagine, since facts are so hard to come by, what would have happened had Shakespeare had a wonderfully gifted sister, called Judith, let us say. Shakespeare himself went, very probably—his mother was an heiress—to the grammar school, where he may have learnt Latin—Ovid, Virgil and Horace—and the elements of grammar and logic. He was, it is well known, a wild boy who poached rabbits, perhaps shot a deer, and had, rather sooner than he should have done, to marry a woman in the neighbourhood, who bore him a child rather quicker than was right. That escapade sent him to seek his fortune in London. He had, it seemed, a taste for the theatre; he began by holding horses at the stage door. Very soon he got work in the theatre, became a successful actor, and lived at the hub of the universe, meeting everybody, knowing everybody, practising his art on the boards, exercising his wits in the streets, and even getting access to the palace of the queen. Meanwhile his extraordinarily gifted sister, let us suppose, remained at home. She was as adventurous, as imaginative, as agog to see the world as he was. But she was not sent to school. She had no chance of learning grammar and logic, let alone of reading Horace and Virgil. She picked up a book now and then, one of her brother's perhaps, and read a few pages. But then her parents came in and told her to mend the stockings or mind the stew and not moon about with books and papers. They would have spoken sharply but kindly, for they were substantial people who knew the conditions of life for a woman and loved their daughter—indeed, more likely than not she was the apple of her father's eye. Perhaps she scribbled some pages up in an apple loft on the sly, but was careful to hide them or set fire to them. Soon, however, before she was out of her teens, she was to be betrothed to the son of a neighbouring wool-stapler. She cried out that marriage was hateful to her, and for that she was severely beaten by her father. Then he ceased to scold her. He begged her instead not to hurt him, not to shame him in this matter of her marriage. He would give her a chain of beads or a fine petticoat, he said; and there were tears in his eyes.

How could she disobey him? How could she break his
heart? The force of her own gift alone drove her to it. She
made up a small parcel of her belongings, let herself down
by a rope one summer's night and took the road to London.
She was not seventeen. The birds that sang in the hedge
were not more musical than she was. She had the quickest
fancy, a gift like her brother's, for the tune of words. Like
him, she had a taste for the theatre. She stood at the stage
door; she wanted to act, she said. Men laughed in her face.
The manager—a fat, loose-lipped man—guffawed. He bel-
lowed something about poodles dancing and women acting
—no woman, he said, could possibly be an actress. He
hinted—you can imagine what. She could get no training
in her craft. Could she even seek her dinner in a tavern or
roam the streets at midnight? Yet her genius was for fiction
and lusted to feed abundantly upon the lives of men and
women and the study of their ways. At last—for she was
very young, oddly like Shakespeare the poet in her face,
with the same grey eyes and rounded brows—at last Nick
Greene the actor-manager took pity on her; she found herself with child by that gentleman and so—who shall measure the heat and violence of the poet's heart when caught
and tangled in a woman's body?—killed herself one winter's night and lies buried at some cross-roads where the
omnibuses now stop outside the Elephant and Castle.

That, more or less, is how the story would run, I think,
if a woman in Shakespeare's day had had Shakespeare's
genius. But for my part, I agree with the deceased bishop,
if such he was—it is unthinkable that any woman in Shakespeare's day should have had Shakespeare's genius. For
genius like Shakespeare's is not born among labouring, un-
educated, servile people. It was not born in England among
the Saxons and the Britons. It is not born today among the
working classes. How, then, could it have been born among
women whose work began, according to Professor Trevelyan, almost before they were out of the nursery, who were

forced to it by their parents and held to it by all the power of law and custom . . .?

Next I think that you may object that in all this I have made too much of the importance of material things. Even allowing a generous margin for symbolism, that five hundred a year stands for the power to contemplate, that a lock on the door means the power to think for oneself, still you may say that the mind should rise above such things; and that great poets have often been poor men. Let me then quote to you the words of your own Professor of Literature, who knows better than I do what goes to the making of a poet. Sir Arthur Quiller-Couch writes: . . . . "The poor poet has not in these days, nor has had for two hundred years, a dog's chance . . . a poor child in England has little more hope than had the son of an Athenian slave to be emancipated into that intellectual freedom of which great writings are born." That is it. Intellectual freedom depends upon material things. Poetry depends upon intellectual freedom. And women have always been poor, not for two hundred years merely, but from the beginning of time. Women have had less intellectual freedom than the sons of Athenian slaves. Women, then, have not had a dog's chance of writing poetry. That is why I have laid so much stress on money and a room of one's own. . . .

I told you in the course of this paper that Shakespeare had a sister; but do not look for her in Sir Sidney Lee's life of the poet. She died young—alas, she never wrote a word. She lies buried where the omnibuses now stop, opposite the Elephant and Castle. Now my belief is that this poet who never wrote a word and was buried at the crossroads still lives. She lives in you and in me, and in many other women who are not here tonight, for they are washing up the dishes and putting the children to bed. But she lives; for great poets do not die; they are continuing presences; they need only the opportunity to walk among us in the flesh. This opportunity, as I think, it is now coming within your power to give her. For my belief is that if we live another century or so—I am talking of the common life which is the real life and not of the little separate lives which we live as individuals—and have five hundred a year each of us and rooms of our own; if we have the habit of freedom and the courage to write exactly what we think; if we escape a little from the common sitting-room and see human beings not always in their relation to each other but in relation to reality; and the sky, too, and the trees or whatever it may be in themselves; if we look past Milton's bogey, for no human being should shut out the view; if we face the fact, for it is a fact, that there is no arm to cling to, but that we go alone and that our relation is to the world of reality and not only to the world of men and women, then the opportunity will come and the dead poet who was Shakespeare's sister will put on the body which she has so often laid down. Drawing her life from the lives of the unknown who were her fore-runners, as her brother did before her, she will be born. As for her coming without that preparation, without that effort on our part, without that determination that when she is born again she shall find it possible to live and write her poetry, that we cannot expect, for that would be impossible. But I maintain that she would come if we worked for her, and that so to work, even in poverty and obscurity, is worth while.

Sources of Selections

ABIGAIL ADAMS
Familiar Letters of John Adams and His Wife, Abigail Adams, During the Revolution, ed. by Charles Francis Adams, is out of print.

MARY WOLLSTONECRAFT
A Vindication of the Rights of Woman is available in a paperbound edition (W. W. Norton & Co., N.Y., 1967). The excerpts used here are from the second edition, published in 1792.

FRANCES WRIGHT
Course of Popular Lectures is out of print.

GEORGE SAND
Indiana is out of print.
Letters of George Sand, selected and edited by Veronica Lucas (Houghton Mifflin Co., N.Y., 1930).

SARAH M. GRIMKÉ
Letters on the Equality of the Sexes and the Condition of Woman was reprinted in a limited edition (Burt Franklin, N.Y., 1970).

HARRIET H. ROBINSON
Early Factory Labor in New England is a report of the Massachusetts Bureau of Statistics of Labor (1883) and is kept on file in some libraries.

MARGARET FULLER
An edited version of *Woman in the Nineteenth Century* is available in a paperbound volume entitled *Margaret Fuller: American Romantic,* ed. by Perry Miller (Cornell University Press, Ithaca, N.Y., 1970). The excerpts used here are from the 1855 edition.

Married Women's Property Act, 1848
This document and much relevant historical material appear in
Ernestine L. Rose, by Yuri Suhl (Reynal, N.Y., 1959).

Declaration of Sentiments and Resolutions,
Seneca Falls
This document is included in *History of Woman Suffrage,* Volume I, by Elizabeth Cady Stanton, Susan B. Anthony and
Matilda Joslyn Gage (Rochester, N.Y., 1881), currently out
of print.

Frederick Douglass
The editorial from *The North Star* appears in *History of Woman Suffrage,* Volume I, op. cit.

Letter from Prison of St. Lazare, Paris
History of Woman Suffrage, Volume I, op. cit. (A more complete version appears in the printed *Record of the Proceedings of the Second National Convention.*)

William Lloyd Garrison
Speech on *Intelligent Wickedness* is from *History of Woman Suffrage,* Volume I, op. cit.

Sojourner Truth
The speeches by Sojourner Truth, *Ain't I a Woman?* and *What Time of Night It Is,* are from *History of Woman Suffrage,* Volume I. The speech *Keeping the Thing Going While Things Are Stirring* appears in Volume II of *History of Woman Suffrage* (Rochester, N.Y., 1881).

Lucretia Mott
Not Christianity, but Priestcraft appears in *History of Woman Suffrage,* Volume I, op. cit.

Lucy Stone
The *Marriage of Lucy Stone Under Protest* and the speech *Disappointment Is the Lot of Woman* both appear in *History of Woman Suffrage,* Volume I, op. cit.

ELIZABETH CADY STANTON

Both speeches to the New York State legislature (1854 and 1860) appear in *History of Woman Suffrage,* Volume I, op. cit. The speech on *Womanliness* appears in *History of Woman Suffrage,* Volume IV, by Susan B. Anthony and Ida Husted Harper (Indiana, 1902). *Solitude of Self,* edited by Harriot Stanton Blatch, was issued separately in pamphlet form; this was the version from which the excerpt included here was taken. It also appears in part in *History of Woman Suffrage,* Volume IV, op. cit.

MARRIED WOMEN'S PROPERTY ACT, 1860

Reprinted in *History of Woman Suffrage,* Volume I, op. cit.

ERNESTINE L. ROSE

Petitions Were Circulated appears in *History of Woman Suffrage,* Volume I, op. cit.

SUSAN B. ANTHONY

The excerpts from Anthony's trial and the speech *Woman Wants Bread, Not the Ballot!* are found in *The Life and Work of Susan B. Anthony,* by Ida Husted Harper, Volume II. A limited edition was published by Arno in 1969.

TENNESSEE CLAFLIN

The articles excerpted here are included in the book *Talks and Essays,* by Lady Cook (née Tennessee Claflin), published in England in 1897, and now out of print.

VICTORIA WOODHULL

An uncut version of her speech *The Elixir of Life* was published in pamphlet form, but is otherwise not available.

JOHN STUART MILL

The Subjection of Women is available in a paperbound edition (M.I.T. Press, 1970).

FRIEDRICH ENGELS

The Origin of the Family, Private Property, and the State was published in a paperbound edition (International Publishers, 1970).

AUGUST BEBEL
Woman and Socialism is now out of print. The excerpt that appears here comes from the authorized translation by Meta L. Stern, published in 1910.

CHARLOTTE PERKINS GILMAN
Women and Economics has been published in a paperbound edition (Harper & Row, N.Y., 1966).

EMILY JAMES PUTNAM
The Lady was reissued in a paperbound edition (The University of Chicago Press, 1970).

SENATE REPORT ON CONDITION OF WOMEN AND CHILD WAGE-EARNERS
Volume IX of this Senate document, from which the excerpt here was taken, may be found at many library collections of government publications.

ANNA GARLIN SPENCER
Woman's Share in Social Culture is out of print.

CARRIE CHAPMAN CATT
Her speech included here was published in pamphlet form and is not otherwise available.

EMMELINE PANKHURST
I Incite This Meeting to Rebellion was reprinted in Emmeline Pankhurst's *My Own Story* (Hearst's International Library Co., N.Y., 1914).
When Civil War Is Waged by Women was published in pamphlet form and is not otherwise available.

EMMA GOLDMAN
A paperbound edition of her essays includes *The Traffic in Women* and *Marriage and Love;* it is entitled *Anarchism and other essays* (Dover Publications, 1969). The excerpts used here are from the 1910 edition.

MARGARET SANGER
Woman and the New Race was republished in a limited edition (Maxwell Reprint Co., Elmsford, New York, 1969).

CLARA ZETKIN

The conversation with Lenin is included in the paperbound book *The Emancipation of Women,* from the writings of V. I. Lenin (International Publishers, N.Y., 1966).

VIRGINIA WOOLF

A Room of One's Own is available in a paperbound edition published by Harcourt, Brace & World, Inc.

About the Author

MIRIAM SCHNEIR was born in New York City. She attended Antioch College and Queens College and worked as a teacher in the New York City public schools and in private schools. Now a free-lance writer, she is especially interested in the fields of education, history (particularly the history of women), and politics. Her articles have appeared in various publications, including *Liberation* and *The New York Times Magazine*. She is the co-author, with Walter Schneir, of *Invitation to an Inquest: A New Look at the Rosenberg-Sobell Case*. She lives in Westchester County.